rebuilt

To
Luke
with blessings?

Michael

"*Rebuilt* is an excellent resource for parishes seeking new ideas and a fresh approach to bringing the faithful closer to Christ in the third millennium."

Most Reverend William E. Lori
Archbishop of Baltimore

"*Rebuilt* answers the most important question challenging our parishes today: How do we form communities of faith-filled disciples called to ongoing conversion and service? It is humorous, candid, and insightful—an exciting and practical guide for clergy and laity who take the New Evangelization seriously."

Most Reverend Joe S. Vásquez
Bishop of Austin

"This story of Catholic parish renewal is a must-read for pastors and future pastors. It provides an amazing testimony to the transforming power of God's love when we say a generous yes to following Jesus in true discipleship, centered in word and sacrament."

Rev. John Horn, S.J.
President-Rector of Kenrick-Glennon Seminary
Archdiocese of St. Louis

"This is an eminently practical how-to book by two ordinary parish leaders doing extraordinary work. They challenge us to learn from their experience of growing a healthy parish built on the radical call of Gospel hope, focused on making disciples, and committed to reaching the lost."

Theresa Rickard, O.P.
Executive Director
Renew International

"Vibrant parishes are essential if we are going to re-propose the genius of Catholicism to the people of our times. *Rebuilt* is much needed and well written. White and Corcoran are stunningly honest, insightful about the real problems facing parishes today, and passionate about helping your parish become the best version of itself."

Matthew Kelly
Author of *Rediscover Catholicism*

"White and Corcoran challenge us to recognize that our parishes have become consumer exchanges, and, as such, have lost their transforming power in people's lives. They remind us that in order to recapture our zeal and enthusiasm we need to return to the basics of proclaiming the Word of God, seeking out those who are lost, and inviting them to come back home and join in the rebuilding."

Rev. Richard Vega
Pastor of St. Frances of Rome Parish
Azusa, CA

"For the reader who doesn't just want to read about a parish success story but wants to have a conversation about how it happened, *Rebuilt* shares how vision, courage, mistakes, success, discernment, and grace shaped a parish's transformation into an evangelizing congregation."

Susan Timoney
Executive Director
Department of Evangelization and Family Life
Archdiocese of Washington

"One would think there are a lot of great books about parishes given their importance. There aren't. White and Corcoran give us a long overdue and frank discussion of parish mission, ministry, and structures. This is a most welcome resource for everyone concerned about Catholic parishes."

Christopher C. Anderson
Executive Director
National Association for Lay Ministry

"Refreshingly honest and down-to-earth story of one parish's journey to becoming a vibrant Catholic community. Practical suggestions offer ways to creatively build up your parish and its mission."

Marti R. Jewell
Assistant Professor of Theology
University of Dallas School of Ministry

"In *Rebuilt*, White and Corcoran show how it's possible to answer Jesus Christ's call to make disciples of all nations by cultivating an infectious energy and enthusiasm in today's Catholic parishes."

Rev. Neil F. Wack, C.S.C.
Pastor of Christ the King Catholic Church
South Bend, IN

"White and Corcoran have detailed what few Catholic leaders have accomplished—how to turn a traditional parish inside out to evangelize in a systematic way." Congratulations on a great book!"

Rev. Robert S. Rivers, C.S.P.
Author of *From Maintenance to Mission*

"White and Corcoran move from analyzing the all-too-typical-problems that they faced in their parish to presenting a clear, detailed, good-humored, and concrete pathway to their destination: a life-giving Catholic parish. The reader finishes this book with hope."

Carol Nevin Abromaitis
Professor of English
Loyola University Maryland

"This is practical theology at its best. Bravo to White and Corcoran who have clearly described the essence of parish life in light of the Gospel mandate, 'Go and make disciples!' All pastors who desire to increase the spiritual health of their parish will find their work easy to read and hard to put down—a real treasure, a pearl of great price!"

Michael J. Begolly
Pastor of Mount Saint Peter Catholic Church
New Kensington, PA

The Story
of a
Catholic
Parish

rebuilt

Awakening the Faithful

Reaching the Lost

Making Church Matter

Michael White and Tom Corcoran
Foreword by Cardinal Timothy M. Dolan

AVE MARIA PRESS AVE Notre Dame, Indiana

Founded in 1865, Ave Maria Press is a ministry of the United States Province of Holy Cross.

www.avemariapress.com

Paperback: ISBN-10 1-59471-386-3, ISBN-13 978-1-59471-386-6

E-book: ISBN-10 1-59471-387-1, ISBN-13 978-1-59471-387-3

Cover and text design by John R. Carson.

Printed and bound in the United States of America.

Library of Congress Cataloging-in-Publication Data
White, Michael.
  Rebuilt : awakening the faithful, reaching the lost, and making church matter /
Michael White and Tom Corcoran.
      p. cm.
  Includes bibliographical references (p.   )
  ISBN 978-1-59471-386-6 (pbk. : alk. paper) -- ISBN 1-59471-386-3 (pbk. : alk. paper)
  1. Church renewal--Catholic Church. I. Corcoran, Tom. II. Title.
  BX1746.W495 2012
  282'.7309051--dc23
                                 2012040940

The parish is where the Church lives. Parishes are communities of faith, of action, and of hope. They are where the gospel is proclaimed and celebrated, where believers are formed and sent to renew the earth. Parishes are the home of the Christian community; they are the heart of our Church.

—NATIONAL CONFERENCE OF CATHOLIC BISHOPS[1]

To

Our Archbishop
for leadership and friendship

The priests of the Archdiocese of Baltimore
for an inspiring example of fruitful service

The founding pastor and members of Church of the Nativity
for a foundation

Ave Maria Press
for a platform

Our collaborators on this project
for wisdom

Our parishioners
for enthusiasm

Our staff
for courage

Our parents
for love

Tom: my wife
for putting the kids to bed so I could write

God
for choosing two thoroughly unlikely, imperfect instruments
to do a great work
thereby proving, beyond a shadow of a doubt,
it's all grace

CONTENTS

FOREWORD

One of the most gratifying tasks I have as an archbishop is visiting our parishes. If I had my way, I would spend more of my time there. In the Archdiocese of New York the parishes come in great variety. Whatever their size, style, culture, or language, these communities are filled with people who love their parishes. The parish is the front-line of the Church and of the New Evangelization!

And that's why I love this book. *Rebuilt* is simply the story of a parish written from the perspective of a parish priest and a lay minister. Father Michael White, whom I have known for many years, and his pastoral associate, Tom Corcoran, write with remarkable honesty and humor, telling us about what happened to them. Through trial and error, success and failure, and with some unexpected experiences along the way, they learned a lot about parish life. Most of all, they learned to fall in love with their parish.

From beginning to end, the authors provide valuable and useful approaches that are easily transferable to other parish settings. It is a rich resource for pastors, pastoral staffers, and parishioners alike. But more than that, this is a book that takes the New Evangelization seriously and points the way forward for others to do the same. The approach you'll discover here is rooted in scripture and is profoundly simple. It is also completely Catholic, seeking at one and the same time to reengage the people in our pews by getting them excited about their Catholic faith while reaching out to those who are *not* there.

The authors clearly have great room in their hearts for Catholics who no longer practice their faith. This is a group that is growing in our country—a sad fact that demands our attention and deserves our very best efforts to reverse the trend and bring them home. We need an evangelization strategy that is intentionally focused on former Catholics, *at the parish level*. Moving forward, such a strategy will more and more become the critical and key question in parish life. This book shapes an answer to that question, and it works. Because of that, *Rebuilt* is one of the most important books for parish ministry in our generation.

If you love your parish, read this book!

Cardinal Timothy Michael Dolan
Archbishop of New York
September 27, 2012

PREFACE

Today, in particular, the pressing pastoral
task of the new evangelization calls for the
involvement of the entire People of God, and
requires a new fervor, new methods and a
new expression for the announcing and witnessing of the Gospel. This task demands
priests who are deeply and fully immersed in
the mystery of Christ and capable of embody-
ing a new style of pastoral life, marked by a
profound communion with the pope, the
bishops and other priests, and a fruitful coop-
eration with the lay faithful, always respect-
ing and fostering the different roles, charisms
and ministries present within the ecclesial
community.

—BLESSED JOHN PAUL II[1]

This is a book about the local community church that Catholics
call their parish. We're two guys—a Catholic pastor and his
lay associate—who have been working in a parish for a few
years. That's probably our essential qualification for writing this book.

Actually, it's our *only* qualification, and to tell you the truth, for a long time we weren't even any good at it.

When it comes to the parish, we have had more than our share of minor disasters and major mishaps. Dumb doesn't even begin to describe the false starts and crash landings we've made. In the process, we've found ourselves stressed out, burned out, beaten up, and put down. There were days when we wanted to quit. There were days that stretched into weeks and months when we wanted to quit. There were times our only prayer was begging God to send us someplace else. There were other times we would have gladly given it all up to go sell hot dogs at Camden Yards. We never imagined ourselves working in a parish, and now we can't imagine working anywhere else. We want to tell you about that.

Just to let you know: We're pretty average people. If you met us, you'd know that instantly. We did not finish at the top of our classes— or even close. Neither do we bring deep wisdom or original insight to this project. We're definitely not visionaries. And yet, we've caught a glimpse of the amazing work God is doing in our parish in which we get to participate. We want to tell you about that, too.

We're writing for pastors, pastoral life directors, associates, deacons, seminarians, religious educators, youth ministers, and volunteer ministers. Even if you've just got a view from the pew but value your local church community and appreciate its fundamental and critical role in your life, then this is a book for you.

We seek to thoughtfully address all of you who are concerned that things in many parishes do not seem to be going well these days. A single, simple fact illustrates the problem: One in three people raised in the Catholic Church has walked away from it, making "former Catholic" the third largest religious designation in the country.[2]

There are lots of people who are ready to tell you why that is so and how to fix it. But many of the arguments we've heard tend to mistake the problem and miss the point. We think the problem is cultural.

Culture is the potent brew of knowledge, belief, and behavior, which everyone in an organization uniquely shares, and it can be the most powerful force in an organization. It affects everything: enthusiasm and morale, productivity and creativity, effectiveness and success. It's more important than vision or mission when it comes to what is going on in a group.[3] *Every* organization has a culture. We think the most acute problem in the Church today is with its culture. And here's the point: It's a parish problem. It really is *the* parish problem.

There are "cultural" problems that parish churches—large and small, old and new, growing and declining, urban, suburban, and rural, northeast, southwest, and everywhere in between, Spanish-speaking, multi-cultural, Asian, African American—all seem to share. These problems will most certainly be exacerbated by the seismic changes increasingly rocking the Catholic Church in this country that, among other things, are leading in some regions to massive parish closings, consolidations, and restructuring.

Things are no longer going as they could or should be going; and fruitful conversation about *why* that is so, or *how* it is related to the exodus of membership, seems to be largely ignored. Gabe Lyons, an author we like, puts it this way,

> Cultures are like clouds. They materialize as byproducts of
> the prevailing conditions. They reveal the world's influen-
> tial currents as they move across the landscape. And when
> you're inside them, it's hard to see what's really going on
> around you.[4]

We offer this book for people out there who have the hunch or perhaps the conviction we have that things could go better. You already know that; you're just having a hard time seeing what's really going on. We write this book to describe our story: what happened to us, what we learned, and what we know about what works in a parish in Timonium, Maryland, at this particular point in history.

As you'll see, we have not concerned ourselves with questions of ecclesiology, canon law, and catechetical practices. We steer entirely clear of difficult but settled issues, and we've tried to tread lightly through the minefield of liturgy. What we are interested in is the "culture" of our parish. The culture is what we have worked to change through a new strategy. Increased membership is the first and obvious fruit. While our neighborhood isn't growing, our parish is. In fact, at this point we've outgrown our current facilities.

> The reason you should read this book is because you too can rebuild or grow a healthy parish.

Other fruits of our new strategy are dramatically increased giving, expanded volunteerism and ministry, and added momentum and enthusiasm. Less measurable, but more important, there is much evidence of a vibrant, authentically Catholic, spiritual rebuilding of our parish. But here's the deal: The reason you should read this book is because, with God's grace, you too can rebuild or grow a healthy parish.

We do not pretend to know anything about your church community, or what would work there. We strive to be respectful of your challenges and your efforts. Of course not every detail we discuss will work everywhere. Our strategy must be translated into *your* setting if it is to work at all. We do not presume to insist that all of our principles are transferable to your parish. But, we're guessing most of them are.

Whatever kind of parish you're in, whatever style church you're leading, whatever the culture of your community, you can grow a healthy parish. By looking beyond the people in the pews to the people who are *not* there, creating a path to help get them there, and leading both parishioners and newcomers to grow as disciples of Jesus Christ, you can rebuild the culture of your parish and make church matter.

To help you along the way, we are happy to offer you web-based tools to get you started. These include "Steps You Can Take in Your Parish" hints, checklists, and other resource materials for free download and "Want to know more/go deeper?" video lessons. All of these are noted throughout part III of this book and available at rebuiltparish. com.

You can do this!

Introduction:
CONVENIENT PARKING

How solitary sits the city, once filled with
people!

—LAMENTATIONS 1:1

Permit us to offer a vast over-simplification, by way of introduction. You could sum up much of the history of the Catholic Church in the United States with a twist on the famous verse from *Field of Dreams*: "They've come; build it." For generations, wave upon wave of Catholics washed ashore and many proceeded to have families, not a few of them large families. When one church filled up, another was built, sometimes just up the street. This is clearly seen here in north Baltimore, specifically the York Road corridor, where a row of Catholic churches is lined up from the Baltimore harbor to the Pennsylvania border.

Most Catholics arrived in this country poor and vulnerable. Many, if not most, were marginalized in American society, as they had been in their countries of origin. The Church, to its everlasting credit, stepped up to meet many of the basic needs these immigrants had. Beyond spiritual care, the Church oftentimes provided health care, education, and networks of social support. Catholics built hospitals, schools,

1

and orphanages, along with churches. The Catholic faithful found themselves in the role of **needy consumers**, and the Church served them well.

As Catholics pursued the American Dream and moved up the economic ladder, these critical needs became less urgent, and people's relationship to the Church changed. They received the sacraments and spiritual guidance; they were given religious instruction and found social support. Their obedience was expected in return for these services, and obedience to Church laws and rules, even local customs, was widely given. The faithful graduated to the role of **compliant consumers** and the strategy of Church leaders became "build it and they will come."

Somewhere after the Second Vatican Council, the role of the average parishioner shifted again. Nobody really knows exactly when, but the tipping point might have been the publication of *Humanae Vitae*, the 1968 Papal Encyclical restating the Church's traditional teaching on the regulation of birth. Other significant developments of this period include the rise of an educated laity, the decline in Catholic school enrollment, the universal disregard of parish boundaries, the first clouds in the coming "crisis" in vocations, and the near total collapse in the practice of confession.

At the same time, the larger culture was being reshaped by the Vietnam War, "white flight," the Civil Rights Movement, the sexual revolution, revolutionary changes in health care, communications, and travel, the questioning of all authority and dependability of institutions, and the accelerated demise of organized religion.

All of these changes within and beyond the Church ushered in the dawn of the so-called "cafeteria" Catholics or what we will be calling **demanding consumers**. This day's dawn increasingly casts light on the new reality: "They're not coming."

And that's just about where our story begins.

Timonium

The church where we serve, Church of the Nativity, was carved out of a large parish bursting at the seams in 1968. It was given birth on the eve of the end of the construction boom that had been exploding in north Baltimore since World War II. Those were also the final days of the European Catholic population expansion that had been effortlessly filling the pews for years before that.

The church was planted by a simple pulpit announcement in the mother parish by the new pastor: "If you live south of Timonium Road you now belong to a new parish. Report to Ridgely Road Middle School next weekend." Imagine making *that* announcement today! In 1968, you could still assume a majority of Catholics in north Baltimore went to church on most Sundays, and you could also assume they would go where they were told to go.

The communities of Lutherville and Timonium, which this church was established to serve, are leafy, affluent suburbs where crime, unemployment, and poverty are rare; where minority residents are few and often more affluent than their neighbors; and where differences are measured by where you went to high school or to which country club you belonged. This is not the land of the super rich, just people with more than enough.

The church was built on a beautiful, wooded campus in the modern "International" style. Perfectly suiting the spare architecture, the talented founding pastor provided an unadorned vision of an efficient operation that got the job done. Lots of big houses were being built in those days, and young families were easily attracted to a new church in their community. It quickly grew in its early years. In many ways, it was successful and even innovative for its time. It had bathrooms, multi-purpose spaces, and accessibility for disabled individuals.

Fast-forward thirty years. We both came to Church of the Nativity unexpectedly, unenthusiastically, and without any intention of staying very long. Neither of us knew anything about running a parish. We had little training and even less interest.

Father Michael: I had spent most of my adult years up until this point in school, studying theology, with a specialization in ecclesiology—study of the Church *itself*—which didn't seem to have any application when it came to running a parish. Except for a short tour of duty in parish work, my only real job was serving as the priest secretary to the Cardinal-Archbishop here in Baltimore. I had lots of interesting experiences in that role, but none that easily translated into parish work, as far as I could see. I was a behind the scenes kind of guy who eschewed the limelight but nonetheless liked to get things done. When the Cardinal appointed me pastor of Nativity, I was sure it was a poor fit, but did what I was told. To be honest, I was unhappy with the assignment. The problems that I discovered here initially made me want to leave, and I kept my eye out for other opportunities, should they come along.

You say goodbye and I say hello, hello, hello. I don't know why you say goodbye, I say hello.
—John Lennon and Paul McCartney[1]

Tom: I was just a year out of college, where I had studied and enjoyed political science. I envisioned a life somewhere in the political world of Washington; however, a brief stint there made me rethink that choice. About that same time, I received a phone call from one of my college professors who was a mentor to me and a close friend of Michael's. Sue must have seen something in me that I didn't see in myself,

> because she introduced me to Michael who eventually offered me a position as youth minister. Since I was engaged to be married, I thought it was a good idea to get a job. But my plan was to stay at Nativity for two or maybe three years, work on a Master's degree in political science (since I still believed that was where my future lay), and then move on to teach.

At best we assumed our tenure here would be a brief transition to bigger or, at least, better things. Who really wants to be stuck in a little parish in the woods? Not us.

Early Observations

Our own lack of excitement and vision about being at the parish perfectly matched the attitude we found here. What we discovered at Nativity in the late 90s was a languid community aging in place. To better assess the situation in our first year, we engaged Georgetown University's Center for Applied Research in the Apostolate to survey our congregation. When asked what attracted them to this church, 96 percent of parishioners identified "convenient parking" as the number one reason they were here. Here are a few others things we discovered.

- Kids hated our religious education program, and it was nearly impossible to find all the volunteer teachers we needed; nobody wanted to do it.
- There was no youth ministry; teenagers and young adults were no-shows at this church.
- The music wasn't bad: It was painfully, ear-achingly, "please, please, please, for the love of God stop!" bad.
- A line-up of rotating priest-celebrants guaranteed an uneven quality of preaching and, sometimes, conflicting messages.

- The experience of weekend Masses was moribund and depressing. We wouldn't have attended this church if we didn't work here.
- The congregation's level of giving wasn't paying the bills (and we had a bare bones budget to say the least). Some recent years had actually seen small deficits. The parish had virtually no savings or reserve. In a well-heeled community we were a relatively poor parish.
- The physical plant was dirty and no longer functional in significant ways. Deferred maintenance seemed to be the maintenance plan. A surprising amount of useable space had been converted to storage space, although no one was sure what we were storing.
- The grounds were neglected and overgrown. The entrance looked as if the place were permanently closed.
- The small staff was divided and deeply dysfunctional. Their work was done in complete isolation one from another. They were a singularly unproductive group, but nearly everything that was done in the parish—from answering the phone to arranging the flowers—was done by them. Gossip and lunch were the only tasks they lent themselves to with enthusiasm. It should be noted, however, that they were paid next to nothing.
- Signs posted everywhere from some unidentified authority issued emphatic instructions always punctuated with exclamation points: "Keep these doors closed at all times!" "Do not move this table!!" "No lemons in the garbage disposal!!!"
- Bulletin boards and posters everywhere tried to attract parishioners' attention to everything from lost puppies to the latest fundraiser. As far as we know, no one ever once paused to survey these posts.
- There was a weekly bulletin, but it was widely acknowledged that "no one reads it." So, most weekends it was read for them from the pulpit following communion. Perhaps that's why most people left after communion.
- The "volunteers" were a law unto themselves, answering to no one (except, perhaps, the former pastor). They included:

1. *The Ushers/Money Counters.* These men (there were no women) were the pastor's police force, invested with the responsibility of enforcing the pastor's house rules.
2. *The Religious Ed Teachers.* Nobody really knew what these women (there were no men) did in their classrooms. And no one seemed to care either.
3. *The Cantors, Lectors, and Eucharistic Ministers.* They had the job of sharing the spotlight with the celebrant and looking like the ultimate insiders.

- Clergy and staff were treated by parishioners as employees—sometimes with hostility, often with indifference, and, when we were doing what they wanted us to, with condescension.
- Complaint was a standard form of communication. Anything from failing to announce the Mass "intention" to the temperature inside the building would bring it on.
- Inexplicably, there was a self-satisfied, self-congratulatory attitude the congregation as a whole seemed to share. Little else united them.
- Besides the people who had been showing up for years, out of convenience or habit, the church was irrelevant and unknown in the community. The number one comment we heard in talking to people outside our congregation was, "I didn't know there was a church back there."
- A new non-denominational church in our neighborhood was meeting in a warehouse. It was half our age, twice our size, and growing. By their own acknowledgement, something like sixty percent of their congregation were former Catholics, including their pastor. As such, they were drawing more baptized Catholics than any Catholic church in north Baltimore.

These discoveries surprised and shocked us. But there was another little known fact that was more shocking still: Our parish was dying.

In what was already at that point a twenty-year pattern, between thirty and fifty people a year were literally dying or moving away, and nobody was replacing them.

And given the obvious age of the congregation, we knew that pace would continue to accelerate on our watch. We were on the path of steady and certain decline. In some ways, it already had the feeling of a deserted place.

> We were on the path of steady and certain decline. In some ways, it already had the feeling of a deserted place.

Privately we blamed the staff for our dying parish, publically we blamed no one, because we didn't even *acknowledge* the problem. We did everything we could to *hide* the problem. Still, we knew we wanted to do something about it.

The way we saw it, our parishioners were like customers, and we were here to serve them. Obviously, since the demographics of the community were stable, and we were in an affluent, robust area (we had a new Macy's down the street), we thought the reason the parish was losing market share was simply because our customers weren't being well served and our product line wasn't that good.

Retail Religion

So we set out to change that. We put effort and imagination into creating programs that would impress parishioners and keep them coming back for more.

For children, we updated the curriculum in the religious ed program and introduced teacher training opportunities. We also developed creative and engaging seasonal events for kids—breakfast with Santa, Easter egg hunts, puppet shows, pageants, and plays.

We started a youth *ministry* program, which was essentially a youth *entertainment* program, with an endless array of activities to "get them involved" (which just meant getting them to show up): youth days, ski trips, movie nights, lock-ins, and dances.

We recruited musical talent to provide professional quality music in a variety of styles for our worship services. We also got into the business of hosting concerts and recitals.

We offered all kinds of fellowship programs: receptions, bus trips, and lectures. We redesigned the bulletin and published a glossy annual report. We started a website (before many churches had websites). We expanded member care as far as we could dream up ways to take it, from hosting complimentary lunches for funerals to coffee service after daily Mass.

It was a waste of time. In hindsight, the situation was reminiscent of the Red Queen's race in Lewis Carroll's *Through the Looking Glass:*

> Now, here, you see, it takes all the running you can do, to
> keep in the same place. If you want to get somewhere else,
> you must run at least twice as fast as that![2]

The more we provided, the faster we had to run just to stay in the same place—but the more we provided, the more was demanded. Just like Alice, who didn't pause to reflect on why she was running an absurd exercise for the insatiable Queen, we hadn't considered why we were doing what we were doing or what we were accomplishing.

Unbeknownst to us, what we were dealing with was a consumer culture. We didn't understand what that was. Consumer culture arose out of industrialization, urbanization, and the emergence of general literacy.[3] It's great if you're a retail establishment making money from it. It's not so great if you're a church. In fact, consumer culture erodes the sustainability of church communities because it allows the congregant to assume the posture of shallow commitment and the attitude of ceaseless demands. Author Rodney Clapp puts it this way:

> The consumer is schooled in insatiability. He or she is never to be satisfied, at least not for long. The consumer is taught that persons consist basically of unmet needs that can be requited by commodified goods and experiences. Accordingly, the consumer should think first and foremost of himself or herself and meeting his or her felt needs.[4]

Probably nothing could underscore this conclusion and that period better than our annual Lenten program. Over the course of about five years we had developed a Friday night Lenten program we called "Family Friendly Fridays." For six consecutive Fridays, we would pile this program on top of everything else we were doing.

It was hugely labor intensive and staff dependent. It included (a free) dinner, childcare, after-dinner entertainment, and then a featured speaker. There was Mass before dinner and Stations of the Cross after the program. We offered live music and even a wine bar. Hundreds and hundreds of people attended. Church colleagues (not always generous in their praise) lauded our program and replicated it in their parishes. Don't ask us what the purpose was because we didn't know. We seemed to just be doing something for the sake of doing something, perhaps to shake off the creeping feeling of irrelevance.

Free Food Isn't Good Enough

Father Michael: My life changed on one of those Fridays. It was the sixth and final evening, and by the time we got to that point, it always seemed as if we had been doing it forever. It was complete burnout every year for everyone on staff.

Anyway, I was serving the dinner (yep, that's what I did) and a lady approached me to complain about the food (the *free* food). And she was noisy and nasty about it. Really mean. She was quickly joined by a chorus of like-minded people who all wanted to complain about the (FREE!) food.

Something snapped; some artery exploded: I knew in an instant (if you didn't count the previous five years) that I could no longer do this. I was wasting my time (this was my *life*, and I was wasting my time). It wasn't just the ingratitude. It was the lack of purpose and the resulting lack of effect.

We were working as hard as we could, and in a non-sustainable way, and it never made any difference. There was never any difference in *anyone* after than before. Now I understood why my predecessor had a door mat that read, *"Go away."*

Part I:

NAMING
THE PROBLEM

1

CHURCH IS NOT EASY

One complex reality. . . .
—Second Vatican Council[1]

Five years! For five years we invested vast measures of time and an ocean of energy in what were our very best ideas in our parish. And it was unsustainable. But that didn't really matter because it was also ineffective. We felt burned out and used up; we felt overworked and underappreciated; we felt sad and sorry for ourselves that all our efforts just weren't working. And then we felt embarrassed that we felt sad and sorry for ourselves.

What Did We Get Wrong?

A lot. Here are ten of the standouts:

1. **We assumed if we did more and did it better, people would grow in their maturity and commitment.**

    That was wrong: they didn't. We had run all the way down the field of retail religion. In the face of a dauntingly consumerist "me-first" culture, we had taken consumers who were just looking for convenient parking and mutated them into ravenous super-consumers who were now demanding dinner.

2. **We thought that if we did more and did it better, people would automatically give more (money).**

    That was wrong: we underestimated how difficult it would be to raise the level of giving; we did not understand how entrenched our people were in their lack of stewardship and how convenient it was for them to remain ignorant of what it costs to run a church. We remained financially unstable.

3. **If we did more and did it better, we took it for granted that people would automatically get involved and help out.**

    That was wrong: we had no idea that most people in our pews were comfortable there and *expected* to be served. (They were, after all, demanding consumers.)

4. **We looked to our stalwart church-goers (senior citizens) as our natural allies as we tried to move forward.**

    Boy, oh boy, was that wrong! We underestimated their intransigence in the face of change. Every time we took a step forward, changed or tried anything, they were a reliable, sometimes hysterical, source of complaint. There was a famous incident our first summer here that we'll never forget. We repainted the hallway outside the office and then re-hung the pictures that had been displayed there; mind you, the *same pictures*, just in a different order. A huge controversy ensued led by a group of seniors. The bishop even got involved.

    We were surprised by their anger, especially toward younger generations, for not sharing their values about church. We didn't understand their deep sense of entitlement to whatever it was they were coming here to get. We failed to recognize that, at this point in history, our senior citizens already represented the first generation of demanding consumers. Previous generations had reduced Catholic Christianity to an exercise in "getting to heaven" by fulfilling the "obligations" the Church placed on them. Our senior consumers continued to operate under an obligation mentality, but according to their own authority and design. In fact, they had further reduced their list of obligations to a simpler set of duties and *expected* the parish to make sure it was easy for them to manage.

5. **Little did we appreciate how detached the second and third generations of demanding consumers had grown.**

We now know they are perfectly comfortable maintaining a loose association with an institution whose organization they do not like and whose teachings they do not accept or respect. They take what they want and ignore everything else.[2]

To their credit, our consumers are specific and consistent in their consumer demands. They want church for their kids—mainly Baptism, First Communion, and a part in the Christmas pageant; they want church as an adornment to their family calendar—Christmas Eve, Easter Sunday, maybe Mother's Day (depending on what time they have brunch reservations); they want Communion when they feel like showing up for Mass (whether or not they're "in communion" with the Church). They want the church building as a backdrop for funerals and perhaps for weddings—but only if the church is pretty (because weddings are destination driven). Beyond that, we're mostly an annoying distraction.

But we were *inconsistent* in our "supplier demands." Our system implicitly understood the "hook" we had into their lives and essentially coerced them to do all the things they didn't want to do: attend regularly, give us money, and keep their kids in religious education.[3] We kept dreaming up *new rules* to try to make the system work for us while they kept figuring out *new ways* to circumvent our rules to make the system work for them. The result was the mutual cynicism to which a consumer mentality can easily lend itself. Author Dallas Willard believes,

The consumer Christian is one who utilizes the grace of God for forgiveness and the services of the church for special occasions, but does not give his or her life and innermost thoughts, feelings, and intentions over to the kingdom of the heavens. Such Christians are not inwardly transformed and not committed to it.[4]

6. **Beyond this basic consumption, we didn't understand how marginalized the whole enterprise of faith and religion had become in the lives of our "parishioners."**

It is now axiomatic for us to say that everything hurts attendance: good weather, bad weather, Ravens home games, a three-day weekend, the St. Patrick's Day Parade, Super Bowl Sunday, road work, Rosh Hashanah, you name it. But in our suburban Baltimore culture the biggest distraction of all is kids' sports programs. Sports rule the weekend schedule and trump everything else going on in the life of the community, starting with church. We're competing with kids' sports, which have become a kind of new religion.

We didn't get that. Church is the last thing to be added to people's to-do lists and the first thing to come off. "Regulars" are probably only once or twice a month attendees. Weekly Mass attendance is rare among "practicing Catholics" in north Baltimore. We didn't get that church is competing for the leisure time and dollars of our congregants, and more and more it's on the losing end of the competition.

We kept trying to market church as something it had no business being—yet another product intended to compete for the "disposable" segment of their lifestyle. Media and advertising have moved consumerism onto a field where church simply can't play. Bestselling author Malcolm Gladwell describes this trend:

> We have become, in our society, overwhelmed by
> people clamoring for our attention . . . this surfeit
> of information is called the "clutter" problem, and
> clutter has made it harder and harder to get any one
> message to stick.[5]

Our little parish didn't have the resources to compete. We were
taking a knife to a gun fight.

7. **Despite our best efforts, we really were not reaching our student
population.**

The young people we did see in church were reticent and dis-
engaged. It just wasn't for them, and they knew it. We blamed the
parents. To the extent that they cared, the parents blamed us.

8. **We didn't understand how profoundly
uninterested the non-church–going
population had grown, how distrust-
ful of any outreach efforts we made,
and how cynical they could be about
all organized religion.**

> We were
> completely
> irrelevant to
> their lives.

Nor did we know that there are peo-
ple in north Baltimore who loathe the Catholic Church and, by
extension, us. Meanwhile, thousands of people in our community
drive past our entrance every day and never, never *ever*, even consider giving us a try. We were completely irrelevant to their lives.

9. **We were not turned toward God. We were not relying on
his leadership. And we were not looking to go where he was
blessing.**

We just kept pushing harder on the systems and the procedures
that had always been in place, even though they were no longer
working.

10. **We thought this would be easy.**

That was wrong: church is not easy. Despite all our work, the parish was still in slow, steady decline.

Why Did We Have It Wrong?

Father Michael: Here are some of my leadership mistakes, inspired by Pastor Perry Noble's blog.[6]

Mistake #1. *Controlling everything.*
That's what a pastor's supposed to do, right?

Mistake #2. *Trying to be perfect.*
I am a perfectionist, and in perfectionist mode I know how things should be done, and it all depends on me. This slows the organization down and damages morale.

Mistake #3. *Spending too much time on details.*
Deep down in the details, where I love to be, I lose sight of where we're going and where God wants us to go.

Mistake #4. *Fixing problems . . . instead of systems.*
Unfortunately, there have been too many times when I have found myself reacting to a problem rather than addressing the process or the system that led to the situation in the first place. It takes a lot more discipline than I usually have to rise above the urgency or the emotion of a difficult situation and try to discern how a broken system needs to be fixed.

Mistake #5. *Trying to please everyone.*

This can be a liability in any sphere. It is a neuralgic problem in church work because we somehow adopt the conviction that we *should* please everyone, that it's job-number-one. It was a hard lesson for me to learn that not everyone is going to like me; I am not going to satisfy everybody. And when I was confronted with demanding consumers, this was a sad lesson that I had to learn over and over again. There were times and seasons of my life where I exhausted myself and demoralized our staff trying to meet the expectations our consumers held and the demands they made . . . just to keep them happy.

Mistake #6. *Putting projects before people.*

On the other hand, I tend to be task-oriented and project-driven. This has created people problems; some people have been ill-served or even lost in the shuffle. Good leaders are going to find the correct *balance* between getting the job done and embracing the relational components, which are sometimes going to slow things down in the short term.

Mistake #7. *Hiring too quickly . . . and firing too slowly.*

When a position was open that I knew needed to be filled, and the right person wasn't available (or I didn't even know who the right person was), I found it hard to wait. My tendency was to fill the role with the best person or the available person and then hope it worked out. Hiring too fast often casts people in the wrong role. It also brought us people I didn't really have any chemistry with (and vice-versa) or people who just didn't fit our team.

I've also made the mistake of waiting too long to let people, who *had* to go, go. I've let problems drag on for years out of fear of conflict, or because I didn't want to confront the sad truth that I'd made a mistake in bringing the person on board to begin with. Sometimes I fell into the trap of overlooking character issues in view of someone's contribution to the organization, and that decision always came back to haunt me. There were other times I thought I could "fix" the person or I just hoped things would get better (I couldn't, they didn't).

Mistake #8. *Wasting time and money.*

Many of my failures and missteps were expensive and time consuming. For instance, I regret how much money we spent, over an extended period of time, trying to build a music program without any clear understanding of what *kind* of program we should have been building for our community.

Mistake #9. *Fearing to lead.*

I am a natural worrier. I am a person who dwells on the worst-case scenario. This is what happens when I let my focus wander from God to the potential problems before me. It's appropriate to plan and take steps to prevent problems. It is necessary to anticipate prudently what can go wrong. But it is sin in my life when this turns to obsessive worry. And it is a failure in leadership when I freeze or fail to move forward.

Mistake #10. *Leading without humility.*

I came to the job of pastor with complete confidence that I knew what I was doing, which I didn't. I held the arrogant but idiotic assumption that after my ordination I was supposed to know it all, so I conducted myself accordingly.

All my education notwithstanding, I was an amateur at running a parish. It's really astonishing how much I didn't know, and it's embarrassing to think of all the effort and energy it took to try and hide that fact and pretend I did. This lack of humility actually blinded me to the severity of the problems I was really facing and convinced me that quick fixes were available. It led me to turn to and rely on false solutions time and again, sometimes making matters worse. But more than emotional immaturity, my pride revealed a spiritual immaturity, an unwillingness to rely on God. I was supposed to be leading a flock of his faithful, and I wasn't even listening very carefully to his direction.

Those were a few of the mistakes made, but if truth be told, this list doesn't even scratch the surface of *the* mistake we were making. There was something else we were getting wrong that was fundamental and critical to the whole enterprise, and we didn't even know it.

2
PHARISEES AT HEART

The pride of your heart has deceived you. . . .
—OBADIAH 1:3

O nce, Nativity was the host site for a pastor's conference about high school youth ministry. You know the drill: In exchange for a free lunch, you listen to speakers discuss new resource materials that they're trying to sell you. Just the sort of thing you've been to dozens of times, but this time was different. There was something wrong. There was a weight to the proceedings that was hard to miss, an eight hundred pound gorilla in the room that nobody acknowledged and everybody felt.

Toward the end of the presentation, during the Q & A session, one uncommonly honest pastor raised a question out of clear frustration and with deep emotion, "Am I the only one who doesn't have a high school program? Am I the only one who can't make it work?" He wasn't the only one, but he was the only one unwilling to pretend. We were all there feigning interest in resources we didn't need for programs we didn't have.

It was amazing to us that nobody was talking about the obvious problems we were facing. But that day *we* started talking about them.

Sure it was disappointing when our initial efforts didn't work. Disappointment is not, however, always a bad thing. In our case it became a kind of catalyst for our competitive natures and core conviction that church ought to work. Christ *promised* it would work.

Despite our original lack of interest, we found ourselves increasingly intrigued by the problems we were discovering and eventually eager to rise to the challenge. How could we stem the decline, revive our parish, and actually start making it grow? In the face of so much failure, how could we succeed?

Blessed Mother Teresa, Success, and Growth

Don't say it, we know, we know! If you work in church you don't like that kind of talk. *"Winning," "succeeding,"* and *"growing"* are dirty words around the church office. We've all heard people, in the wake of dull efforts and dismal failures, quote Blessed Mother Teresa: "God didn't call me to be successful. He called me to be faithful." But maybe she wasn't talking about failure. Maybe she was talking about obedient service, which, in her case (you'd have to admit), was singularly successful. In fact, Blessed Mother Teresa stands among the most successful and innovative church leaders of the twentieth century, having led one of the largest, fastest growing religious movements in the world.

Church communities are living organs. They get bigger and they get smaller all the time. There are churches in seasons of growth because they're in growing communities. Their growth is unintentional or, at least, automatic. Nativity was a church that grew automatically. But when the building boom in this part of Baltimore County ended, as they all eventually do, Nativity became a church in slow, steady decline, on its way to becoming a church in accelerated decline.

That's what happens to churches these days. Organized religion is in free fall, with membership dwindling and congregations dying daily. Today thousands and thousands of churches are in a pattern of accelerated decline, others in slow but steady decline. Some studies estimate that as many as 95 percent of Christian churches in our country are headed in the wrong direction. Even churches in growing communities are no longer immune from attrition and erosion. A lot of churches just aren't going to survive, unless they become intentionally growing churches, not just maintaining members, but attracting them.

Scripture makes it clear that God expects us to be faithful *and fruitful*. Speaking in the temple courts just before he was killed, Jesus tells the unsuccessful religious leaders of his time, the Pharisees: "Therefore, I say to you, the kingdom of God will be taken away from you and given to a people that will produce its fruit" (Matthew 21:43). In the Acts of the Apostles, we read that hundreds and thousands (three thousand in one day) were added to his new community of faith—the Church. "And every day the Lord added to their number those who were being saved" (Acts 2:47).

God doesn't want his Church to fail. And he's assured us it won't. And not even the gates of hell will prevail against it. That's the movement we want to be a part of.

So, how do we do it? How do we make our parish church grow? Wrong question. We don't make it grow; only God does that. As St. Paul teaches, God is the agent of growth in his Church:

> *Right here, right now, there is no other place I wanna be. Right here, right now, watching the world wake up from history.*
> —Jesus Jones[1]

> I planted the seed, Apollos watered it, but God caused the growth. Therefore, neither the one who plants nor the one who waters is anything, but only God, who causes the

growth. . . . For we are God's fellow workers. (1 Corinthians 3:6–7, 9)

In the *Purpose Driven Church*, Rick Warren writes that trying to make your church grow is like saying

> how can we build a wave? The question we need to ask instead is, "What is keeping our church from growing?" The task of church leadership is to discover and remove growth restricting diseases and barriers so that natural, normal growth can occur.[2]

Christ Promised It Would Work

We found ourselves asking the question, "Are we being more obedient to broken systems and the wrong culture than we are to God's will for his Church?"

God's will is growth; God expects us to be fruitful. So, if we're not *fruitful*, don't we have to stop and consider if we're really being *faithful*? If we're not being fruitful, don't we need to evaluate what we're doing wrong, learn more about where God wants us to go, and if necessary, do things differently? We've actually been attacked by members of shrinking churches who have made the assertion that our growth is evidence of our unfaithfulness, and their decline proves their faithfulness. Amazingly, they've got it backward.

If you want to be a growing church, and remain a growing church, you've got to be a healthy church, removing anything that is inhibiting growth, and you don't

> A proud man is always looking down on things and people: and, of course, as long as you are looking down, you cannot see something that is above you.
>
> —C. S. Lewis[3]

have to compromise your faithfulness or orthodoxy to do it. Cardinal Avery Dulles put it this way, "The Church constantly changes to maintain a fruitful dynamic relationship between a people immersed in history and the God who has revealed himself in Jesus Christ."[4]

One of the key factors in moving forward, when we finally did, was our willingness to learn *how* to move forward by turning to people who already were doing so. Strategically, the most important decision we ever made was to go out and aggressively learn from growing churches. If you want to grow, why not learn from healthy churches? If you want to grow, why not do what intentionally growing, healthy churches are doing? Even if it means turning to . . . Protestants!

Without Apology

We consider ourselves to be obedient to the Magisterium, entirely orthodox in our Catholicism, and, in fact, conservative by disposition. We would never compromise our faith or do anything to embarrass the Church or our Archbishop. But why should our Catholicism preclude us from learning and adapting the successful methods of other Christians?

If we call Protestants our "separated brethren," doesn't that mean we already have a familial relationship with them? And perhaps they have something to teach us *if* we're willing to learn. Isn't cutting ourselves off from them and their ideas, especially their *good* ideas, ideas that are working, actually cutting ourselves off from understanding how God is working in our generation? "For the Spirit of Christ has not refrained from using them as means of salvation. . . ."[5] Isn't it pride to ignore what's working elsewhere just because we didn't think of it first?

Fr. Michael Scanlan, T.O.R., former president of Franciscan University, recounts similar thoughts on the necessity of learning from Protestants:

> I came to see that many areas of Catholic life that the
> Protestant Reformation challenged were areas that needed
> change, or at least renewal. Catholics needed (and still need)
> a reaffirmation of the importance of preaching the Word of
> God, of the centrality of God's inspired word in scripture, of
> the need for personal appropriation of God's saving grace,
> of the doctrine of justification by faith, of the need for true
> repentance of sin and not just the sacramental action of
> absolution.[6]

The genius of any successful organization is always going to be in its receptivity to change and openness to good ideas wherever they can be found. Likewise, many of the saints were people who lived and shared their faith in creative new ways that successfully engaged their culture with the message of the Gospel.

Without apology, and eventually without embarrassment, we became students of successful, growing churches. Most all that we have studied are evangelical Protestants, who have more or less cornered the market when it comes to intentional church growth across the American religious landscape.[7] Seventy-five percent of Catholics who have left the Catholic Church to become Protestant have chosen evangelical churches, so it looked like a good place to start.[8] Clearly, they have something to teach us.

Changing Our Minds about Church

Ironically enough, we now find ourselves held in suspect (and sometimes contempt) by *both* conservative and liberal Catholics because of the successful strategies that we have adapted from Protestant communities.

Father Michael: Early on in this process, someone gave me an article profiling the largest church
in the country at the time, a suburban Chicago
church named Willow Creek. The article described,
among other things, a coffee bar in the church
lobby where many parishioners viewed the service on video screens while sipping their cappuc-
cinos. I remember reading that article and actually
putting the magazine down as I tried to grasp the
concept. How was this any different than our own
failed consumer efforts? I didn't know, but intuitively I knew it was.

Tom: A couple of years later I came across an interesting book by a youth pastor named Doug Fields
who served in a church in Orange County, California. At the time I held the position of youth minister
here. Mostly, I kept busy hosting as many programs
as I could manage with little to show for it beyond
my own frustration and fatigue. Doug is an advo-
cate of doing ministry with a purpose in mind, *God's*
purpose.[9] Simple as it sounds, that's exactly what
we *weren't* doing at Nativity.

After reading the book, which immediately
made sense to me, I began evaluating my programs
based on the five biblical purposes for church
ministry Doug outlines: worship, fellowship, discipleship, ministry, and evangelization.[10] I started
changing fun field trips into evangelization events;
we transitioned religious ed classes into fellowship
and discipleship environments. We also began inviting students to serve as ministers and get involved
in worship. These initial efforts were simple and successful in ways that the more labor intensive ones
hadn't been. It felt very different.

A few years into the implementation of this
methodology—which we still didn't even fully

understand—I learned that Doug's church was having a "how-to" conference. I asked Michael if he wanted to go, and he agreed without hesitation. . . .

Father Michael: But definitely with trepidation. From our background, going to a conference sponsored by a Protestant church felt very uncomfortable. We went anyway. It was worth it to us; we were in search of intelligent life on planet church.

When we stepped onto the campus of this church, we were overwhelmed by it. It really was like discovering new life forms. I remember parking the car and approaching what we assumed was the church building, only to find out it was a nursery building, an entire building built just for the Sunday school nursery. And it was big, new, and beautiful. On the other hand, when we finally made our way over to the church, though huge, it was completely unimpressive. Big churches, in my world, meant elaborate churches, churches with fancy finishes, expensive architectural details, and lots of artistic decoration. This was just a Wal-Mart with chairs. The whole experience was a paradigm shift.

Tom: Of course, we approached the conference with the fear of being "outed" as Catholics since we had stepped into an evangelical setting—with Southern Baptist DNA. But getting over the emotional weirdness of another church culture was essential to learning.

Father Michael: It turned out this church was, in fact, one of the most hospitable places I have ever been. Despite my initial unease, I was eager to go back. There was simply too much for me to process in a single visit. I had an early opportunity because they were hosting a conference just for pastors the same spring.

That conference turned out to be as thought-
ful and challenging as the youth conference had
been, and it thoroughly engaged me for several
days. Spending time with about one thousand
mostly Southern Baptist pastors was actually a
lot of fun. But it was on the last day that the main
speaker really turned on the firepower and rolled
out his hell-fire-and-brimstone Baptist best. Perhaps
because it was a Friday afternoon and guys had to
get home for the weekend, or maybe because they
knew what was coming, many people had already
left. I found myself seated in a section of the church
more or less by myself.

And I began to feel like the preacher was preaching to me, I mean *just* to me. I felt like he was looking at me and preaching directly to me. It was very
uncomfortable, and I wanted to leave, but I didn't
feel comfortable doing that either.

Most uncomfortable of all was his message: It
was profoundly convicting. He spoke movingly of
the local church community as the delivery system
for much of what God wants to do in the world.
He described the job of pastor as one of the most
important, consequential jobs on the planet. He
talked about the prideful assumptions, amateurish
approaches, and sad outcomes of many pastors
that are hurting people and dishonoring God.

I think he said, if we're not doing church with
the *purpose* God has set for the Church, then God
will remove his blessings. We will fail, just as God
removed his blessing from the religious leaders
Jesus so vigorously condemned in his day, the
Pharisees. I think he said that a lot of us pastors are
just "Pharisees at heart."

I listened to him with an annoyance that became
anger and then rage. I didn't care if he saw me, I
hoped he did. These deep emotions swept away

my discomfort, and I stormed off. I walked out and headed for my car. Who did he think he was anyway? I'm a pastor. I don't have to listen to this.

I marched off toward the parking lot. But, as we mentioned, this place is big, and I had parked a long, long way from the church. It turned out, by the time I got to my car I had cooled down enough to begin to see through the pride of my heart. I bitterly acknowledged the conviction that everything that guy had said was right and that it should have been directed at me.

Rick Warren had just called me out.

Part II:

FINDING A WAY FORWARD

3

LOST PEOPLE IN
CHURCHWORLD

Even though I walk through the valley of the
   shadow of death,
I fear no evil; for you are with me.

—P<small>SALM</small> 23:4

Tom: You're going to think I'm making this up. I was
attending a meeting for parish staffers sponsored
by a large diocese. The main speaker, who had held
a prominent position in the diocese, began his
remarks, "Since Jesus didn't give the Church a mission statement, I have made an attempt of my own."
   What? Jesus didn't give the Church a mission
statement?

Think about that. Jesus, the Son of God, the greatest preacher
and teacher ever, through whom all wisdom comes, who
endured torture, shed his blood, and laid down his life for the

Church, neglected to tell us what to do as Church. Hmmm. Did *he* forget? Or have *we*?

In his contribution to this discussion, Paulist Father Robert Rivers writes:

> All organizations need mission if they are to stay healthy. Organizational development theory tells us that healthy organizations are ones that have a clear sense of mission. Low morale often results from the aimlessness and malaise that come from the lack of mission. When we have a clear outward focus, some of our internal problems tend to fall into perspective. When we are not absorbed by the mission, these internal problems are magnified.[1]

So What's Our Mission?

That was exactly our problem. We were overwhelmed with the demands of our consumers and ignorant of our real mission. Until our trip to Rick Warren's church, we never even thought about it.

> *Toto, I have a feeling we're not in Kansas anymore.*
> —Dorothy in *The Wizard of Oz*

Jesus actually gave the Church a clear mission, and he couldn't have been clearer. First came the "great command," two commands really, that he told us are more important than all the others.

You shall love the Lord, your God, with all your heart, with all your soul, and with all your mind. This is the greatest and the first commandment. The second is like it: You shall love your neighbor as yourself. (Matthew 22:37–39)

And then, after his resurrection and before he ascended into heaven, he gathered the eleven apostles who still stood with him and gave them the "Great Commission." "Go, therefore, and make disciples of all nations" (Matthew 28:19).

Jesus, who suffered on the cross to regain the authority for humanity that our first parents had surrendered, passed on that authority to the apostles and their successors. And he told them what to do with it: Love God and one another by making disciples. And in case they were wondering how many disciples to make or where, he was clear about that too: Make disciples of everyone, everywhere. The Church has a mission statement: Make disciples. That's it.

Disciples are students. The Church is charged with shaping students for Jesus Christ. And like the owner in the parable of the talents (cf. Matthew 25:24), he harvests where he has not sown and gathers where he has not scattered. In other words, he wants us to do it *for* him and *like* him. He modeled it for us when he walked the earth.

> The Church has a mission statement: Make disciples. That's it.

Early on in his ministry, Jesus needed to instruct his first disciples on this very point. It turns out he wasn't in it just for the hometown crowd and the regulars at the local synagogue. He insisted on reaching those who did not know God. He told them in Luke 4:43, "To the other towns also I must proclaim the good news of the kingdom of God, because for this purpose I have been sent."

All his preaching and teaching, his miracles, his gathering and sending of the disciples, even his cross and resurrection, are part of this basic ministry that is called evangelization. For Jesus, evangelization was his commitment to bring good news of God's kingdom to everyone, including some unlikely people—at least from the perspective of religious people. He said it himself over and over again, "For the Son of Man came to seek and save what was lost" (Luke 19:10).

To Seek and Save the Lost

Lost people aren't evil or immoral or even bad. They're just mixed-up about God. And in this confusion or misunderstanding,

- Lost people might pursue the world and what it offers.
- Lost people come to believe that the way to have a great life is to try to control it themselves.
- Lost people can think that money or sex or power or pleasure or sports will somehow fill the ache in their heart, the hole in their soul for God.

In one way or another, lost people (who may be dechurched people who no longer go to church or unchurched people who never did) try to find a life outside a relationship with God. They miss out on God. And in the process, they usually mess up their lives. Jesus made lost people his priority. And he went out of his way (way, way out of his way) to do it. He spent time where they spent time. He knew how to talk to them and what was important to them. He recognized their worries, fears, sorrows, and sins. He understood their hearts, and he loved them by making an investment in them. Jesus found lost people and then he made them disciples.

One time, Jesus met a man who cheated people for a living and invited him to join his team and become a disciple (Matthew 9:9–13). Afterward, that guy went on to write a book of the Bible.

Another time, Jesus was traveling through a town called Jericho. The citizens greeted him with joy, and he could have gone to anyone's house for dinner. But much to the astonishment of the religious people, Jesus went to the home of Zacchaeus, a very unreligious person. Zacchaeus was a tax collector and likely seen as a traitor to his country and a thief. His neighbors probably mistrusted or even hated him for his wealth. Why did Jesus go to his house? Basically, because he was lost. And Zacchaeus, like Matthew, responded enthusiastically (Luke 19:1–9).

Pastor Andy Stanley at North Point Church in Atlanta writes, "People who were nothing like Jesus liked Jesus."[2] People like the Samaritan woman at the well, who would have been an outcast to most Jews, Mary Magdalene, who had demons cast out from her, and Zacchaeus. To the lost, Jesus reveals the message of the kingdom of heaven, which introduces them to the good news of a life that can be lived more successfully because of a real relationship with the living God.

They liked him, and their lives changed as they became like him. *And then* they brought others to him to begin the process all over again. This is the whole pattern for the life of the Church. From Pope Paul VI's *Evangelii Nuntiandi*,

> Evangelization is in fact the grace and vocation proper to the Church, her deepest identity. She exists in order to evangelize.[3]

No Place for the Lost

Nativity was a convenient outlet for demanding religious consumers, and what they were demanding more than anything else was to just "get it over with" (*it* being Communion . . . to fulfill their obligation . . . for whatever reason they felt an obligation: guilt, fear, or just to get their mothers-in-law off their backs, whatever). It all came down to the consumption of Communion, so the greatest values in our church's culture were simple, easy, and fast. Arriving late and leaving early were the rule rather than the exception. Parking strategically and positioning yourself in the pew to beat everyone else out were the marks of the true masters.

We've actually had demanding consumers who, in their "get it over with" mentality (and startling ignorance of the Eucharistic celebration) tried to insist that we bring Communion to their children in religious education classes. Since they had no intention of taking their kids to class *and* Mass, they wanted to streamline both. We've seen communicants coming to Communion with their car keys already in their hands, forcing us to place the Host alongside the keys. In fact we've watched people who actually *only* came for Communion.

In a minimalist's approach, the music is bare bones, but better yet, there is no music. The preacher doesn't really preach. He just talks (and he doesn't talk long either). Mass is going to be a thirty-minute affair, preferably offered first thing Sunday morning so church doesn't "break up the day" and people can get on with what they really want to be doing: golf, football, having brunch with friends.

Nobody wants to be in the "get it over with" church; it's just better than the alternatives. And there are plenty of them. Consider, for instance, the "militant and triumphant" approach to church culture. This is church for the true believers. Whatever their culture, conservative or liberal, they're alike because they take "liturgy" (at least their version of it) with an uncompromising gravitas that clearly distinguishes them from everybody else. Their style of worship becomes an exaggerated expression of their preferences and those of the people already in the pews. The proceedings are ponderous, which proves they're serious about what they do perhaps and intolerant of what others do. In this approach, the celebrant might even speak theatrically, like the voice of God. It sounds more like he's speaking *for* God rather than *to* him. In between these two extremes, there are lots of other church cultures out there:

- It's all about the building or the history of the congregation, so it's like a museum.

- It's all about being in the comfortable environment of like-minded individuals. Belonging here is a type of currency in your social circle, so it's like a country club.
- It's all about the parochial school. The school trumps the church when it comes to facility use, programming, fundraisers, you name it, so it's all about the kids.
- It's all about a popular pastor or musician, so it's all about a cult of personality.
- It's all about a single issue or program: social justice and service, some political agenda, a particular style of music, so, whatever it is, it's like a boutique.

This is *churchworld,* a comfortable environment for *churchpeople.*

We're not trying to criticize anyone. Our point is that *lost people* won't be attracted to *any* of those environments. In fact, they'll see through them for just what they really are: familiar and fond destinations for the parishioners themselves. This is *churchworld,* a comfortable environment for *churchpeople.*

All Are (Not) Welcome

Churchworld might sometimes be very good at doing what it sets out to do, and churchpeople may love it. Perhaps their church adds profound value to their lives and deserves our respect and praise for that contribution. But churchworld doesn't automatically make disciples, and it is definitely not for the lost.

Churchpeople might not understand that or even think otherwise. Perhaps they see themselves as welcoming, because they run promotions claiming, "Our doors are open," and "Our lights are on," or maybe they hang banners and sing songs proclaiming, "All Are Welcome." But is it so, or do they really mean:

- All are welcome on our terms.
- All are welcome to be present as we meet our needs.
- All are welcome if you dress like us and like the same style music we like and worship according to the same rules we observe (which, by the way, we mostly made up to suit ourselves).

Sometimes it's very subtle. We attended a conference in another part of the country and spent several exhilarating and challenging days in an evangelical church where we felt welcomed and loved. Then, on Sunday morning, we went to Mass. This church was different. They were very obviously working at intentionally welcoming newcomers like us. Good. Then again, maybe they didn't have any choice since the evangelicals next door were hitting it out of the ballpark every weekend and attracting flocks of former Catholics. Either way, it was clear they were trying, but it was also clear that when you entered their church, it was *theirs*. It felt like they expected us to accommodate to their way of doing things, which actually turned out to be difficult to do. Inadvertently, we transgressed one of their idiosyncratic procedures. This is true. Apparently, when presenting yourself for Communion, you're supposed to say your name and name your preference in altar bread (white, whole wheat, or gluten free). We got that all wrong and elicited some dirty stares from the regulars. We did not feel welcome and would not go back again.

Our point is not to disrespect other church communities. It's just that maybe lost people don't feel welcome in these churches because sometimes they're *not* welcome.

And that was truer here at Nativity than any church in our experience. Of course, no effort was made to think from or speak to the perspective of an outsider. And, far from appreciating, much less celebrating them, newcomers and guests at Nativity weren't even greeted or acknowledged. In fact, with predictable regularity, the culture revealed its inbred hostility toward them.

One Easter Sunday morning a "faithful" parishioner arrived for the 10:30 a.m. Mass, as was her custom every week, precisely at 10:25. The only problem was that the church was already full. She was invited to the overflow seating adjacent to the church sanctuary, but that was unacceptable to her. Tearing into a tirade at the top of her voice she screamed, "I'm here every week! This is my church. Who are these people? They never come any other time of the year. Why don't they leave?" When her arguments failed to win her the seat she demanded, she proceeded to rip her offering envelope into little pieces and toss it into the air before storming out.

It's the parish secretary who becomes even more unfriendly when the confused newcomer isn't sure of the right questions to ask. It's the heavy-handed religious education director whose job it is to make sure that "non-parishioners" aren't trying to pull a fast one when it comes to sacramental procedures. It's the pastor who can't resist some kind of passive aggressive comment to the Christmas crowds: "Merry Christmas and Happy Easter, since I know I won't see most of you again until then." Essentially, he's telling regulars, "Don't worry, we'll be back to normal next week," while the message to visitors is, "Don't forget, you don't belong to our club."

> It's just that maybe lost people don't feel welcome in these churches because sometimes they're not welcome.

Sure, lost people might be shallow and unsure in their faith. They are not going to appreciate our procedures and practices, nor are they contributing members yet. But, at some level, these people are seeking God. And if we don't help them find him, not only are *they* lost, *we* are too.

More Than a Mistake

Nativity was never even in the business of reaching the lost. Nativity was irrelevant to the lost. And we *wanted* to be that way. We were proud that we were that way. In fact, we blamed the lost for being lost. It was somehow their fault. They deserved to be lost because they weren't interested in doing church our way. Incidentally, Jesus never blamed the lost for being lost; he just wanted to find them. As long as we ignored his example and held onto our own views, we were abdicating our spiritual leadership. And we'd lost our mission.

Of course you cannot turn your church upside down every time someone new comes in the door, or abandon your values to try to please everyone. Certainly every congregation has a serious responsibility to care for its members and hold to high standards when it comes to the sacraments. That is not being questioned. But, many churches not only care for members, they comfort and coddle them. They pander to them. And then they turn around and challenge the outsiders.

That's backward. We should be attractive and accessible to outsiders and challenging to insiders, helping them to change and grow and move beyond consumerism as the United States Bishops teach in *Go and Make Disciples*:

> Evangelization, then, has both an inward and an outward direction. Inwardly, it calls for our continued receiving of the Gospel of Jesus Christ, our ongoing conversion both individually and as Church. It nurtures us, makes us grow, and renews us in holiness as God's people. Outwardly, evangelization addresses those who have not heard the Gospel or, having heard it, have stopped practicing their faith, and those who seek the fullness of faith. It calls us to work for full communion among all who confess Jesus, but do not yet realize the unity for which Christ prayed.[4]

When we get this wrong it's more than just a mistake, it's a corruption. Corruption results in breaking and destroying something by using it for a purpose other than the purpose intended. This is what happens when we get the mission and purpose of the Church wrong and start using it for something else, like comfortable consumption.

The reason Nativity was failing, the reason Nativity was boring and bland, the reason services were dull and programs poorly attended, the reason lots of our people were grumpy and uncooperative, the reason we were burnt out and increasingly dispirited, the reason everything seemed such a huge hassle, the reason there was so much conflict and contention, the reason the church was dying, was that we weren't focused on the mission Jesus Christ gave us. We were doing a lot of things; we were just doing the wrong things for the wrong reasons and ignoring the one thing we should have been doing. Our parish had become a consumer exchange, and, as such, it had lost its *"transforming power"* in people's lives.[5]

> As long as we ignored his example and held onto our own views, we were abdicating our spiritual leadership. And we'd lost our mission.

We needed to repent and return to the purpose given to us by the Lord. The purpose of Nativity is to reach lost people to help them become disciples, and then to help disciples become *growing* disciples. In other words, a church *of* sinners *for* sinners on the path to sainthood.

And, we were ill serving *both* the lost and the people already in the pews while we ignored our purpose. On the other hand, when evangelization is front and center, the community *and the congregation* are better served.

For missionary activity renews the Church, revitalizes faith and Christian identity, and offers fresh enthusiasm and new incentive. Faith is strengthened when it is given to others! It is in commitment to the Church's universal mission that the new evangelization of Christian peoples will find inspiration and support.[6]

> When we get this wrong it's more than just a mistake, it's a corruption.

A Change in Focus

Over a period of just a couple of years our thinking and feelings did a complete about face when it came to our perspective on doing church. We more or less resolved to challenge the status quo and change the culture. We started deliberately doing things differently. And the main difference was in focus. We were going to start challenging church-people and seeking lost people.

And that . . . was going to make a lot of churchpeople really angry.

4

WAR IN HEAVEN

There is nothing more difficult to take in hand, more perilous to conduct, or more uncertain in its success, than to take the lead in the introduction of a new order of things.

—NICCOLÒ MACHIAVELLI[1]

Father Michael: I vividly remember my first Christmas Eve at Nativity, specifically, the 4 p.m. Mass. Like most everywhere else, this is the service that attracts the biggest crowd of the year, with lots of visitors and newcomers as well as *dechurched* people.

The cantor, someone you did not want to tangle with, was late (as usual) and visibly disorganized as she arranged herself at the podium. As I waved at her from the back to try to get things started, she angrily snapped at me through the microphone, "I start when I'm ready." *Starting*, it turned out, wasn't starting Mass. Instead, to my surprise, we were to be serenaded by her seven-year-old daughter on the violin. (Alas, I will never again be able to listen contentedly to "O Holy Night.")

When we finally did get started I could tell that something was wrong, but it took me a while to figure out what. Guess who had filled the prime seats? The ushers and their families had. They had a smugness that was initially confusing, though later I learned it was an annual tradition, their way of sticking it to the "C & E" (Christmas and Easter) Catholics. When it came time for the collection, I had to appeal for help from the altar, and the guests, standing in the back, had to do it.

After Mass, in the lobby, I was approached by one of our Eucharistic ministers. She shouted in my face, "It makes my blood boil to see *that* in church." *That* turned out to be a young man, dressed in black denim, sporting multiple tattoos and piercings, a really interesting hair color, and, I think, mascara. Everyone, including the young man, heard her. Merry Christmas to all and to all a good night! The message from all of our "ministers" was very clear: This was *their* church, and Christmas Eve was all about *them*.

Some churchpeople care more about themselves than about lost people. But at Nativity it went deeper than that. Not only did they not care *about* them, they really didn't care *for* them either. That Christmas Eve they were telling our visitors, "You don't belong and we don't want you to belong."[2] Of course, why would any of our visitors that evening ever have *wanted* to join our church?

These can be profoundly intransigent attitudes, and challenging them, much less changing them, is more than difficult: It's perilous. Making our mission the one Jesus gave us is a dangerous thing to do.

A Dangerous Thing to Do

In a sense, everything we've said up to this point is simply by way of introduction to our story and what happened to us. It's easy and interesting to go to conferences, read "how-to" books, or just sit around talking about what you want to do. It is a whole different deal to do something.

Little did we know the season of conflict we were marching into.

It's hard to stay focused on who's not there (like the lost). Another author says it better than we can, "The people we need to reach out to are not around to tell us what their needs are. The people who don't feel welcome aren't present to tell us why. The poor who don't feel at home in our church simply remain on the margins."[3]

> We were going to start challenging churchpeople and seeking lost people.

There are also other reasons churches don't do evangelization.

- Resources are tight and already accounted for.
- Everyone at church is busy; reaching the lost isn't on anybody's job description; and there's always another crisis or car raffle to eat up any extra time staff and volunteers have.
- We become insulated from the lost. Churchpeople are friends with churchpeople. We think a lot alike and hang out together. We share a common language and values. Talking to people outside the church takes more effort.
- It's uncomfortable and intimidating to try to do it. Many contemporary Catholics don't have any skills or strategies; they don't know the path to follow to make it happen. And some of what we have seen from other religious groups can be unattractive, even offensive.

- Many Catholics no longer believe in the reality of hell, so what difference does it make if someone knows Christ? No matter that some people's lives are a living hell right now.
- Perhaps more than any other reason, we forget our own desperate need for a savior. So it's easy to forget that everybody else needs a savior too.

Those are all reasons why we don't do evangelization—why we don't even *try*. But there's a reason why people *stop* doing evangelization, why they try to and then give it up, why they fail, why they burn out and lose heart, why they just get disgusted, quit, and walk away.

Think about it. People who don't go to your church will never *complain* about your church. They'll never be in your face wanting to know what you're doing to meet their needs. They won't be contacting the diocesan offices to question your commitment or orthodoxy. Likewise, no official from the diocese will ever call to say, "We received some complaints from people who said they would like to go to your church, but you're not offering a relevant message or an accessible environment." Inevitably, diocesan offices are handed concerns from insiders, not outsiders.

> There's a reason people stop doing evangelization —why they just get disgusted, quit, and walk away.

You'll never be criticized or censured for not doing evangelization. On the other hand, whenever you do introduce it, you introduce change, and when you introduce change people invested in the status quo will *always* complain. When you change anything in churchworld, criticism, complaint, and conflict will usually follow in a forceful, emotionally driven way. And if you start challenging churchpeople and seeking lost people, there will be blood.

Don't get us wrong: At this point we still had no idea what we were doing. We didn't understand what our strategy was going to be. We had nearly no staff or volunteers: The ones we'd inherited were long gone. We were still operating on a shoestring budget, and we were beginning to irritate the very people who were the source of what financial support we had.

But, our biggest problem was that we had no track record. We had no credibility. We were proposing a new order of things, and it was untested in our cultural context. Who would ever believe our "new" ideas were right or that they could work? They *seemed* so wrong to most people, so they must be wrong . . . right?

> **Father Michael:** This was painfully brought to my attention on an occasion when one of our major donors, a man who had been the senior vice president of a huge international corporation, asked to see me. He very cordially told me that if I didn't settle down and leave things alone he would be withdrawing his contributions. He went on to counsel me that change was inherently risky and, in our case, unnecessary. Eventually he did withdraw his support. But the sad irony was that his company meanwhile disappeared and was absorbed into an even larger, and far more creative corporation precisely because it had failed to keep up with the changing marketplace.

Challenging Churchpeople

Notwithstanding all that, we began to move forward.

During Lent of 2004, about a year after our first trip to Rick Warren's church, Saddleback, we decided to begin promoting some of the things we were learning. In what became the last season of our Family Friendly Fridays, we presented material from Saddleback's "101" new members' class, describing God's purposes for the Church: Reach the lost and grow disciples through a focus on worship, fellowship, discipleship, service, and evangelization. The exhilaration we felt after that first night is easy to remember.

Ironically, or maybe predictably, the numbers attending the program plunged as it became clear this was no longer entertainment or "adult enrichment." Some people were offended; others walked out. Over the course of six weeks, we "grew" the crowd from six hundred down to less than two hundred.

> And if you start challenging churchpeople and seeking lost people, there will be blood.

People at Nativity were not accustomed to being challenged; they didn't want to be challenged. And we were presenting a very challenging message, probably for the first time ever in our parish. This essentially stripped away the façade, so common in churchworld, that our congregation was a group of fully devoted disciples whose Christian formation was complete.

One specific challenge we made was for people to begin serving in the parish ministries and begin caring about the lost, because that is a basic, obvious way consumers start growing as disciples. A few people actually stepped forward. It was disappointing that there were not a lot, but at that point we had no real plan for what we wanted people to do nor any strategy for equipping them to succeed. So that turned out okay. We did convince some parishioners to start greeting people at the church doors, a couple of times a month, and several others to help field questions and provide guest information. They sat in a tent outside the front entrance (because we didn't have any other room for their table). The most frequently asked question they got was, "Why are you sitting in this tent?"

Having heard that some churches were finding Sunday evenings to be a popular service time, we had decided to add it to our schedule. Our 5:30 p.m. Mass became *very* popular, especially with youth and young adults, precisely what we had been hoping for. But it turned out to be a lucky break in a way we didn't even anticipate. The time and the demographic of the crowd provided a safe opportunity to begin trying some new things that we thought might make the experience of our parish more interesting or accessible to people who don't like church.

We tested out new technology, lighting, and other environmental elements we'd never even considered using before. We tried different musical styles. We even started using the homily more intentionally to shape our congregation with challenges we wanted them to consider. We began to offer fellowship and hospitality, as well as programs targeted for youth after the Mass.

When our ideas worked, it was great. When they didn't, the young people were forgiving. Sunday evenings became a workshop for change. In fact, this environment was the place where we began to reshape our church culture, and it quickly grew to become a large and vibrant congregation. We were thrilled with this early success but troubled when we learned that some parishioners were critical of the very effort itself and spoke disparagingly about it behind our backs. Because it wasn't focused on their needs, they resented it.

With a boldness we didn't even realize we were exercising, we completed a modest capital campaign during this period and undertook a small but symbolically significant addition to our church building. It put bricks and mortar to some of our more confirmed ideas: wide open spaces to accommodate crowds, more bathrooms, fellowship areas, a café, even a real "Information Center" in the lobby, an entrance plaza, and, most critically, more parking. And don't overlook this point: We did nothing to our exceptionally austere seventies era sanctuary because we prioritized the guest experience over the architecture. Liturgical decorations might delight churchpeople, but they are of no interest to the dechurched.

After these changes, it was impossible to step onto our campus and not know that this was a deliberately different approach to church-world. "Is this a Catholic church?" is a common question at our information desk from first-time visitors (as well as visiting cynics). We certainly don't want to mask our Catholic identity, but the question doesn't really bother us, we don't want to look like "church as usual."

Here, too, critics lined up to denounce what was accomplished because it wasn't all about them. As one man said of our new café, "I don't need it; I don't want it; and I'm not paying for it."

You might be wondering how we pulled off a successful capital campaign when there was growing unhappiness among many members. We don't really know. We'll call it a "God thing." When you start moving in the direction God is giving, unexpected, unexplainable, and amazing things start unfolding. Our boldness simply won respect among new supporters. Brad Powell, senior pastor of North Ridge Church in Plymouth, Michigan, observed this from a similar trial of his own: The right kind of people, the kind who will become a positive force in the church, ultimately respect a leader who leads by conviction rather than following the whims of people.[4]

We need to be clear that we found great and loyal friends as we moved forward, who worked hard, gave generously, and took bullets for us. We'll never forget their support, and we know we couldn't have done it without them. When you start moving in the right direction, the "right" people start stepping forward.

To officially inaugurate our new approach, during Advent of 2004, we decided to present our first ever congregation-wide message series about where we were going. We wanted to go on the record, so to speak. The homily on that first Sunday of Advent began:

John the Baptist is always the herald of the Christmas season, but his message is not one of comfort and joy. Instead, he is as challenging and chastising as any of the Old Testament prophets. In Luke's gospel, he is telling his contemporaries that it is not enough for them to rely upon the accomplishments of their forefathers. It is not enough for them merely to fulfill the regulations and rituals of their religion. To be people of faith and children of God, to be ready for the advent of the Savior, they've got to be producing good works. They had to change.

We are using the Sundays of Advent to reflect together on our parish, who we are, where we have come from, and where we are going, as a meditation and preparation for the Feast of the Nativity. We're going to start asking the question: "How do we need to change?"

We went on to discuss the history of Catholic churches in our community along the York Road corridor of north Baltimore. It is a sad story of more than a dozen once strong, vibrant communities. Some are now shuttered, some others are simply on life support. We described the changing landscape of churchworld and the dysfunction of many traditional approaches. We talked about the purpose of the Church and what was not the purpose of the Church. We clarified our values. We said:

- We believe the authentic Church of Christ subsists in the Roman Catholic Church: We value our Catholicism.[5]
- We believe the people God has led to Church of the Nativity are God's gift to his Church: We value our people.
- We believe God cares about the people in our community who do not go to church: We value those people too.

- We believe that if you want to be a growing church, and remain a growing church, you've got to be a healthy church. We want to be a growing church: We value health.
- We believe excellence in our programs and services honors God and inspires people: We value excellence.
- We believe that in the service of the Lord, we can always do more: We value that challenge.

We said:

> Church of the Nativity is part of the Body of Christ; Christ is our head, leader, and guide. We are all parts or members of his body and servants of the Lord. We believe that the Lord has given us, in our time and in this place, the job of sharing his name with others. We're not in this church to just meet our needs; we're here to meet that need.

> **We're going to start asking the question: "How do we need to change?"**

Then we waited for the response. It didn't come; there was none. It was like our message had largely fallen on deaf ears. In retrospect, some people didn't understand. A lot of people didn't care (at that point), or simply didn't believe we meant what we were saying. And then, of course, there were the "we were here before you and we'll be here after you're gone" gang. One by one, we would find ourselves in conflict with each of these groups as we moved forward.

The conflict came, not when things were *said*, but when things were *done*. What we did was make church all about who wasn't there and started challenging who *was* there to grow. And what we did brought conflict. Every time we moved forward with this agenda we could absolutely go to the bank that there would be criticism and attack.

Rules of Engagement

Here are some of the tactics our dissatisfied demanding consumers used in their war against us:

- **Indirect assault:** This was gossip and slander often accompanied by passive aggressive resistance. It was more widespread and insidious than we realized at the time.
- **Direct assault:** Usually immediately following Mass, this was the most honest form of complaint; but it was emotionally driven, so it was rarely clear or helpful.
- **E-mail:** Closely related to the direct assault, because it's also based in emotion, this attack was often *more* emotionally charged and therefore even *less* helpful.
- **Letter:** It is one of our axioms that *cards* are good, *letters* are bad. If someone goes to the trouble of writing a letter, nine times out of ten it will be a complaint. Complaint letters are invariably written according to the same template:

  1. The writer presents his credentials ("I've been in this parish for forty years!").
  2. The writer presents his issue.
  3. The writer presents every *other* issue he can think of to attach to his issue, as if there was some sort of pattern he is now exposing.
  4. The writer presents his final assertion that "everybody else" feels exactly the same way. It's just that he alone is courageous enough to speak up. Thus does he elevate his complaint to an act of selfless courage.

Oftentimes we received anonymous letters, which is the same style of letter with the gloves off.

- **Letter-writing campaign:** Here someone organizes others into writing about their issue, so that it really *does* appear that "everyone else" feels the same way.
- **Threat:** Usually this form of attack was the threat of withholding money or withdrawing membership from the parish.
- **Threat of legal action:** On two occasions, unhappy consumers brought the threat of legal action into the exchange. In both cases they relied on attorneys who happened to be relatives, so they were just using cheap scare tactics . . . but they were scary.
- **Complaint to the diocese:** Any of the above could also be accompanied by a complaint to the diocese, but oftentimes, veteran combatants just circumvented us and went right to the top. This approach had several advantages. It put us in our place, guaranteed a response from a high level, inflicted obvious discomfort on us, and raised their complaint to a church-wide issue.

So what were they complaining about? Challenge and change. Changes in the Mass times; changes in the weekend schedule; changes in the music; changes in the sanctuary lighting; changes to the focus and content of the weekend message; changes in anything that impacted them or forced them to change their habits; changes that had nothing to do with them and were none of their business; changes in approach and style for which they didn't have a context or referent.

The changes in church life were unwelcome and even perceived as threats to many parishioners. But beyond any of these particular changes was the biggest change of all: the change in culture we were making, challenging churchpeople and seeking the dechurched. More than any other change, this was the one that provoked many of our churchpeople.

Of course the complaints got packaged differently. We were accused of negligence, incompetence, and malice. Supposed violations of canon law, lack of reverence for the sacraments, and disregard for liturgical rules and rubrics were often cited. And character issues were raised. Most complainers probably didn't really care about any of those things (even if they had been true). Their core complaint was always the same complaint. They were demanding consumers whose expectations were no longer being met. In *From Maintenance to Mission,* Father Robert Rivers writes,

> Organizing a parish for evangeliza-tion—moving it from maintenance to mission—requires systematic change in the way the parish func-tions. Unless the pastoral leadership is capable of effectively producing this change, it will not succeed in carrying out the evange-lizing mission of the church. Moreover, becoming a mis-sionary parish touches all the parish's members. Everyone must change.[7]

> *The organizations that need innovation the most are the ones that do the most to stop it from happening.*
> —Seth Godin[6]

Changing our focus from maintenance to mission was both a lead-ership challenge and a management one. In other words, it was about setting the direction and getting as many people headed in that direc-tion as possible, as well as managing the transition. We did an adequate job with the vision and direction part, but we do not for a moment pretend we managed the transition well. We certainly didn't anticipate the difficulties we encountered, and we continued to be surprised as they kept on coming over the course of several years. One of our team-mates, Sean, came to refer to our office as the "bunker."

To be honest, there was some criticism that was heartfelt and sin-cere, and even helpful. There was criticism we richly deserved, even if we didn't see it that way at the time. Through this process, there were many ways we genuinely messed up, and people had every right to complain.

But most of the time it was just hurtful, and some of it was even hateful. We were wounded by the malicious nature of the attacks: the name-calling, the gossip, the stunning slander. Here are some of the hard lessons we learned.

- Pastorally gifted leaders would have assisted people thoughtfully through the process, and made it less painful for them.
- Emotionally intelligent leaders would have taken it all less personally.
- Spiritually mature leaders would have seen the conflict coming, because Jesus told his followers to expect it.

We were lacking on all these counts, but we kept moving forward. We eventually found it impossible to answer every letter and stopped reading the anonymous ones. We gave up on engaging in every argument, converting every critic, trying to win every battle. We couldn't, and it wouldn't have accomplished anything anyway. We stopped hosting town hall–style meetings, soliciting suggestions, or taking polls. They didn't help. They just stirred up people's emotion and energy to fight on.

Nearly everyone who entered the battle eventually left the parish. Oftentimes their shot was really a parting shot. Sometimes, friends left too. They didn't withdraw out of protest, but because they were sick of the conflict in which they found themselves caught. Those departures were the saddest of all, and we mourned their loss. But truthfully there were others whose exit brought a sigh of relief because it meant at least one less battle.

We do not lightly dismiss the pain and the heartache that friends and foes alike experienced in this transition. We are sorry it had to happen, but we're convinced it did, in fact, *have* to happen. You cannot change a culture without conflict.

Status Quo Vs. the Will of God

Religion is not faith. It is a cultural system that collects faith and belief and then aims at supporting and sustaining them. And, like any cultural system, it is inherently resistant to change. The people in the system have what they want, or at least they have *something* that they want. At some level, it's working for *them* even if it's not working. People believe that what they've got is probably better than the risk and fear that come with change.

Besides, they overlook the distinction between faith and religion, so any change to the religious culture can seem like an attack on their faith. The status quo gets confused with the will of God. Challenging or changing anything in churchworld is equated with challenging or changing God! The attacks we experienced were sometimes so vicious because people thought they were defending their faith . . . when, in fact, they were defending the culture of their religion.

> The status quo gets confused with the will of God.

Father Michael: There was so much conflict, and it became so acrimonious and protracted, that I eventually got into therapy. In our very first session, we reviewed some of the specific complaints and the therapist asked me, "Did you really say that parish growth comes through *attrition* as well as *addition*?" Yes I did, and unfortunately—it does.

The Real War

We don't want to overly dramatize our experience, nor demonize the opposition. But, there is another reality at work here as well that should not be ignored and must be anticipated: spiritual warfare. The devil is real, and he really *is* our enemy. The Bible says, "Be sober and vigilant. Your opponent the devil is prowling around like a roaring lion looking for someone to devour" (1 Peter 5:8).

Satan is a major figure throughout the gospels, constantly working against Jesus and stirring up trouble for him. The same is true for the early Church, and they knew it. They understood the reality of their situation.

> Put on the armor of God so that you may be able to stand firm against the tactics of the devil. For our struggle is not with flesh and blood but with the principalities, with the powers, with the world rulers of this present darkness, with the evil spirits in the heavens. (Ephesians 6:11–12)

The Church of Christ is the most powerful force on the planet, and Jesus has already promised that evil, and all its armies, cannot prevail over it. But they'll try. And knowing that, believing it, and preparing for it, will help you arm yourself for the battle ahead.

If you get into the disciple-making business, you will be attacked for it. Attacks will come in many guises, designed to distract you, discourage you, demoralize you, and dissuade you. But you must understand that ultimately the attacks are from the evil one.

It's a spiritual battle. It shouldn't be denied or ignored, but it's nothing to be afraid of either. In fact, it can be confirmation that you're on the right track (not to mention the winning team). Fight this battle on your knees, and you'll win.

Then war broke out in heaven; Michael and his angels bat-
tled against the dragon. The dragon and its angels fought
back, but they did not prevail and there was no longer any
place for them in heaven. (Revelation 12:7–8)

5

PRETTY CHURCHES AND OTHER LIES

Christianity without discipleship is always
Christianity without Christ.

—Dietrich Bonhoeffer[1]

When we came to Nativity it was clear the purpose of the place had become maintenance of the status quo: meeting members wherever they were to help them comfortably stay there. Nativity enabled and even encouraged members to remain demanding consumers, and we ignored everybody else.

Nativity was sinking into irrelevance because we had no vision for reaching the lost and no plan for the spiritual growth and maturity of our members. There was no understanding of even the need for life-change, much less how to effect it.

Avery Dulles proposed that the most fitting description of the Church is the "community of disciples."[2] Respectfully, we would add that implicit in Cardinal Dulles's use of the word "disciple" is the word "growing." The purpose of Nativity is to challenge churchpeople and seek lost people in order to help all of them become a community of growing disciples. Disciples are students who are growing to love God and love others as Jesus taught us.

- It's not about a place; it's about a person.
- It's not about fulfilling obligations or simply supplying the sacraments; it's about following a person on a path.
- It's not about programs or services, or even service; it's about steps along that path of growth.[3]

In other words, it's about conversion and then ongoing conversion. A disciple is growing beyond the sin and the self-defeating behaviors that go with being lost and then beyond the selfishness of consumer religion. A disciple willingly sets out on a path of more and more dying to sin and selfishness so that Christ may live in him or her. That is going to involve action.

Pastor Erwin McManus makes a good point about the fifth book of the New Testament where the Church in its first, purest, and most heroic expression is described. Think about it. It's called *Acts*. They acted; they did things.[4] Specifically, they did what the Lord told them to do. What's that?

> Christianity is not a monument or a museum. It's a movement. It's got to move.

1. **Disciples Love God**

And they do it in the three ways. In Matthew 22:37, Jesus tells us, "You shall love the Lord your God with all your heart, with all your soul, and with your all your mind."

This is a specific strategy. Our minds hold our thoughts and direct our feelings. Our hearts hold our feelings and direct our lives. Our souls hold our lives and direct our destinies. What we worship shapes our thinking, feeling, and living. A disciple is set on displacing the idols of false worship—money, power, pleasure, sex—and restoring God to his proper place. Our thinking, feeling, and being are more and more engaged in a relationship with him.

As Catholics, the Eucharist is "the source and summit" of our Christian life and worship because it is Christ himself. Disciples bring a "full, active participation" to the Eucharistic celebration each week (we'll be talking more about that in subsequent chapters). But "source" and "summit" necessarily mean there has got to be something in between.

Disciples match corporate worship in church with daily quiet time. Disciples are growing in the love of God's word in scripture, obediently spending time there to learn it and learn to hunger for it. Daily Mass, Eucharistic adoration, the Liturgy of the Hours, Marian devotion, especially the Rosary, and regular disciplines of Confession, penance, giving, and fasting can be serious tools for the mature disciple. On the other hand, a few minutes alone with God each day, away from texting and technology, can be a great place to start.

2. **Disciples Love People**

Jesus also commanded, "You shall love your neighbor as yourself" in Matthew 22:39. To love your neighbor *as* yourself, you've got to, well—*love* yourself. Disciples love themselves not by indulging themselves, but rather by taking care of themselves.

Jesus invested time in his own self-care. Time and again in the gospels he withdraws from the crowds and even from his friends for quiet time alone. There he refreshes himself and renews his relationship with the Father. Obviously he pours himself into the lives of others, but only after he allows himself to be filled up. That's the example disciples follow.

While modern society pushes people to their limits, disciples preserve margin in their schedules. Because it is in the margins that rest and refreshment are found and relationships happen. Disciples accept the responsibility to care for themselves in other ways, too, building the energy and resources they need to live as God commands. Physical exercise and good nutrition are part of the process. A weaning away from self-defeating habits like alcohol abuse, nicotine addiction, anger mismanagement, and bad behaviors like gossip, profanity, or pornography, are what disciples do too. As Matthew Kelly aptly sums it up, what we're talking about is a lifestyle change.[5]

Our self-care is preparatory to loving one another. The Church we read about in the Acts of the Apostles was so attractive precisely because they loved one another in a selfless, wholehearted way. And Jesus promises that love like that will be the definitive identification of his followers (cf. John 13:35). It is the most evident fruit of the Holy Spirit and powerful proof of the truth of the message we preach. As Rick Warren says, if congregations actually love one another, "you'll have to lock the doors to keep people out."[6]

Disciples love others beginning with those closest to them each day: their families first of all, but also their co-workers and friends. Their love also finds expression in a specific local church family where they make a commitment and stick to it. People who drift from parish to parish are sometimes just playing games with God and avoiding their real responsibility when it comes to giving and service.

Loving one another is about patience, kindness, and gentleness (cf. Ephesians 4:2), as well as care for others that takes the form of ministry (cf. John 15:12), as we'll be discussing in later chapters. Eventually their love reaches out to everybody they meet, and it finds expression in service and mission.

3. **Disciples Make Disciples**

From the beginning, the whole pattern for *being* a disciple is *making* disciples. When Jesus called the first disciples, he made a single promise to them: They'd be disciple makers (cf. Matthew 4:19). That's what they did and that's what disciples always do. The

Church is in the disciple making business, because we live our faith and grow in our faith by sharing our faith.

Where to Start?

Step #1. Define your mission field.

In Catholic culture, the basic organization of the Universal Church is in "parishes," a term used to indicate a very specific geographical designation. Making disciples of all nations is the mission of the Universal Church, but each diocese and each parish has been given a piece of that mission, a geographical location to help follow and fulfill the mission. We aren't here simply to serve the congregation; we're here to reach those who live within the parish.

Most of our parish at Nativity is in the 21093 zip code (Timonium, Maryland). That's our mission field. It's our job to fulfill the Great Commission in 21093. God has given us this specific locale to reach the lost and to make disciples.

In 21093, there are about 15,000 households, probably 45,000–50,000 people. At this point 8,000 of those people are connected (however loosely) to our church. For purposes of discussion let's be generous and posit that perhaps another 16,000 belong to one of the several other Christian churches in our community. Let's be extremely generous and assume another 8,000 are attending church outside

> *Then Jesus approached and said to them, "All power in heaven and on earth has been given to me. Go therefore, and make disciples of all nations."*
> —Matthew 28:18–19

the zip code. It doesn't matter how you count it, it comes out the same. There are tens of thousands of dechurched people in our zip code. They are the potential disciples in our mission field.

> **Step #2. Describe the "lost" in your mission field.**

Catholic parishes shouldn't have any problem with the "where." But they do have a problem with the "who."

The "scandal of the particularity" is an idea in theology that a particular person (Jesus of Nazareth) has universal significance. God is eternal and therefore not limited to the temporal world. Humans, however, are. For this reason Christ chose a specific point in history and place on the planet in which to redeem us. It doesn't seem fair, but it's how the Incarnation worked. God began his work of saving all people at a defined place and time with some particular people.

> We aren't here simply to serve the congregation; we're here to reach those who live within the parish.

Perhaps the single biggest obstacle to getting started in making disciples is the resistance to getting specific. It doesn't seem fair. But it's how discipleship works. Lifting a page out of Rick Warren's book, *Purpose Driven Church*, we define the lost we are trying to reach in a highly detailed way.

We're looking for Tim . . . "Timonium Tim." Tim is the quintessential lost person in our mission field. Tim is a good guy. If you met Tim at a party, a likely place to run into him, you'd like him. He's educated, well dressed, and successful at what he does. Tim is married with children. He has a beautiful home and a comfortable lifestyle. He drives a nice car.

Tim works hard all week and likes to take the weekends off. On Sunday mornings Tim is on the golf course or on game days at the Baltimore Raven's stadium. Wherever he is, he's definitely not in church; he's never in church, except maybe for a wedding or a funeral. The idea doesn't even occur to him. Tim is culturally Catholic, the product of a parish religious education program or a parochial school. But Tim is definitely not a believer.

His background in the faith is actually more of a liability than an asset because it brings emotional baggage, theological misconceptions, and, perhaps, legitimate complaints. God, faith, church, religion, and *The Da Vinci Code* are all mixed up together in Tim's imagination; and, taken as a whole, the mix is inscrutable. Maybe Tim has formed an attitude of indifference, but, more likely, it's cynicism or contempt. If he's divorced, the situation is further complicated by laws he doesn't understand that seem to judge him unfairly. And he may have a host of other reasons he's mad at the Church.

Tim's a good guy, but he's doing life on his own terms, and, increasingly, it isn't working out so well for him. He's got stress at work and tension and conflict at home. He has financial obligations that are oppressive and credit card debt that is getting out of control. And there are other issues too, like anger, depression, maybe addiction to alcohol, gambling, or pornography. Tim needs purpose; he needs direction; he needs *a savior*.

> We're looking for Tim ... "Timonium Tim."

We actually refer to Tim in our planning meetings and prepare homilies with him in mind. We make programming decisions and even select music based on what he likes, what he'll understand, what works for him. To make Tim a disciple we not only have to know him, we have to speak to him, engage him, and then get him involved. But most of all, we have to love him.

And countless times, after people have come back to church, they've said to us, "I'm Timonium Tim."

Why Tim? How about everybody else out there? Of course we're trying to reach Tim's family and friends, too. But we believe Tim is essential to getting them in the door and keeping them engaged. We're convinced that if we can get Tim on the discipleship path, his wife will happily join him and his kids have a far better shot of staying active through their teen and adult years.

From everything we've been able to observe in parish life, that's exactly how it works. When the Dad takes his role as spiritual leader seriously, families seem to live more God-honoring lives and successfully raise young disciples. On the other hand, when men abdicate this sacred responsibility, or leave it solely for their wives to fulfill, many areas of family life suffer and the family unit can more easily fragment. The children are much more likely to drop out of church if Dad does first. While respectfully recognizing single moms who heroically shoulder the responsibility alone, most of the families in our community are two parent households. So for us, focusing on Tim isn't forgetting about his family; it's raising up a leader for them.

Tim also has more dechurched friends than our members do, so he has the greatest potential to be our next best spokesman out in the community. Tim has access and credibility that we don't have among Catholics who have walked away from the Church in north Baltimore.

Tim is in Timonium, so he's not who *you're* looking for. But there is a specific someone in your community whom you can design your evangelization strategy around. Define his background, his interests, his education, his motivations, his fears, why he doesn't come to Church, and what he chooses to do instead.

Step #3. Design a simple, specific invitation strategy.

Evangelization, as we have noted, has an internal focus (aimed at the people in the pews) and an external one (the people not yet in the pews). The first tends to trump the second. That's why we refer to our internal focus as "discipleship" and reserve the word "evangelization" for outreach. Furthermore, we have become convinced that to make missional evangelization, that is outwardly focused on the dechurched, a dynamic reality in our parish, it must become a *specific* reality.

It has been amazing to us how many of our parishioners struggle with the concept of evangelization, and how much of a stretch it is for them culturally and emotionally. That discovery has led us to the conclusion that evangelization has to be presented in a simple, specific, and consistent way. And it must be vigorously maintained as the number one parish priority. We need to teach evangelization in a crystal clear way and make it a constant theme of our preaching, woven throughout the messages throughout the year. And, at least once a year, we find that we must reintroduce it all over again, as if for the first time. Preaching it once won't work, and preaching it once in a while won't work either. We try to keep evangelization front and center by regularly placing it in the Prayer of the Faithful at Mass and talking about it in the announcements. We plan and rigorously evaluate all our weekend efforts from the perspective and priority of evangelization. And when it comes to Christmas and Easter we turn our preparation and celebrations into church-wide evangelization campaigns.

We define evangelization as a parishioner inviting "Tim" to church on the weekend or to online campus where we live stream on Sundays (more about that later). We try to keep it as simple as that. Our basic strategy is "invest and invite"—a phrase we picked up from Pastor Andy Stanley.[7]

We encourage people to be on the lookout for and get to know lost people in their kids' sports programs, through the Home School Association, or at work. Pray for them; spend time with them; even consider fasting for them. Look for other ways to sacrifice for them, too. At Nativity, we ask our disciples to give up pew space at optimum times, park off campus, and walk to church so Tim has no trouble finding a parking spot or a seat.

Disciples bring their faith into everyday relationships. They are people of character and courtesy and so many other qualities that shine out and wordlessly influence potential disciples. When words are welcome, disciples share their story of conversion and how their faith works for them. And then, when the opportunity arises, and it always does, disciples invite potential disciples to church. During our new member orientation, we gather information on how new members have found their way to us. Nearly *all* the newcomers to our church in recent years (700 this past year alone) have come to us from dechurched backgrounds because of a personal invitation.

> Our basic strategy is "invest and invite."

Matthew Kelly organizes his approach in four steps: (1) nurture friendships; (2) pray for the people you're trying to reach; (3) share your own life-changing story; (4) invite your friend to church.[8] Essentially, it's the same method Jesus used. When Andrew and John first met him and wondered who he was and what he was up to, he didn't make a case for his mission; he didn't even get into his message. He didn't tell them everything that was ahead and what would be required of them. He simply said, "Come, and you will see" (cf. John 1:39).

What Doesn't Make Disciples

Once we get Tim in the door, we've got a shot at getting him and his family on the path of discipleship. But before we describe that path, we want to be honest and go ahead and admit what *didn't* make disciples at Nativity, which would be *most* of what we had been doing and *much* of what we had initially held as values.

1. **Just Showing Up**

   Attendance at church is no measurement of discipleship. However impressive our Mass count, it doesn't mean we're making disciples. A perceptive pastor we know quips, "My church sleeps eight hundred."

2. **Looking for Magic**

   Nativity was a sacramental machine: Mass every day, twice a day in Advent and Lent, and eight times each weekend, baptisms, confessions, weddings, funerals, daily devotions, anointing, and adoration. It's all good stuff, it's how some Catholics grow spiritually. For others, it's what they do *instead* of grow. And sometimes it can begin to look like magic. Many mistakenly think, "If I just work it long enough I'll earn what I'm after: a spouse, a job, successful surgery, kids who *finally* listen to me, eternal life."

   For certain, the sacraments give us grace to put us in right relationship with God and his life in our soul, nourishing and strengthening us for our discipleship walk. But they're not meant to replace it.

   Daily Mass serves as a great example of the false thinking here. Some of the people who attend Mass everyday are saints and serious disciples. Others are surely headed in that direction, but not necessarily so. In fact, in our experience at Nativity some daily Mass goers were isolated from parish life, and seemed quite selfish in their attitude toward the parish. In an unexpected way, these people were actually the ultimate consumers because they were consuming the most, while giving the least.

- It's the guy who shows up at Confession every week (but never in his own parish) to confess the exact same sins he fully intends to return to in the week ahead.
- It's the lady who stealthily stuffs the pew pockets full of leaflets promising wonders and cures if you'll just join her in praying wacky prayers before passing them on with similar promises.
- It's the couple that buries St. Joseph statues (upside down) all over the back yard to try and sell their house at asking price (they have kits on the Internet for as low as $9.95; you get the statue, complete with burial instructions and a body bag).

No wonder there are Christians who think Catholicism is a cult. Magic doesn't make disciples.

3. **Knowing Stuff**

> **Father Michael:** When I was in college I had several math and science core courses I had to fulfill in order to graduate. When I finally finished those requirements, I vowed I would never again go near anything resembling those subjects. I didn't much like them to begin with, and I had been schooled to hate them.

We found that many people in our community are like that when it comes to their Catholic faith. They've been educated in Catholic schools for years, and they have been exposed to a lot of content. But we have become convinced that for more than a few of them, this experience reduced Christianity to a school subject, which they had to take and did not like. And once they got out of school, they were done with it.

Unfortunately, the same was true for our religious ed program. At Nativity, after kids figured out school wasn't fun (at about third grade) and parents got what they came for (First Communion), the resistance grew and the class numbers dropped. Typically fourth grade had half as many students as second grade—a not uncommon reality in many parishes. If a kid actually made it through Confirmation, without learning to resent us, the angels rejoiced. But that was definitely the end of the line. As in so many other places Confirmation became graduation because it was often the last time we saw our young people.

By the way, in our community we've found that the graduates of our Catholic schools and religious education programs often walk away with a remarkably superficial understanding of Catholicism and a profound ignorance of scripture. Not to mention that many of them don't know the Lord in a personal way. Disciples are students, and they're life-long learners, going deeper than just mastering content.

Knowledge is important. Paul teaches us to be transformed by the renewal of our minds, to let the truth in to change us, to reshape us, to move us to a new place (Romans 12:2). We need to have the right brain food to change. But knowledge alone cannot be our goal. As St. Paul also teaches, knowledge of God without love is nothing (cf. 1 Corinthians 13:2).

> It's amazing how much you don't know about a game you've been playing all your life.
> —Mickey Mantle[9]

The biblical idea of knowledge goes much deeper than just cerebral understanding. It implies intimacy. To know in biblical terms means we really experience something in our hearts as well as our heads. In all aspects of our personhood, it is knowledge that leads to love, while love, in turn, makes us want to know more. Transformation and life-change must be the goals of discipleship, and simply sharing knowledge doesn't make disciples.

4. **Obeying Rules/Fulfilling Obligations**

Obsession with religious rules and liturgical rubrics, or policing your pastor to make sure he's as obsessive-compulsive as you are about them, won't make disciples, just Pharisees.

In fact, an exclusive or excessive focus on the fulfillment of rules and obligations cultivates a deep sense of consumerism. Rule-focused churchpeople form the impression that they've done *their* part; now you owe them. When parishioners say to you, "I've been a good Catholic all my life," it's often a preamble to what you owe them as a result of their rule keeping.

5. **Hanging around Church**

You don't become more like Jesus simply hosting or participating in lots of church programs. There were plenty of churchpeople at Nativity who spent all their time at church and whose characters were never transformed into Christ's character. Not incidentally, their personal and family lives were oftentimes deeply dysfunctional.

Likewise, being in the Knights of Columbus or the Rosary Society is great, but it's not, in itself, discipleship. In fact, sometimes membership in these para-church organizations becomes a substitute for active church membership—an excuse for not going on Sunday, getting involved in parish life, or even actually belonging to a specific parish.

6. **Self-Serving Service**

The best example of this non-discipleship making activity in our experience was the money counters. Every Sunday, more or less the same group of guys gathered for coffee, donuts, gossip, to complain about us, and to get a peek into what everyone was or wasn't giving. It wasn't discipleship; it was a men's club.

7. **Trading Money for Influence**

Usually you think of contributors as supporters, but we have seen people use money to try to get us to do things they want us to do or stop doing things they want us to stop doing. Bribery is not discipleship and its not stewardship either.

8. **Making the Donuts**

Discipleship is not just about going through the motions of doing church, however faithfully the motions are undertaken. Some of you will remember the old commercial for Dunkin' Donuts where the haggard baker wakes up and mumbles, "Time to make the donuts," then shuffles off zombie-like to work. When we first came here there was a very low-energy staff person who always greeted everyone on Sunday mornings with a similarly mournful lament. Others at Nativity shared this lack of vision, had no direction, and just completed tasks over and over again, days without end.

9. **Building Pretty Churches**

A recent article in a national publication detailed the plan of a pastor to dismantle an entire church building in one part of the country and reassemble it in another part of the country, at an estimated cost of $12 million. The building is strikingly beautiful but now shuttered.

The assumption implicit in his plan is that the building he is moving will make disciples. It's a lie, it won't. It didn't where it was (that's why it's empty and for sale), and it won't in a new location. This pastor is in a fast growing part of the country, so he won't have any trouble filling it at first, but his pretty building won't make disciples.

Most pastors want to build or renovate a church. It is the easiest project for which to raise money, and the most gratifying to accomplish. But beautiful churches don't make disciples. If they did, Europe would be filled with them.

The pastor and martyr Dietrich Bonhoeffer expressed in a classic and unforgettable way the distinction between mere church goers in pretty Churches and true disciples.

> Cheap grace is the deadly enemy of our Church. . . .
>
> Cheap grace means grace sold on the market . . . . The sacraments, the forgiveness of sin, and the consolations of religion are thrown away at cut prices. Grace is represented as the Church's inexhaustible treasury, from which she showers blessings with generous hands, without asking questions or fixing limits. Grace without price; grace without cost! . . . Cheap grace is the grace we bestow on ourselves.
>
> Cheap grace is the preaching of forgiveness without requiring repentance, baptism without church discipline, Communion without confession . . . . Cheap grace is grace without discipleship, grace without the cross, grace without Jesus Christ, living and incarnate. . . .
>
> Costly grace is the Gospel, which must be sought again and again, the gift which must be asked for, the door at which a man must knock. Such grace is costly because it calls us to follow, and it is grace because it calls us to follow Jesus Christ. It is costly because it costs a man his life, and it is grace because it gives a man the only true life. It is costly because it condemns sin, and grace because it justifies the sinner. Above all, it is costly because it cost God the life of his Son.[10]

So What?

Okay, so how do you reach lost people and set them on the path of discipleship? Where do you begin to grow disciples? That's what the rest of this book is about.

And it all starts just where you'd expect. You see . . .

Part III:

DEVELOPING
THE STRATEGY

6

"IT'S THE WEEKEND, STUPID!"

Among the many activities of a parish, "none is as vital or as community-forming as the Sunday celebration of the Lord's Day."

—BLESSED JOHN PAUL II[1]

Father Michael: Last summer I joined a large group of extended family and friends at the beach. There were, on and off, about twenty-five to thirty of us. Come Sunday morning, some slept in, some worked out, two went running, one read the newspaper and watched the Sunday-morning talk shows. Most of the group undertook an obligatory annual ritual of pancakes at Uncle Andy's Pancake House.

Want to know what this crowd of mostly Irish- and Italian-American, largely parochial school educated, cradle Catholics did *not* do? Go to church.

You might wonder what I did about this dechurched epiphany in the heart of my own family? I breathed a sigh of relief. Thank goodness they didn't go to church, at least to the parish church in this town. I know what I'm talking about. I went.

Back in the day, this church would have been mobbed on summer Sunday mornings. Not any more. There were plenty of empty seats. And, the congregation was old, old, old.

At the door a grumpy usher grunted at me. Everyone else avoided eye contact and ignored me. More than most churches in my experience, this congregation exuded a huge "us versus them" culture (which seems ironic given that they're in a resort community). A hundred little details (the devotional prayers insiders prayed before Mass that the rest of us didn't know or the weird way they passed the offertory basket) underscored for me as a visitor that I did not belong.

There was no opening hymn, because the organist hadn't shown up on time. The organ was in the sanctuary, so you could see she wasn't there, and you could also see when our luck ran out and she did show up (during the homily). When the music came, it was old school stuff which everyone knows (and no one likes). Nobody sang or even pretended to try, except the organist herself who also served as a kind of Wagnerian cantor (she definitely didn't need that mike). And she seemed fine with the "no one else is singing but me" part; really, she did.

The lector read the readings in a way that convinced me he'd never laid eyes on them before. The celebrant was not the pastor, but some other priest who did not bother to introduce himself. He sort of assumed we knew who he was, but it didn't matter. Who he was or what he had to say seemed deeply irrelevant to the assembly. As became clear, he was a visiting missionary, there to raise funds for his mission, though he never told us a single thing about it.

He began, "Your pastor loves you, so he told me not to talk for more than five minutes."

The fellow in front of me replied in only a half-whisper, "If he really loved us, he'd tell you to shut up." The preacher then proceeded to quote a different gospel than the one we'd just heard, which is usually a clear indication of a canned talk. It quickly became obvious that was exactly what we were hearing. Next he told a string of groan-inducing jokes and then turned on the guilt about hungry children. (Maybe he helped feed kids somewhere).

At the same time ushers were handing out pledge cards to relieve the guilt and support the mission. Instructions for filling out the cards took up the rest of the homily (it turned out to be twice the length promised). Here's the thing: Virtually no one paid any attention. They stared at the ceiling, the stared at the floor, they talked to one another, they gave a glance to the card then dropped it on the floor, but they paid no attention to the presentation, and, as far as I could see, no one actually made a pledge.

Then we powered through the rest of the Mass as if the building was on fire. When I returned to my seat from Communion, almost the entire section I was seated in was gone. Finally the remaining faithful were inundated with a string of announcements, which were actually, unbelievably, more fundraising appeals, this time for the parish itself.

At the dismissal, instead of some charge to go in peace and serve the Lord or announce the Gospel, the celebrant says, "Don't forget, at the beach, it's always Happy Hour." Really? Did you just give them permission to start drinking?

Why would I want any of my dechurched family members to have set aside their various weekend activities to witness this gathering of the Body of Christ? The last place I would want to reintroduce them to worship was this half empty church for a half-hearted exercise in fund raising and a full miss when it comes to what the Christian community is supposed to be about when it assembles.

Meanwhile, just down the street at Uncle Andy's Pancake House, enthusiastic crowds formed a waiting line that snaked all the way around the block. Hmmm . . . Uncle Andy's got pancakes. We've got the living Word of God. What's wrong with this picture?

Your Number One Opportunity

In his book, *Amusing Ourselves to Death,* Neil Postman criticizes the newscaster who invites us to "tune in again tomorrow night!" after sharing a half hour of murder and mayhem. Postman asks, "What for?"[2] More bad news? Why should people come to church or come *back* to church if their experience week after week is unhelpful, or maybe even offensive? Who could blame them for finding other things to do?

A national campaign invites non-practicing Catholics to "come home." But what in the world are they coming home to? If it's more of the irrelevant experience that drove them away to begin with, we could be doing more harm than good.

The weekend experience is the number one opportunity for people in the community to connect with church. And almost everyone who actually does come in contact with the parish does so on the weekend.

In that brief time, they will decide if it's worth it to come back or not. If the experience is boring and bad, then they won't.

And yet, in our parish here in Timonium, very little time or attention was given to the weekend. Even after we had come to understand our mission and made significant progress in moving forward with a disciplined strategy to fulfill it, we still didn't get this point. We continued to treat the weekend as an afterthought; the music was whatever the musicians felt like playing; the celebrants determined the weekend messages; and, especially telling, most of our staff took weekends off. We were too busy Monday through Friday to worry about Sunday.

And worse than just ignoring it ourselves, we also gave our weekends away. Requests to use our pulpit to raise money for missions or special collections, or anything else, were always favorably received and gladly given (it was less work for us). Really, anybody could show up in our lobby and make it all about them and their deal: the Girl Scouts sold cookies, the youth group sold cakes, the Knights of Columbus solicited new members, and the Ladies Club promoted their fashion show. And of course, whatever they were doing inevitably involved plastering promotional posters on the front doors and annoying people with announcements after Communion. Additionally, on any given weekend, groups from outside the parish might be hosting *their* events on *our* campus: We even had a children's theatre company trooping through for a while, because it was easy additional income. All of this was diverting attention and energy from what should have been our focus.

> We just decided to stop doing a lot of things we had been doing and instead concentrate on the weekend.

One of the most important strategic decisions we made was to declare war on distractions and focus our staff and resources on the weekend—from the perspective of *lost people*. We just decided to stop doing a lot of things we had been doing and instead concentrate on the weekend. In an adaptation of James Carville's famous assessment of the 1992 election, "It's the economy, Stupid!" we've come to rely on Pastor Ed Young's axiom, "It's the weekend, Stupid!"[3]

Blessed Pope John Paul II very simply taught that the Eucharist builds the Church.[4] The Church is formed and grows through the Eucharist, and mature Catholics understand what they are giving and what they are given in the Eucharist. They rightly hold the Eucharist as the "gift par excellence."[5] In it, they are nourished and grow as disciples.

"The Eucharist is 'the sum and summary of our faith,'" says Pope Benedict XVI.

> The Church's faith is essentially a Eucharistic faith, and it is especially nourished at the table of the Eucharist. . . . For this reason, the Sacrament of the Altar is always at the heart of the Church's life: "thanks to the Eucharist, the Church is reborn ever anew!" The more lively the Eucharistic faith of the People of God, the deeper is its sharing in ecclesial life in the steadfast commitment to the mission entrusted by Christ to his disciples.[6]

But let's be honest. Many of the people coming to church these days do not understand the Eucharist and are simply not engaged in it. And all the cultural Catholics in our community, who aren't even showing up, have simply walked away from the Eucharist entirely. They have tuned the Church out, and no matter how beautifully or faithfully we celebrate the Eucharist—and we should celebrate it beautifully and faithfully—it's not getting them back. The sad irony we have found in discussion with former Catholics, who have decamped to evangelical churches, is their nearly uniform explanation, "I just felt like I wasn't being fed."

To begin to reverse this situation in our community, we started looking beyond the Liturgy of the Eucharist to the elements of the weekend experience that could have the greatest impact on the dechurched and those new to the discipleship path. We have been criticized and mischaracterized on this point so we want to be clear. The Eucharist is central to our parish and our weekend worship. What we are talking about is simply acknowledging where people are, *meeting* them where they are *in order* to lead them more effectively and successfully into a fuller appreciation and celebration of the Eucharist. We were going to start focusing on the weekend from the perspective of lost people.

What does that mean? Basically, it's about just a few things. In this chapter we'll discuss the two that will impact your guests first. Get them right and you'll be shaping a great weekend experience.

Music Is Water

Focusing on the weekend from the perspective of lost people means . . . "It's the Music!" The weekend experience should be a form of transportation, taking the participant on an emotional, intellectual, and ultimately spiritual journey to the higher things of God. The United States Conference of Catholic Bishops' *Sing to the Lord* says,

> God has bestowed upon his people the gift of song. God dwells within each human person, in the place where music takes its source. Indeed, God, the giver of song, is present whenever his people sing his praises. A cry from

It wasn't that complicated. We just took a hard-nosed look at what we were doing and decided to focus entirely on those few things we knew we could do better than anyone else, not getting distracted into arenas that would feed our egos and at which we could not be the best.
—Wells Fargo Executive[7]

deep within our being, music is a way for God to lead us to
the realm of higher things.[8]

We like to say that music is the water on which the experience sails.
"Music does what words alone cannot do. It is capable of expressing a
dimension of meaning and feeling that words alone cannot convey."[9]
More than any other element in the church's weekend experience, it
is the music that can touch and change people's hearts—for better or
for worse. Historically at Nativity, music was a huge problem.

As is typical in many places, the program included some musical
options: three weekend Masses were designated as "cantor and organ,"
one as "choir," one "folk," and, blessedly, one was "quiet." The folk
Mass was far and away more popular than the other musical choices,
perhaps because it was easiest to listen to or the easiest to tune out.
The group tried their best, but they struggled. Their presentation was
flawed and the music they played was dated and uninteresting. At the
other masses, the music was worse—far, far worse.

Many of the choir members were more convinced of their own
skills than they had reason to be and their accumulated sound was
grievous. Most of the cantors were prima donnas in clear performance
mode. The organist was a wonderful person who struggled mightily
with a poorly designed organ. Traditional hymns, as well as more
recent additions to the compendium of sacred music, were simply
slaughtered Mass after Mass, week after week. And no one sang, and
we really mean *no one*! If someone sang, you knew they were a visitor
and everyone stared at them until they shut up or went away. Not
surprisingly, on some weekends the most popular weekend Mass was
the one without music.

Early on, we had a town hall meeting to listen to the range of concerns we had inherited. While most people were generally apathetic
toward the parish, that evening turned into a virtual riot of bitter
complaint all about the music. And we had to agree with much of

what was said. They were right. We had terrible music, and it made the weekend experience terrible. And that made people angry.

Want to know what we did about the problem? Absolutely nothing. We didn't want to hurt anybody's feelings (if you don't count the parishioners as anybody), so we did nothing for two years. Then, when we just couldn't endure it anymore, when even *we* didn't want to come to our church to listen to this noise, we dared to do the unthinkable: We talked to the musicians. We sat down with our musicians and actually started a conversation with them about music. Unfortunately, but not surprisingly, they were deeply resistant to our interventions, and we found it painful even to try to move forward.

Eventually we hired a "music director," which felt like a huge step, because we were raising the program to a "professional" level, and, more importantly, we could hand the whole problem off to him. It didn't work. The guy was a brilliant talent who seemed hell-bent on overwhelming our parishioners in a style of music we came to call "dissonant and difficult." He resisted and resented our requests. "I'm not a jukebox," he'd snap and hold the preferences of the congregation in contempt. And far from taking care of our problems, his direction seemed to magnify the drama. A parting of the ways was inevitable, but it took us *another* two years to face that additional pain and do what we had to do.

> Not surprisingly, on some weekends the most popular weekend Mass was the one without music.

Speaking only from our own experience, a big problem with church music was the musicians themselves. More than a few of the professionals were high maintenance individuals. Some of them came at a high price, had more than a little trouble staying within their budgets, and did not work well with others. Sometimes they sported the cynical attitude, "I will do what I want to do, and you will pay me for it." The volunteer musicians could hold an even *bigger* sense of entitlement and be more demanding. Either way, the music program was all about the musicians. We can easily remember the discomfort we felt one Fourth of July weekend when the new music director played on and on through a "French atonal" Communion meditation (don't worry if you don't know what that is, we didn't either; just think merciless). Meanwhile the parishioners who actually stayed anxiously checked their watches while they waited to get to the pool or their holiday cookouts. It was a complete cultural disconnect.

Bad to Worse

But it wasn't all their fault by any means. We were to blame too, because when it came to music, like so many things, we didn't know what we were doing anyway. We just kept wandering through a desert of bad choices as we tried to find our way forward. In our lack of understanding, we actually made the music program more difficult and labor intensive than it already was. Many Catholic churches in our region of the country have two styles of worship music, the "guitar Mass" and the "organ Mass." Recently it seems that many mainline Protestant churches have also taken up the practice of providing options. Signs outside more traditional style churches now commonly announce the addition of a "contemporary" service in addition to the "traditional" service, presumably to attract newcomers without alienating regulars. Good luck to them, because different musical programs start making things complicated. Believe us, we know. In what turned out to be, hands down, the dumbest idea we ever had, we took the "options" idea and *expanded* it.

Father Michael: This was such a bad idea I'm still embarrassed to discuss it. We developed what I absurdly called a "menu of musical options." This was an unbelievably transparent effort to pander to demanding customers, with not just two or three but *four* distinct musical programs at different liturgies every weekend. For a period of time we offered a "choral Mass" with vested choir and classical choral musical offerings, and a "traditional" Mass with more standard organ hymns. Then there was something we called "familiar contemporary," which was folk music, and "current contemporary," which was Gather-style music.

Maybe it's not necessarily a bad thing to have different musical options in your setting. Maybe. But we doubt it. In our experience different options created competing systems. These systems were in competition for limited resources and shared space, and created logistical problems from Mass to Mass. Most consequentially, they divided the congregation along the fault lines of musical preferences.

It was another exercise in consumerism. And, like all such efforts, it was actually counterproductive to growth efforts because newcomers don't base their attendance on musical styles but on service times. If they don't like the music at the time they prefer, they go elsewhere or give up. We wanted an effective music program, but we had no conception about what that meant.

Father Michael: I approached the music program armed mostly with my own preferences and predispositions. I love classical music and, in church, choral music. We had an extraordinarily gifted choir director here for a while who fielded a world-class men and boys choir, and I loved it. I just couldn't get anybody else to want it. Hopefully there will always be a place for such music, but at that point Nativity needed a different approach.

Our original cantors had a slender repertoire of ubiquitous fare: "Gather Us In" and, of course, "Mass of Creation." The folk group liked the familiar old folk music they grew up with in the 1960s and '70s like "Let There Be Peace on Earth" and "They'll Know We are Christians By Our Love." Meanwhile, if you asked the average person in the pew at that time what they wanted, they would have provided a very simple and specific list of easy listening music with a sentimental bent: "Ave Maria," "On Eagle's Wings," "God Bless America," "I Am the Bread of Life," "Be Not Afraid." Actually, it was unnecessary to ask them because when they didn't get what they wanted, they let us know after Mass. That's what customers do.

The musical battles we had—and boy did we have battles—were all about personal preferences with consumers and suppliers fighting over the product lines each preferred. But what we still didn't get, even after all our effort, was that neither the elitist music of the musical professionals nor the sweet and comfortable choices of our congregants would ever attract "Tim."

There was another problem with some of our more contemporary music. As Thomas Day, in his very insightful book, *Why Catholics Can't Sing*, describes, there is an issue that takes the discussion out of the arena of "mere taste":

And that is the tendency of this music to let the congregation become the "Voice of God." In other words, the composer sets the text so that the congregation sings God's words, usually without quotation marks, in a somewhat bored, relaxed, almost casual style. This is startling and unprecedented in the history of Christianity. The words sung by this God/congregation always seem to be reassuring everyone that they live lives of unfailing, heroic saintliness and that they have purchased their own salvation through their good works.[10]

In other words, not all of our music was worship music. We worked hard to build a music program, and we intuitively understood how important it is, but despite our best efforts we couldn't get it right. We had a music program, first a bad one and then a better one and eventually a great one. We had a music program; what we needed was a *worship* program.

The point isn't about building a music program anyway. It's about moving the congregation beyond the position of musical consumers, who are either delighted or comforted or bored or offended by the music, and helping them become worshipers. At the same time, it's about growing musicians from performers with a "gig" mentality into worship leaders. And, it's about worship through song.

> We had a music program; what we needed was a *worship* program.

Disciples Sing

"Sing" is one of the most commonly used words in the Bible.[11] God's people are supposed to sing. "Serve the Lord with gladness; come before him with joyful song" (Psalm 100:2). Singing is the elemental form of worship. It's what Moses and Israel did in response to their saving passage through the Red Sea; it's what David and the people did as they brought the Ark of the Covenant to Jerusalem; it's what Jesus and his disciples did the night before he died (the Last Supper wasn't a "quiet" Mass). Liturgical music should lead us into song, and we should sing throughout the liturgy *and* beyond.

> Inspired by sung participation, the body of the Word Incar-
> nate goes forth to spread the Gospel with full force and
> compassion. In this way, the Church leads men and women
> "to the faith, freedom and peace of Christ by the example of
> its life and teaching, by the sacraments and other means of
> grace. Its aim is to open up for all men a free and sure path
> to full participation in the mystery of Christ."[12]

In other words, singing and discipleship go together. Disciples are
moved to worship and then motivated to service particularly and powerfully through their sung participation in worship.

When we finally figured out this little fact, we at least knew where
we needed to go; we just didn't know how to get there. Prayer would
have helped, and eventually that's where we turned. We prayed and
fasted (a little) and waited. No kidding, one day, Easter Sunday as it
turned out, a fellow named Al came walking through the door of our
office and told us that he had been leading contemporary music at a
parish in Texas. He was moving to our community to be closer to his
family, and he would love to help us out. And he did. Starting out
small, he helped reshape our program in a big way.

Looking at our program today, we have five nearly identical services
led by Al and the band he has built and, more recently, a second band
led by Rob. Both bands include drummers, keyboards, bassists, and
various others as needed from Mass to Mass and week to week (we
were surprised to learn how much musical talent was just sitting in our
pews). Typically the bands play current "praise and worship" music
because that's a style of music we've found is attractive and engaging
to Tim and his family. And, of all the musical genres we've used, the
vibrant and joyful cast and smooth melody of this contemporary style
also has the power to get them singing.

"Praise and worship" music is a kind of adult alternative rock (with
Christian lyrics). Is it appropriate? We think so in our setting, and

we think we're on solid ground liturgically, too. The Second Vatican Council noted:

> There are peoples who have their own musical traditions and these play a great part in their religious and social life. For this reason due importance is to be attached to their music, and a suitable place is to be given to it, not only in forming their attitude toward religion, but also in adapting worship to their native genius. . . .[13]

The Council Fathers were thinking principally of the importance of music when it comes to evangelization and worship in mission territory. Exactly our point: Timonium, Maryland, in the twenty-first century *is* mission territory. And music that matches the culture is a powerful and effective missional tool.

Sometimes we also include updated versions of more traditional hymns. And on Christmas Eve, and during Holy Week, our choir director, Rich, fields a full-fledged traditional choir to provide the familiar favorites and classics, which everybody (Tim included) always wants on those occasions.

We are *not* advocating any particular style of music. In the multicultural reality that is American Catholicism that would be absurd. Besides, in Catholic worship the *Novus Ordo* can accommodate many different musical styles as long as the music fulfills three basic criteria as outlined by Cardinal Joseph Ratzinger, now Pope Benedict XVI:

- It is related to God's Word and *"God's saving action."*
- It lifts the human heart toward God.
- It more effectively unites the individual with the larger community.[14]

Beyond that, it's just about discovering the music that works in your community—not the personal preferences of the pastor and the music director, not the demands from the pews, not even the stated preferences of the majority. The music must be all about attracting the lost and growing disciples through worship.

> Timonium, Maryland, in the twenty-first century is mission territory. And music that matches the culture is a powerful and effective missional tool.

The music that we use is selected with the input of several people on staff including, but not limited to or directed by, the musicians. It usually remains consistent from week to week in the course of a season, which, we've found, *dramatically* increases participation. We used to be somewhat sheepish about repeating music, but the results speak for themselves, and as people become familiar with the message behind the music they're growing in their discipleship.

We no longer have a "quiet" or "low" Mass. We stopped doing it a couple of years ago, and it was one of the best decisions we ever made. At Nativity, the quiet Mass was keeping alive the "get it over with" mentality among a lot of the people who were showing up with no intention of participatory worship.

Once we invited a friend, a minister from another denomination, to join us for Mass. He used a great analogy, comparing the music of the service to a movie soundtrack. If carefully and thoughtfully selected, music can shape the experience of the story or, to return to our original analogy, take the parishioners on a journey to higher things.

We try to make sure the music is connected to the liturgical action. There must be direction and flow to it, contoured to the ritual itself. Just as the liturgical year brings what has been called "progressive solemnity" (that is, some feasts call for greater or more solemn celebration), the same can be said for the Mass itself.[15] Inherent in the celebration of the Eucharist there is a "progressive solemnity" and it can be powerfully underscored with music. We think music at the entrance rite wants to communicate a feel of arrival, perhaps even urgency, drawing people into an "event" experience. Music at the offertory can begin to lead people deeper into the mystery itself. At Communion, softer or more poignant, music can be truly uplifting and inspiring. The closing wants to be a high energy send off.

We use two otherwise unexpected elements in our creative and contemporary approach to the weekend experience to underscore this very point—Gregorian chant and *silence*.

Gregorian chant, the music proper to the Roman liturgy, powerfully anchors our weekend experience in our tradition, and we use it for the acclamations of the Eucharistic prayer and sometimes as an introit and counterpoint to the opening or Communion music. It somehow seems to very effectively summon our congregation into the very heart of the mystery we celebrate. Far from turning Tim and his family off, we've found it can actually bring them into the unfolding action, leading them step-by-step through the progression of the solemnity. Churchworld can look canned and corny or, alternately, showy and insincere to lost people, at least that's the attitude they have coming in the door. Infusing our weekend service with the spirit of mystery inherent in the Roman liturgy, as incomparably expressed in Gregorian chant, can serve as an antidote for that perception.

> Music can shape the experience of the story or, to return to our original analogy, take the parishioners on a journey to higher things.

The power of music can be matched by the power of silence. We've said we're not fans of a "quiet" weekend Mass, but the deliberate and creative use of silence, as introduction or punctuation to the spoken or sung word, can dramatically enhance the worship experience.

> Music arises out of silence and returns to silence. God is revealed both in the beauty of song and in the power of silence. . . . The importance of silence in the Liturgy cannot be overemphasized.[16]

A Communion song, sung with spirit, softly landing into a shared silence can be the most dramatic and impactful moment of the whole weekend experience. But we've found silence is strong and most effective for our congregation in the context of music. Because the music is powerful, so is the silence. Use music to manage the silence.

YOU CAN DO THIS!
Steps You Can Take in Your Parish

To get where you need to go isn't about talent or luck or even money. It's about consistently following a few basic principles:

- Make sure you have the best musicians you can find (paid or volunteer) and use them; do the difficult thing and ask people who are holding your program down or even making it worse to step aside. Face the hard facts and lean into the conflict in order to advance your program.
- Raise your music and musicians up in prayer. Fast for them.
- Whatever the style, make sure your music is worship and your musicians are worship leaders.
- Take care with the selection of your music and do it in view of the liturgy as well as the lost. You need to be talking to your musicians about the music. It's not about what you like or they want; it's about the lost.

- Don't be afraid to repeat music from week to week. In loving ways, encourage your congregation to sing and sing with them.

Literally, after air quality, music is the single greatest environmental factor for your community, because it determines how people feel in your church. It has the power to make them feel like pampered customers or dissatisfied ones. It also has the power to make them feel like they're part of the movement of growing disciples that we want our parish to be. Furthermore, and emphatically, we are convinced that churches will remain consumer-driven as long as people aren't singing. It's not exactly clear to us *why* that is so, but congregational singing seems to be a reliable bellwether for church health. We like to say coming to church and not singing is like going to the gym and not working out. You've gotta sing!

Over these recent years, we've watched with growing enthusiasm as our congregation has at least *begun* to sing. When a parish is worshiping God together through song, in a sincere and selfless way, it is transformative.

> We are convinced that churches will remain consumer-driven as long as people aren't singing.

Sing to the Lord a new song; his praise in the assembly of the saints. . . . A song is a thing of joy; more profoundly it is a thing of love. Anyone, therefore, who has learned to love the new life has learned to sing a new song, and the new song reminds us of our new life. The new man, the new song, the new covenant, all belong to the one kingdom of God.[17]

Accessible and Attractive

Focusing on the weekend from the perspective of lost people means . . . "It's all about the ministers!" We're definitely not interested in pandering to the consumer demands of members, because we don't want them to remain consumers. But that's where people start. So, we do want to engage our potential members by offering an attractive and accessible weekend experience.

Our parishioners who serve as volunteer ministers remove some of the obstacles and make that happen. Little things can get in the way. If you can't find a parking spot, don't feel welcomed, or sit in a dirty pew, it can be difficult to focus on God. Little things become big things. In a subsequent chapter we'll discuss the priority of making members ministers and how to do it. Here we want to introduce the main "teams" of member-ministers, who make the weekend happen.

In our community, people tend to bring their cars with them when they come to church. So we've got to take care of their cars before we can take care of them. For us, the whole weekend experience and all our ministry efforts begin with our **Parking Team**. They direct traffic, manage flow, assist with special needs, and make sure we're accommodating the maximum number of cars. But more importantly, our parking ministry is also about establishing a welcoming, festive environment as people enter our campus, wordlessly communicating, "We're waiting for you. We're glad you're here."

Once inside the building, our **Host Team** goes ahead and adds words to the welcome. Their goal is to greet *everyone* who comes through any of our doors, demonstrating in a convincing way our enthusiasm for their presence with us. There is nothing quite as welcoming as people who are happy to see you. At this point in their experience guests are probably smiling and we've already begun to successfully preach the gospel.

We've worked our way out of the old idea of ushers and promoted hosts as aides who assist and accommodate guests. But hosts are also charged with performing the tasks formerly associated with the ushers, like taking up the offering. They're also on hand to "control" the house. The attractive environment we're aiming to have will only happen if it's a *controlled* environment.

The Host Team has a plan for greeting and seating. They also serve as problem solvers for problem people and the inevitable bad behavior encountered in dealing with the public. The weekend experience in your church can be damaged, even destroyed, by misbehavior. Mass is no place for screaming infants who cannot be comforted or big babies who want to answer their cell phones. When necessary, hosts will invite people to step out of the sanctuary. Whatever they're doing, hopefully they are shaping an environment in which adults and young adults can get some distance from the rest of their lives, relax, and focus on God.

Besides directional questions, the Host Team doesn't try to answer all the questions; the **Information Team** does. Stationed in the lobby with their own desk and laptop, they handle—you guessed it—*information*. The team provides visitors with details about programs and services, and helps members sign up to take their next steps in discipleship. When we first started the information desk, the volunteers didn't really know much about the parish, but we equipped them to say, "I'll find out." Eventually the team developed, and now constantly updates, a comprehensive manual of the information they need. The team leader attends the weekly staff meeting where we

> Mass is no place for screaming infants who cannot be comforted or big babies who want to answer their cell phones.

prepare for the weekend and then, in turn, updates her ministers. At this point, they know more about what's going on than we do.

By the way, an unintended and happy consequence of this ministry is a tremendous reduction in foot traffic in our office Monday through Friday. Currently, we don't even employ an office receptionist or secretary. The Information Team handles everything from Mass cards to baptismal certificates on the weekend.

YOU CAN DO THIS!
Steps You Can Take in Your Parish

Start putting together, in one place (a binder or on your laptop or website), information that parishioners actually need and want: how to register, how to get envelopes, how to sign up for programs, service, and events . . . everything in one place.

Find three or four people in your parish who you wish there were more of: friendly and enthusiastic people you would like to represent you; recruit them to be your Information Team. Here's how you do it: Tell them they can actually stop doing everything else they're already doing, and you promise not to ask them to do anything else as long as they're in this service. Make the upfront investment in them you need to, so that you're setting them up for success. Meet with them regularly, make sure they know about everything that's going on.

Find a space in your lobby or near your front door or at least in a highly visible and accessible place. Put a table there. Try to find a nice table, or a nice cloth for the table. Do not clutter the table top with a lot of junk, just a few relevant and timely things you might have on hand (like your bulletin). Put everything else you need *under* the table. Have a sign that lets people know what's the purpose of the table.

- Note: No chairs, your team needs to stand.
- *Nota Bene*: Do not sell stuff at this table or use it for fundraisers.

Create a schedule for your team and try to make sure people don't have to serve alone. Help your team understand, they're not hosting a watering hole for insiders. They are the front line when it comes to evangelization and discipleship.

Our **Café Team** manages the café. They sell coffee, tea, juice, and bottled water all weekend long; bagels and donuts Sunday morning; snacks, sandwiches, and pizza in the afternoon. To keep things simple, we only serve prepared food. Besides brewing coffee, there is no cooking in our café. And we only offer hand-held food so people can stand. We don't want the number of seats to limit our capacity, and we don't want to become a dining room for regulars (thus creating a new class of consumers). The goal is an easy and accessible fellowship environment for as many people as possible. And although we aim at breaking even, our café is *not* a fundraiser.

Besides the obvious work of running a café, our team is tasked with interacting with the parishioners and visitors in a more personal way than our other teams do. We have developed a culture where people are willing to hang around after Mass. We don't do any large social gatherings, like dances or dinners, because they're a lot of work, and people in our congregation don't need another event on their schedules (and, in a later chapter, we'll discuss why we don't like fundraisers).

Besides, we've found an easier way to provide fellowship that engages hundreds more people than old-fashioned, labor-intensive, and stand-alone events. The weekend is *when* fellowship happens; the café is *where* it happens; and the Café Team is *how* it happens.

The more time people spend on campus the more likely it is they'll buy into the message of the Gospel and get involved in the ways we want them to get involved by going deeper into the message. The biggest wins of the weekend are overhearing people in the café after Mass talking about the Gospel message.

Invest and Invite

These four teams or ministries form a continuum; they work together in a strategic way. The Parking Ministers are communicating with people in a friendly, helpful, brief encounter. The Host Team is interacting with as many people as they can, in a one on one way, but also only briefly. Yet, these two ministries together ensure that most everyone who visits our campus on a weekend will have at least two friendly interactions with someone while here.

> The biggest wins of the weekend are overhearing people in the café after Mass, talking about the Gospel message.

The Information Team and the Café Team are going deeper with people who, for whatever reason, are looking for more in their experience. The Information Desk is a destination for people to get to know us better and get involved. In the café, our ministers create fellowship that can actually begin a conversation and lead to a relationship.

More recently we have begun working on a fifth ministry that would complement, perhaps complete, this effort. We don't even have a name for it yet. These ministers are given special training to assist people who would like to avail themselves of pastoral care immediately following the service. They can be a shoulder to cry on, a friendly ear, a comforting embrace for people's emotional response to the service, and a safe spot to unpack some of the baggage they carried in with them. They're not counselors or therapists; they're pastoral ministers who provide support and prayer. The priest doesn't have to be the only one in the parish available to listen to and care about the people in the pews.

All our weekend ministers are part of the "invest and invite" evangelization strategy we discussed earlier. It works like this: If you actually go to the effort of inviting a visitor, you can have utter certainty that they will be well received which, in turn, motivates you to make more invitations!

Clean Your Nursery

In addition to all the liturgical ministers needed for the Mass, we have other weekend ministries too that take care of technology and operations. Our **Operations Team** sets up and breaks down for programs and services. They wash windows, vacuum carpets, and keep the place clean throughout the weekend. This is incredibly important work and can be done by your parishioners.

If you come to our church midmorning on Sunday, perhaps a thousand people have already been through our building. Without on-going maintenance, trashcans are full, glass doors are smudged, and children's spaces are dirty. People do not want to bring their kids to dirty children's spaces. Besides, poor maintenance erodes our credibility.

A pastor we know tells the story of visiting a church that had begged him for consultation and coaching (because things were not going well for them). He arrived just a little early and decided to wander around on his own. The first thing he came across was the nursery, and it was filthy. He turned around and proceeded to leave. At that point his hosts were just arriving. He told them on his way out: "Here's my advice: Clean your nursery. Don't tell me how much you love Jesus, just clean your nursery!"

YOU CAN DO THIS!
Steps You Can Take in Your Parish

We urge you to consider what your facility looks like to a newcomer or first time visitor. Is it neat and orderly and, most importantly, clean? How your building looks will tell guests more about you than anything you can say from the pulpit. Whether your church is beautiful matters not in the least to the lost; that it is well maintained is critical.

Our weekend ministers also include the **Tech Team**. They handle the basics: what you *see* and what you *hear*. How many times have you been in church and you couldn't see what was going on or hear what was said? How crazy is that?

Tech includes our camera crew as well as the people who work the "board," putting audio and visual together. Currently, we have several "video venues," which are what we call worship areas outside our main sanctuary where the service is broadcast. These areas provide overflow seating and accommodate special needs, like people who choose to keep their small children with them. At the same time video venues offer a more relaxed seating choice for dechurched newcomers not yet familiar with the order of service or comfortable in the sanctuary. We have also begun live streaming our weekend message on our website (as an even more accessible place to invite the lost). The point is, what the Tech Team produces *is* the weekend experience for many people.

In the main worship space the team gives shape to the service experience through sight and sound. As noted previously, our church is a '70s era minimalist structure; the interior walls are a drab brown brick. A couple of years ago we got a green light (from the Archdiocese) to dramatically change this environment by hanging large 9x16 foot screens on either side of the altar. Under the direction of the Tech Team, we began to project Mass. *That* certainly stirred up a lot of comment and criticism, but the end result is positive and powerful, drawing people deep into the liturgical action. By the way, if you visit St. Peter's in Rome or St. Patrick's in New York, you'll see the same thing.

Irresistible Environments

Little things are big things. Make it easy to park, greet people, cultivate a friendly environment, provide uplifting music, and you'll have the framework for a great weekend experience. Andy Stanley sums up these weekend efforts in terms of creating, what he calls, an "irresistible environment." Referring to his incredible church north of Atlanta he writes:

> The reason [our] volunteers do what they do . . . is because [they] understand that we're not simply parking cars . . . we're creating irresistible environments. When people come into those environments, there's kind of an 'aha' moment as they begin to connect [. . .] with the relevance of the gospel and the relevance of scripture as it relates to their everyday experience.[18]

Our weekend ministers and musicians are shaping an environment that's attractive and, eventually we hope, irresistible.

Want to know more/go deeper?

Listen to Barry, our weekend director, talk about what he does on the weekends and how we put it all together. Go to rebuiltparish.com, click "Chapter 6," and then click "The Weekend Director."

Adults Don't Always Come Alone

There is a flipside to everything we've said here about shaping the weekend environment for adults. Without this other element, you'll never have an attractive—much less irresistible—environment. That's because you've got to . . .

7

MOBILIZE THE NEXT GENERATION

The Church looks to the young; or rather the Church in a special way sees herself in the young.

—BLESSED JOHN PAUL II[1]

Just outside the main sanctuary at Nativity there is a glass-enclosed space that is perfect for additional seating, especially for people with special needs, like moms and dads with noisy babies. Considering that this church was built in 1970, it was an impressive innovation.

However, for some reason, *who* sat there, or rather who was *allowed* to sit there, was a point of contention and even conflict in the congregation. One of the first parish council meetings we attended was an unfriendly debate on this topic. Apparently there was the more liberal view, "It doesn't matter," and the conservative approach, "No one should be sitting there, because they *belong in church*!" Although no conclusive decision was reached one way or another at that time, the conservative faction (i.e. the ushers) made it as difficult and unpleasant as possible for anyone to be there. For starters, there were no chairs.

> **Father Michael**: One Sunday I observed the ramifications of this conflict. A mom came in with an infant in a carrier, in one hand, tugging a toddler in the other, as well as hauling all the mom stuff moms lug around. She had to walk to a small closet on the far side of the space, where it was necessary to pull open a heavy metal door, hold it open because it had a closure, then reach in to pull out a metal folding chair, drag the chair back out into the room and set it up. In the midst of this process, the toddler took off, the infant started screaming and she discovered the chair was broken. She abandoned the project and wordlessly departed.

Little Kids are a Big Deal

Focusing on the weekend from the perspective of lost people means . . . "It's the kids programs!" We're convinced that weekend programs for children that stand alongside of, or in addition to Mass, aren't just a good thing; they're critically important to creating an irresistible environment for parents (or grandparents) with young kids. One of the major reasons families drop out of churchworld these days is because it's too difficult for them to go to Mass on a weekly basis. It just doesn't work out trying to bring small children into an adult worship event.

The Mass is neither children's ministry nor "family time." It's time we give to God. We're firm believers that children should be introduced to the Mass and learn to worship there. But we also believe that happens most successfully in age-appropriate environments that help them learn how to worship.

Without programs for children, families have no choice. How often have you seen a parent unsuccessfully trying to keep a toddler occupied and quiet, all the while eliciting dirty stares all around (some of them coming from the altar). We force small children to try to sit through a service that is incomprehensible to them. And then we're surprised when they grow to hate it and stop going at their earliest opportunity. We are accomplishing the opposite of what we're trying to effect. This is a part of our culture that we have to change.

> **The Mass is neither children's ministry nor "family time." It's time we give to God.**

Tom: On the flip side, being a parent with small children is one of the most challenging seasons of life. Believe me, I know; I've got five under ten.

New parents find themselves at an important transition in their lives, often one that involves revisiting and reconsidering discarded religious practice. They're waking up to the dawning reality that parenting is no easy thing to try to handle alone. Almost intuitively they're coming to the realization that instilling moral values and virtuous habits in children requires an authority greater than their own. Most parents, even if they're dechurched, are interested in exposing their children to some kind of basic faith experience. For all these reasons, they're drawn to church. Responding to those feelings and felt needs with programs they can use is a formula for success.

Though your community might be different, we believe the greatest opportunities for the Church to connect with the dechurched in Timonium is by helping those families with their families. A colleague of ours, Carol, likes to say, "Do something for my kid and you do something for me."

> "Do something for my kid and you do something for me."

Of course we provide the necessary sacramental preparation, and in a subsequent chapter we'll be discussing our children's religious education program. Here we just want to talk about the weekend programs we've developed for kids.

Our programs aim to be safe, and all our ministers have the necessary child protection screening and background checks. We want our programs to be accessible to newcomers and first time guests so there's no sign up, kids can just show up instead. And we hope they enjoy their time with us and want to come back—it's really okay to have fun in church. Meanwhile, confident their kids are cared for, parents and grandparents can relax, enjoy a break from their children, and enter more fully into worship themselves.

Kidzone

We start children's programs at six months in what we call "Kidzone." For our youngest children, we just want to make sure church is a place where they're known and loved, a place they love to come to. But it's not babysitting. From their first visit, kids are hearing scripture, singing worship songs, and listening to puppets tell Bible stories, which is the weekend "message" for them. And they're not in a nursery. They're in a *worship* environment, and they're learning from others, kids and adults, *how* to worship. Kidzone is open at every Mass, for children up to age three.

YOU CAN DO THIS!
Steps You Can Take in Your Parish

You are a DRE with a strained budget, limited space, and no weekend kids' programs. Whatever the arrangement of your physical space, there is probably a room you could use as a nursery, at least on Sunday morning, at least for one Mass.

- Identify that space.
- Clean it.
- Childproof it.
- Supply it.
- Staff it.

You are aiming at establishing a clean, safe, inviting environment for kids. If you can make it colorful and attractive, all the better. Get some people who love to decorate to help you come up with a plan that is easy to assemble on Sunday and easy to store during the week.

Practically speaking, used toys and books in good condition are a great place to start in terms of supplies. You'll have no trouble getting these donated. When it comes to staffing, don't look to Moms (give them a break). Talk to empty nesters and high school students about taking care of the nursery. Of course, make sure your volunteers have the necessary background checks and child protection training before you begin.

Invest in your volunteer ministers, schedule in time to spend with them at least once a month for coffee and brainstorming about programming for your new nursery: worship music, videos, fun faith-based exercises and activities. There are great, free activities online too! Some of our favorite ideas have come from searches on Google.

Before the beginning of Mass, let people know about your nursery and how they can use it. Make it easy for them to find.

All Stars

Three- to six-year-olds go to "All Stars." We call it a "play-worship-learn" environment because we want each of those elements to help move kids to the next element. The playtime is a fellowship time, leading into a worship experience that includes music and Bible teaching (we try to work from the lectionary readings whenever possible). After worship, the kids are introduced to small groups for the day's lesson.

Time Travelers

We call our children's Liturgy of the Word program "Time Travelers" because we think that sounds more interesting to kids. But we're also making a point about what we Christians believe: We want kids to get the idea that the Word of God is alive and that they can live that Word. In Time Travelers they go "back" to the Bible stories and biblical teachings to hear a message that's relevant in their lives today and tomorrow. The Bible readings are always based on the Lectionary and the message is consistent with the homily at Mass. Usually the message is told by costumed characters from the Bible story itself (if your parish is like ours, there are people in your pews who would *love* to do this.) Our program takes place in an old classroom adjacent to our sanctuary. We call the space "Time Travelers Theater," which sounds like a fun place kids would want to visit. Any space can be adapted. Besides the message, we also include high-energy worship led by a "worship leader." Time Travelers is for children in grades one through four.

Want to know more/go deeper?

Meet Lisa, our director of children's ministry, and let her give you the details about our kids environments. Go to rebuiltparish.com, click "Chapter 7," and then click "Weekend Kids Programs."

Children's Ministry exists to help kids live, pray, and grow in their relationship with Jesus Christ. Kids programs don't have to be expensive, and, contrary to our previous experience, you really can get adults and young adult volunteers involved. It's an especially great place to engage teenage girls and empty nester moms; but, we also go out of our way to encourage men to volunteer because of the impact their presence has on boys. People love to spend time with kids, and if you set them up for success in your programs, they *will* get involved.

Once they're in the door, great children's programs will ensure that the kids keep their parents coming back. A pastor we know tells the story of witnessing a parent dragging a kid out the front door of the church repeatedly pleading, "We've *got* to go." Finally the kid breaks away and screams, "I want to go back in the damn church!"

> Great children's programs will ensure that the kids keep their parents coming back.

The experience we're going for is well expressed in this letter—typical of many more we have received.

Dear Nativity,

I just wanted to thank everyone at the church for being so welcoming and friendly to our family. For us, the barrier that Nativity has removed is the frustration we've experienced with having our three children attend Mass with us. We had taken many months off from attending any church because we had become so frustrated, continually trying to keep our children quiet or occupied, while getting nothing out of it at all, except irritated with one another.

Someone recommended Nativity, so we gave it a try. On our first visit, a very friendly person led us around and showed us where we could take our children. She was welcoming and helpful, and our kids were so comfortable with the experience they wanted to come back. Every time that we've entered or left church, someone has smiled at us and greeted us, and that means so much. The parking volunteers were helpful, dedicated, and friendly.

> *The way to get started is to quit talking and begin doing.*
> —Walt Disney[2]

The hospitality and service, the fellowship, and the incredible organization have convinced us that Christ's presence is alive in this church. The program for our twenty-month-old is wonderful and safe, and All Stars for our four- and five-year-old children has helped enrich their church experiences.

Thanks to Nativity, my wife and I can now sit as a couple for an hour, worship, sing, and renew our spirits just enough to make it through another crazy week! We look forward to every Sunday now, and we plan to start getting more involved, which I've come to believe is the only way to keep our faith alive.

Care about Student Programs

Focusing on the weekend means . . . "It's the Student Programs!" Specific programs for teens and pre-teens are a key element in our weekend experience. Their very place on the schedule underscores that we care about young people as much as anyone else in the parish and actively seek to engage them in the life of the Church.

We have a program for high school students and a separate one for middle school, because if you put them together you end up with a middle school program. In other words, high school students need their own program. More recently, we've divided the middle school program into two programs: fifth and sixth graders in one and seventh and eighth graders in the other. The more age-specific all kids' and student programs are, the more attractive and successful they likely will be.

Our current youth program suffers because it must share space with children's programs—which means they can't run simultaneously—which in turn means families with children in different grades have to make multiple trips. One day we hope to change that, but right now we offer children's programs on Sunday morning and Saturday afternoon and student programs on Sunday afternoon. Ideally, our middle school programs would be available on Sunday morning, but no matter how much space you have, high school needs to be in the evening because they don't do Sunday mornings.

The weekend experience for student programs includes fun fellowship time, with lots of adult ministers, men and women, available to interact with students on their arrival. There is no sign up, just show up and bring a friend if you like. Next comes worship, led by student bands and then a message usually offered by our Youth Minister, Chris. His message is based on the readings of the lectionary and closely parallels the homily at Mass. We call this our "crowd" program, and while it is definitely not intended to be a substitute or alternative for the weekly Eucharist, it is a great complement to it, and it is a good place for dechurched kids to start.

The main purpose of Chris's message is to set direction for the conversations we hope happen next in small groups. After the message, students break off into small groups to go deeper and make life application. These are single sex groups of six to eight each led by a couple of adult leaders. The groups themselves organize any in-week activities, like service trips, sports programs, and fun stuff. We'll be saying more about small groups in a subsequent chapter.

We've acknowledged that when we came here, teens and students were largely absent. Years of our best efforts and it was still hard to get anything more than a Confirmation program going. Students just aren't interested, and increasingly, their parents don't care or at least don't care to fight that battle. And we'll go ahead and admit that we continue to struggle with student ministry: Motivating them to come, getting them to come back, and keeping them engaged are no small things. On the other hand, one of the truly astonishing things to us about all of the successful churches we studied was their successful youth ministry. What's their secret? Turns out its not rocket science, just some basic steps instead of games or guilt.

1. **Build your children's program.**

    The reason we didn't have a youth program is that we had boring and bad children's programs. Build your children's program. Children's ministry is forming the future students in your youth program. If they have a great experience in your church as kids, they'll want to continue coming when they're older. It just becomes a part of their lifestyle instead of a class to pass or a requirement to fill. A great children's program is building a great youth program. That's why our children's director and student director work very carefully together and even share an office.

2. **Make your youth minister high profile.**

    Next to the pastor, the youth minister should be the highest profile member of your team, well known to the whole congregation. Why? Because it is easy for the youth minister to get lost in the crowd, and then your youth ministry program will get lost too. Think about it: Little kids could care less who the director of their religious education program is. But it is the youth minister who must sell the program to students. Currently, Chris does the announcements at many of our weekend Masses, even when they have nothing to do with youth ministry. Everyone knows him and it helps that he can be quite funny. (He also thinks he's cool, but that is open for multiple interpretations.)

Want to know more/go deeper?

Let Chris introduce himself and some of the lessons he's learned in building and maintaining a great parish youth ministry. Go to rebuiltparish.com, click "Chapter 7," and then click "Chris Speaks!" You can also go to Chris's blog, "Marathon Youth Ministry," at christopherwesley.org.

You probably want your director to be a young adult. This is just going to look more accessible to the students. A young adult is also likely to bring energy and a flexible schedule to the job. If your director is a guy, find a young woman to assist him (or vice-versa.) Students need same-sex role models in this position. Make sure your director is exactly the type of adult parents would want in their kids' lives. And he or she needs the full support of the pastor and direct access to him.

At the same time, go out of your way to ensure high school students themselves are prominent throughout your weekend experience, in the liturgy and in all the ministries.

3. **Make your youth programs accessible.**

The mantra for student programs here is "no sign up, just show up." There are no books, classrooms, or anything else that begins to look like school. In our high school program there are also no fees or registration, students are welcome to come anytime, and they can always bring friends. When a teen can bring a friend, it makes a big difference, especially in a community like ours where students are going to so many different schools.

4. **Make your programs excellent and attractive.**

   The same rules apply for student programs that apply to adult programs. Music, message, and ministers have to be of a consistently high quality. Young people recognize and value quality and it gives credibility to your message.

5. **Keep turning the flywheel.**

   Too often parishes put a lot of effort and expense into a youth *event*, and are disappointed in the attendance. So they stop trying. Or they try something for a season and burn their volunteers out and then give up. Don't just do events, don't worry about having any particular style of program. It's not about events, and it's not about programs. It's about getting students on a discipleship path and creating the environment in which they keep moving down that path worshiping God, enjoying fellowship with other believers, growing in knowledge and love of their faith, serving others, and sharing their faith.

> It's not about events and it's not about programs. It's about getting students on a discipleship path.

Make that a part of your culture, keep turning that flywheel.

When it comes to student ministry, the problem *and* the way forward are perfectly summed up by next-generation spiritual-growth author Reggie Joiner:

> Eight out of ten students participate in church during their teenage years, but most of them will take a permanent detour from active faith at some point soon after they get their driver's licenses, . . . pronouncing Christianity boring, irrelevant, and out of touch.
>
> We've tried too long to educate their minds instead of engaging their lives. The more we try to change the way

we do church so this generation will join us, the more they seem to stay away.

Some of us are convinced the system is fundamentally flawed because we don't know what our goal is. . . . What if our goal should not be to get them into church? What if the same energy could be applied to mobilize them to be the church?[3]

The goal in our weekend student programs is to influence and motivate young people to be the Church right now.

YOU CAN DO THIS!
Steps You Can Take in Your Parish

You're a pastor or pastoral life director and you have no youth ministry beyond a middle school Confirmation program. Start talking to your eighth graders about staying involved next year, plan something in the spring that's just for them, to introduce them to the idea of high school ministry.

Look for high school students who are already coming to Mass. Invite them to do things at Mass: greet at the door, serve as lector, altar server, or usher. If they play music maybe they can help out there once in a while, but take care that you're not dropping them into a bad ministry culture.

Be on the lookout for an adult you know who has a heart for teens and can connect with them. Invite him or her to serve as a volunteer director, and to be available to the teens who are serving. Let your new director do the announcements after communion or before Mass. Give the people in your congregation a face and a name to connect with in the youth ministry. Above all else, make sure this is someone you can pour time and energy into, especially if he or she is a young

adult. The most important thing you can give any youth minister is your attention, support, and love.

And One More Thing

The weekend matters a lot. More than almost anything. Almost.

There is one other element to your weekend experience, and it is so important it eclipses everything else. If you don't get this one right, all your other efforts will suffer, your hard work won't really pay off, and your parish probably won't grow. That's because focusing on the weekend from the perspective of lost people means you've got to do one other thing . . .

8

MAKE THE MESSAGE MATTER

"Teach, delight, move."

—CICERO[1]

O ne of the greatest preachers in the history of Christianity, St. Augustine was the first to deliberately apply the principles of Ciceronian rhetoric (teach, delight, move) to Christian preaching. For Augustine, preaching is fundamental to the work of the Church, its purpose being to engage and teach people with the Word of God in order to *change* them. And that's what we see from the very beginning as the apostles followed the example given to them by Jesus: They engaged and taught people in order to change them to become more like Christ. That's it. The Word of God has the power to change people.

In the history of the Church the great periods of reform were marked by the renewal of preaching. The founding of the Dominicans and the Franciscans, the Reformation and the Counter-Reformation, the Jesuit movement, the missionary efforts of the Church in North and South America, Asia, Africa, and now today a more evangelically minded Catholic community have all been exercises in effective and relevant preaching.

Again and again in the game-changing epochs there is a rediscovery of the importance of preaching in the life of the Church and an accompanying restoration to its primacy of place in the work of the Church.

The Table of God's Word

The Second Vatican Council led the way in a contemporary Catholic revival:

> The treasures of the Bible are to be opened up more lavishly, so that richer fare may be provided for the faithful at the table of God's word. . . .
>
> By means of the homily the mysteries of the faith and the guiding principles of the Christian life are expounded from the sacred text; . . . the homily, therefore, is to be highly esteemed as part of the liturgy itself.[2]

I fully intend to preach the Word of God to you until there's a difference between how you walk out of here and how you walked in here.
—Pastor T. D. Jakes[3]

Catholic Christians call it the "homily," and Protestant Christians call it the "sermon." We've come to refer to it as the "message." For a few minutes each week, we get to share the life-changing Gospel of Jesus Christ. It is an unparalleled opportunity to help church members go deeper. Next to the sacraments, preaching the Word of God is one of the most important things you can do to grow disciples, and it's even more important when it comes to reaching the lost. For lost people as well as those new to the discipleship path, the weekend message is *the* defining element of the weekend experience, because they don't yet understand or appreciate the Eucharist.

When we first came here, we didn't get that. Week after week we just gave our pulpit away to whoever happened to be helping us with "weekend coverage " (as the practice of bringing in outside clergy to assist with the weekend Mass schedule is usually called). Whatever they decided to say was entirely up to them and fine with us, as long as they did it in less than eight minutes. Typically, we didn't even know what they were saying. And sometimes, as we've noted, there were even conflicting and contradictory messages. Over the years, our preachers tended to fall into one (or more) of the following styles:

> For a few minutes each week, we get to share the life-changing Gospel of Jesus Christ. It is an unparalleled opportunity to help church members go deeper.

1. **Bible Study for Believers**

   Because the Second Vatican Council encouraged Catholics to get into scripture, in the subsequent decades many preachers started really digging deep into the text—certainly a great development. However, one preacher here used his homily solely for exegesis and textual criticism. Some churchpeople loved it, because it was interesting to them (and perhaps it made them feel smart). For lost people it might as well have been Greek.

2. **Church Chat for Church Ladies**

   Chatty news, gossip, and insider jokes that take the place of God's word characterize this approach. For the lost, it is an unmistakable reminder that they don't belong.

3. **Sermons for Seminarians**

   Father Michael: This was me, looking back at my preaching. I was trained to preach (such as it was) in seminary, and my audience there were other seminarians. Lots of theology, fine theological nuances, fun facts about the Liturgy, great moments in Church history, all are big values here. Sometimes homilies that fall into this category, to be fair, can be terrific and in the right setting (like a seminary) very effective. But not only is this kind of sermon sending the lost the clear message they don't belong, it is also a reminder to them *why* they don't *want* to belong.

4. **Convincing the Convinced (Yep, "Preaching to the Choir")**

We know a guy who fervently preaches each week exactly what his congregation expects to hear and already believes. Obviously this message will be well received by the people already in the pews. But when you're always telling people what they *want* to hear, instead of what they *need* to hear, you can be sure you're not preaching the whole Word of God. This is a formula that ensures you are not helping people grow. There was a priest here who regularly preached the obligation of weekly Mass attendance and the importance of "dressing properly." The suit and tie, never-miss-a-Sunday crowd was always pleased and happy to convey their "You tell 'em, Father!" attitude. Only problem was that, 'em were never there.

In this category we'll also include preaching politics. Some guys, especially if they've been in a place for awhile, and share the politics of their congregation (or think they do), will preach their political or social agenda. Nothing will turn the lost off faster, even if they agree with you, because it is exactly what they expect church to do, and they resent it.

5. **Nagging the Uninterested**

> **Father Michael**: In my home parish growing up, the parish had incurred an enormous debt building a new church. Week after week the pastor would climb into the pulpit to nag everyone to give more, which apparently had no effect.
>
> A preacher here seized any opportunity to point out the shortcomings of the congregation in an ineffective though deeply demoralizing way. Those in this category scold or embarrass to try to get people to do what they want them to do. Their basic argument is obligation and guilt. Unfortunately that's not enough to motivate uninterested people, and nobody is more uninterested than lost people.

6. **Boys' Club Banter**

There is a parish we have sometimes visited, and the guy always begins with jokes. Always! The jokes are all stale, sometimes offensive, oft repeated, and completely gratuitous. They have nothing to do with anything except perhaps helping to hold onto the myth of a Catholic culture that has long since disappeared. Of course, his congregation *loves* it. We'll include under this category purposeless storytelling, movie reviews, book reports, and extended asides for news and sports.

This is the basic message of the "get it over with" mentality. Since what we are doing as an assembly is only an obligation to be fulfilled, the preacher does everyone a favor and makes it as painless as possible. The approach ensures a positive response after Mass from the ushers with comments like, "That was a good one, *Padre!*" For lost people, who have no sense of any obligation, this genial entertainment is worthless (maybe even embarrassing). Besides, it underscores the fact that, just as they suspected, there really is nothing of substance for them in churchworld.

7. **Hamming It Up**

One priest we know was the complete entertainer: He sang; he danced; he told stories; he could make you laugh and cry and then sent you out wanting more. Great job, great talent, but the message was all about him: his problems, his concerns, his dog (he even brought his dog with him a few times). Lost people probably enjoyed it like everybody else (especially dog lovers), but they didn't get any closer to God's word.

8. **Canned Ham**

Packaged sermons! Referring to experiences that were obviously not in his experience, making points he probably did not actually understand, and speaking in a style not really his own, this poor guy even used words he didn't know how to pronounce. He was a lovely man but his appearance in the pulpit became groan-time for everyone, churched or dechurched.

9. **Dishing Leftovers**

Ceaselessly recycling his old stuff, this fellow just mailed it in. And if he didn't care, why would the lost?

10. **Let's Pretend (I Have a Message)**

Week after week, one guy used to fake it. Really, he did. He simply had no message. He never prepared to preach and had nothing to say. Instead, he just talked off the top of his head, repeating platitudes, axioms, and truisms about God that all amounted to nothing. It was like soap bubbles. Just try to grasp them. His homily appeared to be something, but it was nothing. He constantly introduced his flimsy assertions with the phrase, "Our God is . . ." and he always left you with the feeling our God is pretty much nothing. The phrase became loathsome to us. And the lost will avoid it along with everyone else.

11. **Public Confession/Public Boasting**

Some preachers use the pulpit to unburden themselves of their own worries or concerns, or even their shortcomings and failures. This is Jimmy Swaggart crying, "I have sinned."

> **Father Michael**: A pastor I know was, to his great credit, a recovering alcoholic. But, every Sunday was some version of his own addiction and recovery story. It was doubtlessly a great help to him (and most likely others too), but it didn't have any reference to God's word.

On the opposite end of this spectrum is the preacher who constantly boasts about his accomplishments, or tries to make himself look smart and important. A guy we've heard regularly regaled the congregation with his awards, his degrees, Greek and Latin phrases he had memorized. It was absurdly boastful and yet tedious and inane at the same time. He didn't understand that nobody cared. And why should they? Furthermore, pomposity and pride, in place of preaching, is a lot of what lost people hate in organized religion.

12. **Let's Just Be Friends**

This was the fellow who wandered up and down the aisle, removing his glasses to wipe away tears and addressing everyone in a soft, velvety voice. The message was "we're all friends." Nothing wrong with that, until he starts equating the sum total of the Gospel message with feeling good and being happy. It's vacuous and actually discouraging to the lost who aren't looking for friends; they're looking for God.

Discipline Builds Skill

Preachers bring their particular personality to the presentation, and they are right to do so. Also, the natural pull for any preacher is settling into a style that works for him and then sticking to it. Likewise, identifying reliable resources and streamlining the approach are going to provide a more dependably successful formula for getting the job done week after week. That's nothing to fault; it's what any craftsman does. It's just an efficient approach to a difficult job. It is about becoming a skilled craftsman. The Bible tells us:

> Do you see those skilled at their work?
> They will stand in the presence of kings. (Proverbs 22:29)

But why is the homily/message used for purposes other than its real purpose? Why can the message become so trite and formulaic? Why is everything prioritized above preparation? Why is it so easily treated as an afterthought?

Because preaching God's word and preparing to preach God's word demand discipline, and discipline is no fun.

Think of the long, lonely laps of an Olympic swimmer or the steady, solitary commitment of a distance runner, the focused, sometimes forced, effort of any athlete in training. That's message preparation. It is long and lonely, solitary and steady, focused, and sometimes forced work. It is not easy or always enjoyable, and day in and day out it brings no rewards and zero job satisfaction. It doesn't even seem important.

Father Michael: I remember the woman who came into my office, unannounced, saw me working on my homily and said, "Oh, good, you're not doing anything," as she sat down and proceeded to interrupt me in my work.

It's more interesting to deal with crises and emergencies; it's more gratifying to meet people's expectations and demands. There is so much else that can come and take your time that you want to address. That's the way it's always been.

The Acts of the Apostles tells us that the Church of the apostles was exploding with growth because the grace of God was powerfully at work in the *preaching* of the apostles. But in Acts 6, we read that some of the churchpeople started complaining. One group felt under-served by the apostles (sound familiar?):

> So the Twelve called together the community of the disciples and said, "It is not right for us to neglect the Word of God to serve at table. . . . We shall devote ourselves to prayer and to the ministry of the word." (Acts 6:2, 4)

It is not right to give up preaching the word. They don't say that other forms of ministry and service are unimportant. They're only saying that the service of the Word of God is *more* important, and it is something only *they* can do. Others could, and eventually did, serve at table. Likewise, for us it is not right to give up the preaching (and preparation for preaching) of God's word to take on tasks that parishioners could be doing for one another.

Father Michael: People don't show up on Sunday morning because I'm a good counselor. Being a great administrator or manager won't fill the pews. Trying to meet the expectations of everyone in the congregation will never grow the church. Aside from the celebration of the sacraments, I have come to see the preparation and presentation of

the weekend message as the most important thing
I do. It is my point of greatest impact with the largest circle of people—the message is the number
one place where the lost get connected and members are challenged to change.

On the surface, it can be difficult to believe the message matters.
After all, it's just words. And nobody's paying any attention anyway,
right? But, over and over again, scripture describes the power of words.
To begin with, God *speaks* the world into existence with his word. And
we've been made like him, so our words have power, too.

That is not suggesting that "saying it makes it so." A lot of preaching, of whatever school or style, is all about
telling people what they want to hear. Those
are just empty words, and they have no
effect beyond pleasing parishioners. We like
to remind ourselves around here that, "Saying it *doesn't* make it so."

> The message
> is the number
> one place where
> the lost get
> connected and
> members are
> challenged to
> change.

We can't speak nothing into something
like God does, but our words have the
power to build up and the power to tear
down. Our words can change and transform. The Bible says, "Death and life are in
the power of the tongue" (Proverbs 18:21).

Words have power, and *God's* word has *God's* power. And when we
speak God's word we unleash God's power.

Indeed, the Word of God is living and effective, sharper
than any two-edged sword, penetrating even between soul
and spirit, joints and marrow, and able to discern reflections
and thoughts of the heart. (Hebrews 4:12)

We see this demonstrated throughout scripture. God sent Moses to Pharaoh, and when he speaks God's word, God's power is unleashed in the plagues of Egypt (cf. Exodus 7–12). Peter speaks the Word of God to the crippled beggar, and he is healed (cf. Acts 3:1–8). God leads the prophet Ezekiel to a valley of dry bones. These bones represent the spiritual dryness of Israel that had become completely hardhearted. God tells Ezekiel,

> Prophesy over these bones, and say to them: "Dry bones, hear the word of the LORD! Thus says the Lord GOD to these bones: Listen! I will make breath enter you so you may come to life. I will put sinews on you, make flesh grow over you, cover you with skin, and put breath into you so you may come to life. Then you shall know that I am the LORD." (Ezekiel 37:4–6)

Ezekiel speaks the Word of God and gets to see the power of God. That's the deal. When you are faithful to the Word of God, you get to see the power of God at work in your life.

Faithfully proclaiming God's word effectively unleashes God's power in your congregation. It is the power to change people's lives: healing what was broken, curing what was sick, raising up what was dead. God's word brings about change when we take the time to introduce people to its relevance and meaning in their lives.

> When you are faithful to the Word of God, you get to see the power of God at work in your life.

Speaking God's word in your church will change the people in your church. Then it will change your church; it will breathe new life into it; maybe it will resurrect your parish from the dead.

The clearest, most striking example of this, for us, came in the finances of the parish. We'll speak more of this in a later chapter, but our point here is that by actually preaching what God says about money, new life was breathed into our financial situation. And the level of giving has continued to grow, even in a time of economic turmoil. There was no campaign; we didn't bring in consultants to tell us how to do it; we just started using God's word; and *then* we started to see God's power at work. We weren't a "rich" parish where the money funded our church growth strategy. The money didn't fund the strategy; it followed it, and it came in response to the preaching.

New life was breathed into our volunteer ministry after we started consistently preaching what God has to say about serving. Discipleship, daily quiet time, singing at Mass, and every area of growth in our church is unmistakably the fruit of preaching.

A Path to Better Preaching

When Jesus finished these words, the crowds were astonished at his teaching, for he taught them as one having authority, and not as their scribes.
—Matthew 7:28–29

That's the key. In a setting like Nativity, we were too often speaking only from our own authority. We weren't really relying on God's authority. And in the process we were limiting our effectiveness *and* our church growth.

In looking at the most successful churches in the country, we discovered that their approach was very different from ours, and we began to challenge and change some of our assumptions. Here are the principles we now rely on.

1. **Preach to yourself.**

    Prayer should be foundational to all preaching and preparation for preaching. At the same time, and if you're actually trying to apply what you preach to your own life, your preaching will always be authentic. The first life that should be changed by your preaching is your own. Your preaching must come out of lived experience of trying to walk with God, learning from him, and being transformed into his image. That's why preaching and preparation for preaching should find its foundation in prayer.

2. **Preach to your community.**

    In the same vein, we have to be very deliberate about preaching to our people. Preaching to the community means we need to connect with our community on several levels. Aristotle noted that when someone is speaking, an audience determines whether or not they will listen to the speaker based on *ethos*, *logos*, and *pathos*.[4]

    Ethos asks questions like, "Are you ethical?" or "Are you telling the truth?" As preachers, our lives need to be transparently authentic if anybody is going to listen to us.

    Logos asks, "Do you know what you are talking about?" As preachers, we must base our message in God's word, and the Church's Magisterium to answer this question successfully.

    Pathos asks the question, "Do you care about me?" or "Are you speaking in my best interest?" To answer this question, we're going to have to know our community and how to connect with them emotionally. Overlooking the emotional connection of a message will mean people shut down and turn the message off. Effectively engaging the emotional content of the congregation's life will take work, because it's about entering other people's worlds and working from the perspective of their experience.

    Arguably the most important and powerful element in making an emotional connection with an audience is through humor: not jokes, not comedy, not camp, but definitely making people laugh. The ancients referred to the fluids of the human body as our "humors." They thought that the right balance and purity of humors was the key to good health.[5] While we now know the human body doesn't work that way, it is still true to say that the balance that comes from the attitude of good humor is healthy. Laughter makes even bad circumstances better.

Humor is based in truth, and it happens when people recognize a true pattern or are surprised when that pattern is reversed or interrupted. And *then* they laugh, and *when* they laugh they relax . . . and listen. Using humor in the message, by exposing our humanity, poking fun at ourselves, or exaggerating our shared experiences, is a powerful way to engage an audience and help them hear a difficult or challenging message. Humor can win you a hearing.

On the other side of the emotional spectrum are the congregation's concerns and sorrows. There was a terrible tragedy in our part of town a few years ago: A young man murdered his family. Really shocking, horrifying news, but when Sunday morning came we proceeded with business as usual. A distressed woman asked after Mass why we hadn't mentioned it. Believe it or not, we hadn't even thought of it. We have discovered how much we don't know about our community, the great deal we have to learn, and how easily we become insulated from the culture around us. We're constantly amazed at the disconnect that we sometimes still experience between what the people in the community are interested in or concerned about and where our heads are.

We need to preach to our community by tracking on what has them distracted or worried. Ignoring current events just makes us more irrelevant to people's lives.

3. **Preach one message.**

Around here it is axiomatic to say, "one church, one message." We work hard to try to offer the same message at every weekend Mass.

Father Michael: Accordingly, September to May, our "peak" season, I usually preach all weekend Masses, regardless of who is the celebrant. That is uncommon I know, but it ensures that the whole congregation is hearing the same message each weekend. In recent years, while continuing to grow, we have reduced the number of weekend Masses, discontinuing underused ones, in part to help make this value more sustainable.

If that is not a direction you want to take, or if you have associates and regular weekend assistants who also preach, your homilies can be coordinated with some additional effort. Having your whole community hear one message is well worth that effort. One message keeps the parish focused on one theme, facing the same challenges, growing in the same direction.

4. **Preach messages in series.**

A "message series" is about exploring a single theme over the course of multiple weekends. This is a common practice in the evangelical churches we have studied. But if you think about it, the idea makes so much more sense in liturgical churches that have the liturgy's seasons and the lectionary's cycles of readings. It is interesting to explore the themes that are woven through the Church year in our series.

Preaching in series makes preaching prep easier, because we're not starting with a blank slate every week. It also encourages people to keep coming back to hear the rest of the message. Typically, at this point, we do a "back-to-school" style series in September, a stewardship series in October and November, an Advent series preparing for Christmas, and a series in the New Year about resolutions and life-change. During Lent, we try to stretch the congregation with a discipleship series challenging people to go deeper, and then at Easter we give a more celebratory series. Over the past few years, we have an expanded series throughout the whole year to include summertime. These past few summers we've relied on a two-pronged approach: a biblical series and one focused on the Eucharist.

We find that our most effective series are closely associated with the lectionary, which in turn is closely in sync with the seasons of the year and relevant to our people emotionally and experientially. In other words, a message in December is going to be different in style and substance from one in July. We've found that the four-to six–week series are the most successful. Any longer and it begins to feel too long; any shorter and it doesn't get enough traction.

5. **Preach the purpose of the message. Preach life-change.**

Augustine said teach and engage in order to change people, to help them move intellectually and emotionally from where they are to where God wants them to be.[6] We are trying to help parishioners change the way they think and the way they feel about God's word so that he can shape them according to his will. In the process, their lives will change. The purpose of preaching is to change lives.

6. **Preach the outcomes of the message.**

What, specifically, do you want them to change? What *is* the message, and what do you want them to *do* with the message? Aim at nothing and you will hit every time. Often messages succeed in hitting nothing because there is no target, no win. For homilies to be effective, we've learned to take time to figure out the target we're trying to hit. When it comes to preaching, Andy Stanley asks, "What do you want them to know, what do you want them to do?"[7]

We try each week to answer those questions as clearly as we can, because if the answer is cloudy in the pulpit, it will be a dense deep fog out in the congregation. And it is amazing how often we struggle to come up with an answer, how frequently we find ourselves on Monday morning asking, "What did we want them to *know*; what exactly was it that we wanted them to *do*?"

In the last year or so, we have also added some comments at the very end of our service, much as many parishes have announcements. We call them "endnotes." But our announcements don't try to sell anyone anything or necessarily highlight upcoming events. Instead, we very deliberately, sometimes playfully, underscore, one more time, what we want them to know and what we want them to do. By the way, it's an excellent opportunity to introduce your staff to the congregation. The pastor doesn't have to be the only voice they hear.

> **What do you want them to know, what do you want them to do?**

7. **Preach the announcements.**

We have come to include church-wide goals in our message series, asking the question, "How will the church be different *after* than *before*?" A stewardship series is obviously going to look for increased giving. One January we had a series about what God wants from us, and the church-wide goal was more people in ministry. We did a series looking at Acts of the Apostles one Easter, and the goal was for everyone to read the entire book. We did a series on emotional health and challenged everyone to go to confession one weekend (hundreds did). It is very energizing to preach a message series and have these kinds of outcomes to show for our efforts.

8. **Preach other people's messages.**

Plagiarism is a serious ethical violation. But it is not plagiarism to avail yourself of the tremendous resources that other preachers out there are only too happy to share. As Rick Warren says, "We're all on the same team." Reading and *listening* to the messages other preachers make available for this purpose can be a great way to grow your repertoire, not copying or aping but adopting other people's messages and making them your own. We have found that our most successful messages and series are based on other people's material we have adapted from other preachers and aligned with our liturgical readings. Of course, this means we have to acknowledge that other people out there are better at this than we are. The more we study others, the more talent we uncover.

9. **Preach prepared.**

If you consistently step into the pulpit only after rock solid preparation, if your congregation can go to the bank on your preparation, if they know they can invite friends and will not be disappointed, you will have their attention. You won't need "attention getters" to try to trick them into paying attention to you. People notice when you put time and energy into your message, and they will appreciate it. By the way, the best way you prepare for next week is by reviewing last week. And the very best way to review is to watch a video or listen to a recording of your homily. You will begin to grow exponentially as a speaker when you do.

Want to know more/go deeper?

See Michael and Tom talk about message preparation and series preparation. Go to rebuiltparish.com and click "Chapter 8," then click "Message Preparation."

---

10. **Preach God's word.**

Make sure it is all about the Word of God and nothing else. When we are faithful to the Word of God, relevancy follows naturally. As an Oklahoma pastor puts it, "It's ludicrous to say that you can't have relevant preaching if you're giving good exposition of the text. That's stupid. We don't have to make the Bible relevant. If we're faithful to the text, it can't help but be relevant."[8]

And preach *all* of God's word, the comforting parts and the challenging bits, too. In the twentieth chapter of Acts, Paul delivers his final message to the Church of Ephesus, knowing that he will never see them again. He says, "I did not shrink from proclaiming to you the entire plan of God."

Father Michael: What an awesome responsibility, what an incredible opportunity, to share the whole counsel of God with people! That responsibility and opportunity deserve our very best, sustained efforts.

Frankly, at Nativity, the homily was the most dreaded portion of the service and probably *the* major reason people stopped coming to this church. No, actually I'm going to go ahead and assert it absolutely *was* the major reason people were leaving. And oftentimes they were leaving to find churches that had a relevant, engaging message, even if that meant giving up the sacraments. Our preaching should be leading people into a deeper appreciation and celebration of the Eucharist, not alienating them from it.

Currently, my weekend message is about twenty minutes long. And I do not apologize for that. The message matters . . . a lot. The hard truth is, your church won't matter in your community until your message does. Look at the rest of the story in Acts 6. The apostles appointed people to take care of the ministry needs that had been taking them away from the pulpit. In other words, they staff up and then return to "prayer" (the Eucharist and the liturgy) and the "ministry of the word" (preaching). So, what happened? "The Word of God continued to spread, and the number of the disciples in Jerusalem increased greatly" (Acts 6:7).

God puts a high priority on the preaching of his word. And when we do preach it, his word spreads. And the number of disciples increases. Your church grows!

YOU CAN DO THIS!
Steps You Can Take in Your Parish

- If you're a pastor, sit down and map out a message series for next Advent or Lent that establishes consistent themes, clear challenges, and attractive outcomes.
- If you share your pulpit with an associate or regular assistant sit down together and plan for the series.
- If you're a Pastoral Life Director, invite your celebrants to plan the series and facilitate the discussion.
- Look for free resources (like message outlines and promotional art) on other churches' websites. Try LifeChurch.tv.
- Promote your series as a series and get people excited about it. Make it feel like an adventure you're all taking together.

Short Shelf Life

Father Michael: All that said, let's be completely honest: Even the most brilliantly worded, finely crafted, totally engaging, and effective homily has a shelf life of about two days. By Tuesday, everyone's more or less forgotten what I said on Sunday. By Wednesday, I've forgotten. That need not be depressing because our weekend message should not be presented as the final word on any topic. Instead, it's a starting point; it's the place to begin the conversation. The very best compliments I get, the ones I value the most, occur when people tell me they discussed the message in the car on the way home, that it was the topic of conversation around the dinner table or the water cooler, that people were talking about it at the pool on Sunday afternoons. We want the conversation to continue throughout the week because discipleship isn't just a weekend exercise. We just want to get the conversation started.

As important as they are, the weekend experience and its message aren't enough. To keep the conversation going, you've got to do something else; you've got to . . .

9

BUILD FROM BELOW

Put on then, as God's chosen ones, holy and beloved, heartfelt compassion, kindness, humility, gentleness, and patience, bearing with one another and forgiving one another, if one has a grievance against another; as the Lord has forgiven you, so must you also do. And over all these put on love, that is, the bond of perfection.

—Colossians 3:12–14

B lame it on the 225 stations you have on premium cable. Or maybe it's your crazy schedule and your kids' sports; perhaps it's all the fault of endless mobility and terrible traffic; and let's not forget the ceaseless distraction of seemingly ever-present screens that bombard us with information—useful or not. Whatever the cause, Americans are increasingly disconnected from a sense of community. And beyond the inevitable loneliness and isolation that it causes, it could be bringing even more serious consequences. In his fascinating book, *Bowling Alone*, Robert D. Putnam argues, "Our growing social-capital deficit threatens educational performance, safe neighborhoods, equitable tax collection, democratic responsiveness, everyday honesty, and even our health and happiness."[1]

The basic problem is that we're made for relationships, quite literally: "The Lord God said: It is not good for the man to be alone" (Genesis 2:18). We need relationships and we'll look for them in artificial ways if we can't find them for real, as the phenomenon that is Facebook dramatically underscores. We're made for relationships because that's how God made us. And scripture tells us that our companions will definitely influence the quality and direction of our lives.

> Walk with the wise and you become wise,
> but the companion of fools fares badly. (Proverbs 13:20)

If you examine your personal history, you will find a story of relationships. We grow and develop and change with others. And in whatever endeavor we want to succeed, we'll also need friends to support and encourage us. That's the way it works in life. And what's true for your life in general is also true for your faith life; it's all about relationships.

Tom: Looking back on my own history, I was lucky to have great examples of faith in my parents and my grandfather, as well as a solid Catholic education. But it wasn't until I met my future wife that my own faith became a vital and active part of my life. With Mia, I found someone with whom I could discuss and share my faith, be held accountable, and grow.

Personal, Not Private

The Christian faith is certainly held in a *personal* way, but not in a *private* way. We see this from the beginning as Jesus calls twelve apostles to live and work together. Likewise, the life of the Church we read about in Acts was a *common* life.

> All the believers were together and held everything in common. . . . Every day they devoted themselves to meeting together in the temple area and to breaking bread in their homes. They ate their meals with exultation and sincerity of heart, praising God and enjoying favor with all the people. (Acts 2:44,46–47)

Without Christ-centered friendships, our walk of faith will most certainly be a slower, less steady one, and we're far more likely to fall and fail. When we have friendships in which Christ is a central part, we connect with him in a way we will not on our own. In other words, we grow in faith *relationally*.

> For I long to see you, that I may share with you some spiritual gift so that you may be strengthened, that is, that you and I may be mutually encouraged by one another's faith. (Romans 1:11–12)

Historically, in most US parishes friendship and fellowship were promoted through various fraternal societies, guilds, and clubs. These organizations have dramatically declined in membership during the last few decades and in many places have entirely disappeared. Perhaps this is because their original purposes became unclear, or because their rituals and rules do not appeal to contemporary taste. Maybe they've just fallen victim to the same generational changes that have depleted the Shriners and the Elks. In any event, along with their demise, the Church's sense of community has certainly suffered.

Parish churches in many places, especially in the part of the country where we live, were also more firmly imbedded in compact suburban or dense urban neighborhoods where everyone tended to know everyone else. Fellowship and support happened more effortlessly in these settings than it does in the cultural landscapes where many parishes operate today.

For these reasons, as well as the unprecedented lifestyle changes related to both mobility and technology that all Americans are experiencing, parishes are simply no longer the social centers they once were. The Friday night CYO dances and Sunday afternoon parish picnics are only a fond memory to many and a quaint historical curiosity to others. But the result is the same: Increasingly, parishioners don't know one another. At Nativity, people might have had friends who happened to be *in* the parish, but it seemed like very few people had friends *from* church. The proof of this was obvious at weddings, baptisms, and funerals. Beyond those directly involved, we rarely saw many parishioners at those ceremonies. In other words, our parishioners' friends weren't our parishioners.

> People congregated at Nativity, but the congregation wasn't a community.

People congregated at Nativity, but the congregation wasn't a community. In fact, much of what was in the culture here actually worked *against* the idea of community. There was no time or place to do it; there was no plan to make it happen. People came late and then left early. They did not greet one another; the Sign of Peace was a halfhearted, halting exercise. We recall a story told by others: A visitor is seated alongside a lady piously fingering her rosary through the Mass. At the Sign of Peace, the visitor turns to exchange greetings. The lady briefly looks up from her rosary to say, "I don't go in for that crap."

There was never any emotional connection among parishioners (if you didn't count tension in the parking lot). That's not surprising really, as consumers rarely care much about one another.

This is not very affirming to parishioners, and it's terribly unattractive to the lost. Probably a huge reason people who don't go to church *say* they don't go to church is that churches often feel unfriendly.

Unfriendliness is also unhelpful to our purpose. If we're challenging people to go deeper in their faith but providing no support system to sustain that exercise, it won't work. If we're inviting them into a countercultural lifestyle and then sending them back out into the culture to try to do it on their own, it won't happen.

Neither does community happen by accident, nor even easily. And in large churches, set in sprawling suburbs, it's not going to happen at all unless it is a deliberate exercise. Furthermore, it looks like our parishes will be getting even *bigger* in the future (at least geographically) through the consolidations, twining, and mergers that are happening in many parts of the country and the rapid growth of the Church in others. What is that going to do to the already strained sense of community in many places?

We must make our large churches more personal, providing fellowship and consistent member care. And in parishes of any size we need to encourage relationships that support congregants in their faith. In an age of technology and increasingly superficial personal relationships we must strive to provide a community of friendship in faith just as the Church

> Sometimes you wanna go where everybody knows your name, and they're always glad you came. You wanna be where you can see our troubles are all the same, you wanna be where everybody knows your name.
>
> —Gary Portnoy[2]

historically provided desperately needed resources for its impoverished immigrants. At the same time, we need a strategy to make community happen. Our strategy at Nativity is small groups.

Small Groups

It might look like a new idea that emerged in the Post–Vatican II era, but small groups are as as old as the New Testament communities. It might sound like another "Protestant" idea we're just slavishly aping, but it's completely Catholic. Blessed John Paul II taught:

> So that all parishes . . . may be truly communities of Christians, local ecclesial authorities ought to foster . . . small, basic or so-called "living" communities, where the faithful can communicate the Word of God and express it in service and love to one another; these communities are true expressions of ecclesial communion and centers of evangelization, in communion with their pastors.[3]

Here again, it all started as a youth movement. We began using small groups to replace our dysfunctional high school religious education program. Immediately, it was a hit, breathing new life into what had been a moribund enterprise.

Next, we moved on to adults in a modest way. In the spring of 2005, we formed two groups with some adventurous people who were willing to learn along with us for a season or so. It turned out we had a lot to learn. One of the groups disbanded before we even finished the exercise, and in the process the woman who was serving as our volunteer leader quit (and left the parish too; we still don't know why). It didn't feel very successful. But we kept trying and learning, and just a year later, boldly, we invited the whole parish to try a small-group experience just for Lent. For the content of this exercise we used Rick Warren's *40 Days of Purpose* campaign.

That was encouraging because a large number of people gave it a try, but it was short-lived success. Our first full season for groups came two years later with far less participation. In the beginning we were naïve enough to believe that running a small-group program would be a no brainer. What's the big deal? Just get some adults together, invite them to talk about faith, and it'll all work out. As we've said, church isn't easy and this exercise turned out to be one of our greatest challenges.

Frankly, we've found that small groups are a tough sell in a Catholic setting. Making an additional time commitment each week for church or even considering the value in doing so seems to be the initial stumbling block. But there are others: welcoming people into your home, talking about your problems, even acknowledging you have problems—it's just not what people want to do. And it's definitely not what Catholics have been taught to do.

> We need a strategy to make community happen. Our strategy is small groups.

Administratively, it is a labor-intensive enterprise, whatever the size of the program. Groups will always be in movement: merging, growing, dividing, and disbanding. They will constantly encounter logistical problems and personality clashes. And they're emotionally messy.

But through a lot of deep disappointments and some solid success we've continued to work at it. We talk about groups and promote them all the time. And once a year, usually in January, we have a church-wide small group "launch" for new groups, leaders, and members.

Today we have groups for men and women, seniors and young adults; we have couples groups and singles groups, we have groups based on affinity, like mom's groups, and groups that gather according to the convenience of their location or day and time.

Along with our weekend "crowd" programs described previously, students also meet in small groups. The high school program that started it all continues strong, and now we have another for middle schoolers. The groups have been very successful in engaging young people at a whole new level of young discipleship and, at this point, are really the heart of our youth programs.

Just this past year we also began transitioning our program of religious education for first through fourth grade into a small group program instead of a traditional classroom instruction style. While it is a brand new effort, it has been met with great enthusiasm by kids as well as their parents. In fact, our kids have become some of our biggest fans of small groups because they're a lot more fun than Sunday school.

Want to know more/go deeper?

See Chris and Lisa talk about small groups for students and kids. Go to rebuiltparish.com, click "Chapter 9," then click "Kids and Students, Small Groups."

Group life is not everything we want it to be, but it is definitely a defining part of our culture. We're glad it is, because the rewards for parish fellowship and discipleship are inestimably valuable.

What We've Learned about Small Groups

1. **Small groups are small.**

C. S. Lewis argues in *The Four Loves* that the best place to support a friendship is in a small circle of friends.[4] Likewise, faith-based relationships need to be sustained and strengthened in groups that are small. Ideally a group wants to be made up of six to ten people. Any more than that and members start getting lost in the crowd and stop talking. And then they stop coming. Getting too small is another problem: Two people are a couple, not a group, and three or four people can find themselves with too much pressure to speak.

Since small groups are congregated with people whose life situations are constantly changing, the composition of groups will constantly be changing, even in a healthy group culture. Groups expand and contract, and the key for leadership is going to be managing the process, dividing groups that have grown too big and merging groups that have become too small. Groups will always resist these interventions, but that's what leadership is there to facilitate.

2. **Small groups are integrated into the life of our parish.**

This is extremely important: Small groups are not intended to be stand-alone communities, silos for independent efforts, parachurch gatherings for special interests, or circles for idle conversation and parish gossip. These are dangers that must carefully avoided or they will do harm to the fellowship of your parish. Groups arise out of the communion of both the parish and the universal Church, and they must remain *in* communion with their pastors, as Blessed John Paul II taught. That means they're moving and growing in the same direction as the whole community, and *group* members are contributing *church* members. That's why we actually look to groups to staff our parish initiatives like service projects. Groups that serve together in a particular ministry or mission are more solidly connected to one another and to parish life, too. Small groups have been invaluable in giving parishioners a vested interest in the life of the parish and moving them beyond the role of spectating consumer.

The key to make this happen is going to be the small-group leader. More and more we have been coming to understand how important our leaders are to the success of the group and their connection back to the parish. Connecting, supporting, training, and equipping the leaders as ministers and shepherds of the group are the keys.

3. **Small groups are our delivery system for pastoral care.**

Small groups are the place where our great big church can get small and personal, where we're known, loved, and cared for. As such, we like to say that small groups are our primary delivery system for pastoral care. If they're in a small group, people can get the pastoral care they need, and so much more than our staff could ever give them. Unfortunately, from time to time, someone will bring to our attention their disappointment about the *lack* of care they've experienced in our parish. And inevitably we learn they weren't in a small group.

In a parish of our size, no matter how much attention the staff lavishes on pastoral care, people will fall through the cracks. This is liable to happen, but with small groups it doesn't have to happen. We'll go even further and assert that the day has passed when clergy and staff are solely, or even primarily, responsible for all such efforts in the life of the parish. Emphatically, this expectation needs to end! It's just setting us up for frustration and failure, and it can't be sustained anyway, given current forecasts for vocations.[5] Besides, if we're really going to be the Church that Christ calls us to be, we *all* need to care for one another. The Bible commands us to do it.

> **Tom**: Perhaps the main reason people don't care for one another is because there is no system for them to do it. But care can easily happen in small groups. Here's an example a group leader recently shared with us:
>
> > A woman joined our group who had been carrying a very large burden for a long time. Her husband has been in a bad place physically,

emotionally, mentally, career-wise, you name it. But he had been insisting that no one know about his problems and so she had no real support. When she joined our group, I got the sense very quickly that she was holding something big back. The comments she made were like someone dipping their toe in the water to feel the temperature but never actually taking the plunge. After months she finally opened up to our group, which was a huge step. Some of the women gave her very tangible, practical steps she could take to pursue health and healing in her marriage. Things have not improved yet, but she comes to group knowing that she is accepted, supported, loved, and prayed for; and she leaves group with hope and resolve.

Parishioners absolutely *can* provide pastoral care for one another, and they *will* if they're in a small group. Looking after members who are sick; checking in on people dealing with family problems; offering the helping hand that's sometimes needed to get through a difficult week; providing a meal or a ride; watching the kids or walking the dog during a period of loss, these are little things that can be big things of great value in the life of the whole parish community. And when, from time to time, tragedy shows up, you've already got a team ready to help.

We know of a group who learned of a member's inoperable cancer and moved in to support and care for him and stand with his heavily burdened caregiver wife. Day after day they were there for them, laughing and crying with them and loving them all the while. What more effective pastoral care could our parish possibly offer?

Father Michael: I presided at a heartbreaking funeral for a baby girl. In spite of the sadness, it was an extremely beautiful service, mostly because of the mom's small group. Those ladies just stepped in and took care of everything. They greeted guests, made and handed out programs, and generally ensured that everything ran smoothly. One of their number offered a eulogy that was truly amazing (think about it, a eulogy for an infant).

Afterward, they went home with the family and stayed with them that day, as well as the difficult days that followed. The family was completely surrounded by the love and support of that group and with a depth and breadth that our parish staff could never have provided. For me, it was one of the most striking examples ever of our church being the church we're supposed to be.

4. **Small groups are about life-change.**

Everything that we're discussing when it comes to parish life has to do with life-change. But small groups promote life-change at a fundamental level that rarely happens in a weekend congregation, and will not happen elsewhere.

The power of small groups comes from forming relationships in which *conversations* lead to *conversion*. God made us to learn from other people's experiences and examples. When people sit in a circle and listen to other people's stories, they grow in an understanding of what works in life and how life itself works. As one author describes it:

> It is no etymological fluke that conversation and conversion have the same roots in the Latin. Throughout our lives our conversations change us and move us and often convert us. The root

connection between conversion and conversation
is more than fun with words. The etymological connection tells an important truth. It tells us a story
about our humanness. And our divineness.[6]

Our format for small-group meetings is as simple as can be. Groups gather in members' homes (not at church, which would be unnecessary work for us). There is usually up-front time for social-izing and refreshments, perhaps food. Next comes brief prayer time, followed by some opening questions that we provide to get members on the same page and thinking about the meeting's topic. Sometimes this is followed by a DVD presentation we've prepared. There are also plenty of free resources that many churches make available.

Our message, typically given by Tom, parallels the weekend message Father Michael gave the previous Sunday, but probably with a different approach. So, by the time members start their discussion, they've already heard two messages on the topic. The point of the discussion is not an intellectual exchange of ideas; it's a *sharing from the heart* about where members are on this specific topic—practical things like money, marriage, or anger—and where they need to go. Before leaving, the group prays together. We suggest that gatherings typically run ninety minutes. It's amazing what can happen in ninety minutes of honesty and transparency.

Tom: A friend of ours shares this life challenging experience when it came to her career:

A few years ago I was very unhappy at work and it seeped into other areas of my life and dominated my thoughts. Thankfully I had the support of my group every week who encour-aged me. This helped me hear and eventually follow what God was calling me to do—start my own business. I never in a million years would have thought it was my path. But thanks to the message series at Nativity and the support of my small group, I finally realized it, made the decision to quit my job and start my own business. I have never been happier.

Father Michael: I was in a group a few years ago (our staff members belong to groups), and a guy courageously shared with us that he was struggling with a serious porn addiction. Another guy in the group had already been through the same thing and could discuss with him, step by step, how he tackled his problem. This turned out to be a life-changing exercise when it came to the guy's marriage. I've seen examples of groups helping people to quit smoking, lose weight, get in shape, restore broken relationships.

Tom: One of my favorite examples of this kind of modeling life-change came from a small group I was a part of. A member told the story of how his relationship with one of his daughters improved from a critical decision he made. She had gone away to college and was having a difficult time. She called home to share her struggles, and her father decided he would drop everything and make the five-hour drive to her school to demonstrate his love and support. The next morning, he showed up outside her dorm. Instantly, she understood, in a new way, his love for her, and, afterward, their relationship, which had been tenuous, was transformed. About a year later, another member of the group found himself in exactly the same situation and immediately knew what he had to do.

A group leader shared this example of life change:

> A member of our group has been struggling for over
> eighteen months with his business: His partner is
> driving the company under; he has had to lay off
> half his employees, and his personal money is tied
> up in the company. His brother-in-law, and good
> friend since grammar school, is suffering from an
> addiction, creating great stress for his sister and
> nephew; his interventions have not been successful.
> His son has begun to experience significant depres-
> sion as a result of the death of a close relative. He
> has a strong marriage, but feels the need to protect
> his family from all that's going on. When he first
> came to the group two years ago, he would often
> "pass" when we went around the circle at the end
> of group to pray. Now, he'll often start our prayer
> circle; his prayers, clearly from the heart, are some
> of the most moving and powerful in our group.
> Last week he talked about his need for the group,
> "It's the only place I have in my life where I don't
> have to put up a good front." His courage and faith
> have touched all of us deeply.

In a sin-stained world, all of us have struggles. We are not always the person we *want* to be or even the one we *appear* to be. Neither do most of us have any place to bring our struggles and problems. We have nowhere to share our joys and sorrows. We're taught to hide our hurts and hang-ups and to fudge on our faults and fears. Especially in church settings, we wear masks or create images that are time-consuming to maintain and ultimately too fragile not to eventually fail. It's a heavy burden. Ironically, when the mask sometimes slips and people are exposed for who they really are, they often walk away from churchworld because they no longer feel worthy or welcome. Just when they could use the help of a church family the most, they give up on it because everyone's found out their secret: they're not perfect and their lives are messy.

In a small group we can trust people to know our story and accept us despite our imperfections. Small groups are the opportunity for us to do what the Bible tells us to do for other Christians, "Bear one another's burdens, and so you will fulfill the law of Christ" (Galatians 6:2).

Small groups are definitely a place we can find support, but they're *not* "support groups." Neither are they talk-therapy exercises or 12-step programs. They are not meant to be platforms for individuals to focus only on their own needs in a way that dominates the life of the group.

Since groups are about doing life together, we encourage members to be as real and authentic as possible, to be honest about *who* they are and *where* they are in their walk with the Lord. Members love and support one another whoever they are, wherever they are in their journey. Group members also hold one another accountable to change and growth.

If we're going to be serious about life-change, serious issues will be raised. That is why confidentiality is key. Confidentiality creates a safe environment where members can be honest. Lack of it can kill a group's trust, and then it will kill the group. One thing that helps foster this safe and comfortable atmosphere is that we encourage the groups to remain stable. Members remain in the same group for an agreed-upon period of time. When individuals are not hopping from group to group but are committed to specific others, the level of comfort rises with this sense of stability.

5. **Small groups are our schools for discipleship.**

Small groups are about life-change, but the biggest change we are looking for is growth in disciples. The primary purpose of our small groups is to help people become growing disciples of Jesus

Christ. Healthy churches aren't just growing; they're growing disciples. Small groups are our schools for discipleship.

We hope this especially happens through the application of God's word to their daily lives. But, we don't push Bible study, or any kind of study, *per se*, because when people start focusing on content, they can easily stop sharing themselves. Our small groups are "schools" not in the sense of adult education or even just faith formation—they're about *life transformation*.

Tom: From our small-group experience, probably the most remarkable story of conversion, life-changing outcomes, and discipleship concerns our friend, Jack. This was a guy trying to put his life back together after a painful divorce and an unexpected transition in his career. Jack was in the pew but skeptical of many of our new initiatives. When it came to small-group life, his skepticism was deeply cynical.

However, after repeated invitations, Jack reluctantly gave it a try, mostly just to prove that he was right, we were wrong, and small groups were a deeply dumb idea. But little by little, the experience opened Jack's mind and then reshaped his heart. He started caring about the guys in the group; he found himself

> Group members hold one another accountable to change and growth.

moved that they cared about him. He began to value the refreshment he felt from getting things off his chest and out in the open. He found himself changing and growing. Jack grew to be an enthusiastic group member and a more committed disciple. Eventually, he became the group leader and even a member of our steering team. When, recently, we had the opportunity to add a

Small-Group Director to our part-time staff, Jack was the logical choice. In view of his complete conversion from persecutor to champion, we call him the "St. Paul" of our small group program.

Want to know more/go deeper?

Listen to our small-group team leader discuss getting and keeping people on a discipleship path through small groups. Go to rebuiltparish.com/chapter9 and watch the video "Small Groups."

YOU CAN DO THIS!
Steps You Can Take in Your Parish

- Start a small group with a few of your parishioners who are willing to give it a try. Meet weekly September through May, with a break for Christmas.
- The small-group resources our groups use are available for free on our website. This will keep you focused on the Sunday readings. Bring your bibles (and use them). If you want to go in another direction, there are lots of other great resources (start your search with Ave Maria Press).
- Select a group leader, whose job is to make sure no one dominates, everyone talks, and the conversation doesn't get stuck in content. Be open, be honest, be loving.
- Keep inviting other parishioners to join you, but don't let people just come and go. They have to make a commitment to show up. When you grow beyond a dozen members, divide into two groups. The leader will have to be the one to encourage the members to do this. Repeat

the process. But be sure to stay in close contact with new group leaders.

- Encourage your pastor to mention small groups from the pulpit, as a way of beginning to plant it in the culture of your parish.

Partners on the Path

Discipleship is all about simple steps, and when we've got partners on the path, the journey is less difficult. In a certain sense, just being around other people who are even *trying* to live the Christian life will make the effort easier. Authentic relationships rooted in a growing relationship with Jesus Christ is what small groups are about. And we're convinced it's the way forward for the whole Catholic Church.

> The Church of the future will be one built from below by basic communities as a result of free initiative and association. We should make every effort not to hold up this development, but to promote it and direct it on to the right lines. The Church will exist only by being constantly renewed by a free decision of faith.[7]

While we work to shape a culture that promotes, assists, and supports small groups, it is ultimately the work of God. Jesus taught:

> If you love me, you will keep my commandments. And I will ask the father; and he will give another Advocate to be with you always, the Spirit of truth. (John 14:15–17)

The central doctrine of Christianity is the truth that in God there are three persons: Father, Son, and Spirit, one God, three distinct persons. This is a mystery to be held and celebrated, even though we cannot grasp its full meaning. But the mystery itself reveals something critically important about *how* God exists and operates: in intimate relationship—as community. The Trinity is a communion of persons and, as such, is the original small group. Ultimately, small-group life seeks to reflect the life of our God, who is one in three.

There's Sharing and Then There's Sharing

When it comes to growing disciples, it's definitely about sharing your life . . . but that's not all you've got to share. Turns out there is something much more difficult to share than just your life.

10

DON'T ROB GOD

The payment of tithes is due to God and those who refuse to pay, usurp the property of another. Those who withhold them or hinder their payment shall be excommunicated, nor be absolved of this crime until after full restitution is made.

—Council of Trent[1]

Jesus talked about money all the time. Why? Because he understood how it dominates our thoughts, holds our hearts, and stands as a big obstacle to a relationship with God. So much so, he told us flat out you just can't serve both. You've got to choose.

> No servant can serve two masters. Either he will hate one and love the other, or be devoted to one and despise the other. You cannot serve God and mammon. (Luke 16:13)

On one occasion someone seeks his assistance with finances, and here is Jesus' advice: "Take care to guard against all forms of greed" (Luke 12:15).

Greed, or avarice, is the love of money and wealth in an inappropriate or even destructive way. It comes in different forms, so we must be on guard to recognize it. In Catholic moral theology it is treated as a serious vice because it raises money to the purpose of life itself.

If greed was a problem in a poor, agrarian community two thousand years ago, it must be exponentially more so in our contemporary consumer culture. Billions of dollars are spent each year on advertising and marketing; new technologies, styles, flavors, models, and brands hit the stores daily. And every day our culture reminds us of what we don't have, encouraging us to believe that if we had it, we'd be happy. We buy the lie and spend like no others in human history.

Catholics, like everyone else, have gotten into deep credit card and other consumer debt. Many have leveraged themselves into mortgages they can barely afford to pay. One pastor describes the experience of visiting his parishioners in their enormous McMansion homes that are almost completely unfurnished because, presumably, they've run out of money. Another pastor we know calculated that if his parishioners were simply giving to the church the same amount they were paying in *interest* on their credit card debt, their parish income would triple. This is a problem for communities at all economic levels.

Some of our parishioners, even if they make a lot of money, are not in a position to give us anything, because they've already used it up on themselves. Mismanagement of personal finances and debt are serious sources of stress in many people's lives and a major factor contributing to the staggering divorce rate.[2]

People aren't just swimming in a sea of materialism, they're drowning in it. When it comes to money, people don't know how to *live* because they don't know how to *give*. The antidote to greed and the way out of debt is *giving*.

Giving Is Incredibly Important

As we have studied what others have written about parish ministry, we have been consistently surprised and eventually shocked that money is not usually discussed. Neither does either one of us remember money or giving ever being treated in any of our years of Catholic school education, including seminary. What is Church teaching on giving? What does the Bible say? Who knows?

Our experience seems to underscore some serious misunderstanding and, consequently, faulty teaching and preaching, as well as flawed money raising methodologies, in many Catholic settings. So, not surprisingly, Catholic giving at the parish level is abysmal, consistently at or near the very bottom of giving levels among Christians. It is a scandal that dishonors God and belies a certain level of immaturity.

Giving is incredibly important when it comes to growing a healthy parish for two other reasons. The first one is the obvious one, which many Catholics blissfully ignore: It takes money to run a parish. You can't turn on the lights, heat the building, or provide programs without it. All your ministry costs something, and lack of giving will cripple or even kill your efforts. Most critically, you need money to pay a church staff. Catholics are accustomed to getting church for next to nothing because parishes and schools used to be staffed with people who basically worked for free. That was a nice arrangement, but its day is done.

> Catholic giving at the parish level is abysmal. . . . It is a scandal that dishonors God and belies a certain level of immaturity.

As we move forward, parishes will be primarily staffed by lay people, the majority of whom will have to be paid. And if our parishes are going to be successful, parish staffers will have to be paid competitively or the best people won't come to us or stay very long.

So the issue of parish funding is a serious and increasingly critical one. The failure to get it right could lead to the same kind of financial crisis in parishes that is currently eviscerating Catholic school systems across the country. Maybe that crisis is already upon us.

Giving is even more important when it comes to discipleship. One time, a young man approached Jesus about becoming a disciple. He seems to have the right stuff. It looks like he's got it all together—except for one thing. When Jesus says to him, "Go, sell what you have and give it to the poor, and you will have treasure in heaven. Then come, follow me" (Matthew 19:21), the man walks away from that advice. Matthew tells us he leaves with sadness, because he had great wealth. And, as far as we know, he never becomes a disciple. Elsewhere Jesus tells the story of the rich fool who is only wealthy in ways that won't last and actually "not rich in what matters to God" (Luke 12.21). Our money and our discipleship go hand in hand.

Despite the common misperception, based on so much nagging out of need and a focus on fundraising, this topic is largely ignored in the pulpit as a spiritual issue. Why?

Pastors and parish staffs themselves may be poorly educated in what God's word teaches, and may be unconvinced of the spiritual value of giving. Introducing the topic to an equally undereducated and disbelieving congregation will cause conflict. Besides, frustrated and fatigued by so much ecclesial mismanagement and scandal, and the financial calamity they have wrought, many Catholics just tune out. So, it's easier for everyone to ignore it.

Carnivals, Christmas Trees, and Spaghetti Dinners

We have nobody to blame but ourselves. Here again, Nativity is a textbook lesson in what *not* to do, both before and after we arrived.

This church began meeting in a junior high school gym. From the outset, pastor and congregation alike set their hearts on erecting a church building as quickly as possible. This is a common mistake, though an understandable one. Churchpeople want to build churches even before they're needed or financially sustainable. Certainly it relieves them of the tedious task of weekly set up in a borrowed space. But more compellingly, the church building defines who they are as a community. It's a mistake to think this way because a community's identity should define it's space. But unfortunately, it's a consistently repeated mistake.

The ensuing scenario at Nativity was also typical: the young congregation, still trying to grow, saddled itself with a huge debt which quickly dominated parish life. When gifts and offerings failed to provide the income necessary to service the debt,

> *Build your people before you build your steeple.*
> —Rick Warren[3]

they turned, urgently, to fundraisers to make up the difference. The fundraisers became the focus of parish activity, eating up staff and volunteer efforts, and probably precluding a lot of other more missional things from happening. And when even the fundraisers weren't enough to pay the bills, the parish offered a "bond program." This was a resourceful but breathtakingly unbiblical approach in which parishioners *loaned* money to the parish, instead of *giving*.

Over the years, these various approaches completely confused the parishioners about giving and the parish continued to struggle with its finances. To clarify the situation, so the legend around here goes, one Sunday, parish leaders took to the pulpit and made it simple for everyone to understand. They announced, "All we need to make this place work is eight dollars a week from every family." In other words, they reduced the offering to a simple admission price. Ironically, the upshot of this strategy was actually a reduction in some weekly offerings! Apparently the people who paid the most attention to it were the ones giving *more* than the eight dollars.

When we first came to Nativity we didn't think much about money. We had no appreciation for its importance aside from what we could do with it. Nor was there any message for our congregation when it came to giving, beyond "*we want more.*"

There seemed to always be a fundraiser going on. As we saw it, fundraisers were an obvious way to supplement our "income" and get stuff we wanted that couldn't be accommodated or justified in the budget. One spring we were trying to raffle off a car, which we had purchased for that purpose. Our initial efforts didn't even yield the sticker price, so we had to keep extending the drawing to sell more tickets. All the while the car continued to sit out in front of the church, a big, bright, shining indictment of how much we didn't get it.

In addition to our lack of knowledge and understanding was our own lack of giving. Neither of us ever gave much financial support to the church. We never even considered it. Few others on our staff gave either, and some of our more active parishioners considered their *service* their offering. Once, during a particularly annoying fundraising campaign, one of our major volunteers declared, "I'm not contributing a dime, because the time I give you has a cash value of at least $20,000 a year!" The financial strain of the period tempted us to just ask for the cash instead.

And, on the other hand, when it came to our personal finances, we were both pretty lost: stupid spending, credit card debt, lack of financial planning, and no savings. These things are not unrelated.

A parish we know claimed on their street sign, "We're a tithing parish." Who were they trying to convince? And then they belied their own propaganda because right next to that sign was another one—advertising bingo. Sorry, you can't have it both ways.

To host their regular fundraisers, quarterly spaghetti dinners, a small church took on a huge debt to build a church hall and catering kitchen.

Their dinners are justifiably famous throughout the community, but, at this point, ironically, they're barely raising enough money to meet their monthly payments on the new construction.

A church elsewhere in our region hosts ceaseless fundraisers—big, ugly, labor-intensive fundraisers—one after another. A summer carnival is followed by the fall festival; the Halloween haunted house comes next, then the mother of all Christmas tree sales closes out the season. It's what they do. It's just not what the Lord told us to do.

Fundraisers can be fun. They can provide fellowship. Sometimes they're a function of a community's social or ethnic culture, and even a source of pride. As such we respectfully acknowledge their attraction.

But, fundamentally, fundraisers are about an exchange of money for something, or the *possibility* of something, in return. As such, they are a consumer exchange. And often, they are so consummately consumer driven that they almost create a parody of the Church of Christ. Raffles, auctions, silent auctions, sales, dinners, dinner theatre, dances, 50/50s, bingo, tuition incentives—none of these is how God teaches us to fund the work of his Church.

It's like fruit. Fundraising is all about going for the "fruit," plucking it off the branches, shaking it out of the tree, gathering it up from the ground. It is sometimes successful short-term but it is a losing long-term strategy when it comes to church funding. At some point, we'll have taken all the fruit off the tree; we can even damage or kill the tree with overaggressive harvesting (professional fundraisers call it "donor fatigue"). We can go for the fruit . . . or we can plant fruit-bearing trees. These are two very different exercises, leading to two different outcomes. Successful church funding should be about planting fruit-bearing trees—parishioners who are givers. Fundraising raises funds. We should be raising givers.

Raising Givers

Our education actually started with the teaching found in the third chapter of the book of the prophet Malachi. God says to the people of Israel,

> Since the days of your fathers you have turned aside from my statutes, and have not kept them. Return to me, and I will return to you, says the LORD of hosts. But you say, "Why should we return?" Can anyone rob God? But you are robbing me! (Malachi 3:7–8a)

God tells the people of Israel that he has given them a law to follow, which they are ignoring. Their disobedience has taken them far from him and the blessings he wants to share with them. In fact, he accuses them of robbery. How can you rob God? It is not that difficult.

> And you say, "How have we robbed you?" Of tithes and contributions! You are indeed accursed, for you, the whole nation, rob me. Bring the whole tithe into the storehouse. . . . try me in this, says the Lord of hosts: Shall I not open for you the floodgates of heaven, to pour down blessing upon you without measure? (Malachi 3:8b–10)

God promises blessing in our churches and over our lives if we'll just honor his word. Ignoring it, on the other hand, is effectively cutting ourselves off from his blessings. Unfortunately there are thousands of financially struggling churches, of all denominations, whose troubles sadly illustrate this truth. Notice how God says, "Try me in this." He is asking us to test him. When it comes to our money, God wants us to test him and

> Fundraising raises funds. We should be raising givers.

see if he will not be faithful. Just try it and see if he won't work his blessings in your life and the life of your parish. It's a challenge.

After reading that passage, it's easy to agree with Mark Twain's assessment: "It ain't those parts of the Bible that I can't understand that bother me, it is the parts that I do understand."

The Tithe

The tithe is the gift of 10 percent of what we have or earn, given to honor God. Counted in the tithe are all our gifts to the poor as well as our offering in our place of worship. Catholic school tuition is not counted in the tithe (sorry). Tithing is established as the consistent standard for worship-giving throughout the Bible beginning in Genesis. In the context of his worship, Abraham gives the priest, King Melchizedek, a tenth of what he has. It is the king's share and a sacrificial offering (Genesis 14:18–20). Later we learn this is how his son Jacob worshiped too:

> Then Jacob [said], If God will be with me and will watch
> over me, then the Lord will be my God and this stone that
> I have set up as a pillar will be God's house, and of all that
> you give me I will give you a tenth. (Genesis 28:20–22)

Many Catholics hear "tithing" and freak out, "Isn't that an Old Testament concept that Jesus abolished?" Or, they conceive of it as something that Protestants do, and that we've somehow outgrown.

Father Michael: The first time I deliberately talked about tithing in a homily, a lady accosted me afterward, wagging her finger, scolding, "I never want to hear that word again in this church." And, believe it or not, I acquiesced to her demand; for a long

> time, I never used the word. I just ignored that part
> of the Bible.

The argument that the tithe is an Old Testament command superseded in the New Testament is convenient but wrong. Jesus said he came not to abolish the law, but to fulfill it. In Matthew 23:23 and in Luke 11:42, Jesus explicitly addresses tithing and commends it. In other passages, he raises giving to God to a whole new level. He praises Zacchaeus for promising to give at a 50 percent level (cf. Luke 19:9–10), and the poor widow who gave at the 100 percent level (Mark 12:43–44, Luke 21:3).

God doesn't just want us to give a tithe. He wants us to recognize him as the owner of everything and to diligently embrace our role as stewards of what we have and hold on his behalf. And eventually, one way or another, he's taking it all back. Tithing is just the threshold— the place to get started.

Historically, the issue became confused where, in some countries, tithing was automatically included in the civic tax. People didn't have a choice; they had to pay it. As historical developments in much of Europe and North America brought the division of Church and state (and with it the end of state funding for churches), the tithe was often lost sight of, or no longer understood. In Ireland it came to be deeply resented along with the established state *protestant* church, which the tax funded.[4] At one point resentment actually fermented into a revolt dubbed the "Tithe War." Meanwhile, in other European countries, state funding, where it still exists, can inhibit congregational giving. In this country, besides all the fundraisers, tithing was eclipsed by the endless campaigns that funded the buildings needed to accommodate the Church's growth. The ongoing muddle between parish funding and school funding doesn't help either.

Yet, tithing is imperative if we are to open ourselves and our parishes to the blessings promised in Malachi. It is a teaching that must be retrieved and relearned if we're truly shaping consumer Catholics into disciples, and if parishes are to be revived and genuinely rebuilt in a way that conforms more closely to the Gospel.

But this is not easy, after generations of misunderstanding.

Start with Yourself

We had to start somewhere, so we started with ourselves. Giving to God first forced us to place every other expense after our offering. And both of us can honestly say that as we started tithing, we also found ourselves eliminating debt and building savings. More recently, we've challenged the rest of our staff to set out on the tithing path. And now some of them tithe and others are percentage givers working toward the goal of tithing. Not coincidently, because of increases in our congregational giving in recent years, we have been able to raise, and continue to raise, staff salaries. These things are not unrelated.

After we changed our hearts, we were in a position to challenge and change others through a clear, consistent message not clouded or confused by fundraisers or random appeals for special needs. In this process, we've aimed at raising disciples who are givers and tithers. While we actively

> Tithing is just the threshold—the place to get started.

and enthusiastically encourage members of our church to tithe, at this point, besides our staff, probably very few do. That's okay—for now. We just want to get them on the right road headed in the right direction, if for no other reason, at least to set the next generation up for success.

As a way of moving forward and continuing the dialogue, we encourage people to honor the biblical standard on which the tithe is based. We challenge members to become:

- Planned givers (designating money in their budget to give)
- Priority givers (giving to God first before other expenses)
- Percentage givers (giving a percentage, not a dollar amount)
- Progressive givers (increasing the percentage regularly)[5]

Rather than just turn people off with a message that might be impossible for them to hear, "give 10 percent," these steps allow us to engage everyone in a stewardship process. We simply challenge people to take the step that's the next step for them.

If you're just throwing pocket change into the basket on Sunday (some people call it "tipping" God), plan your gift instead; make it a priority as you budget your other expenses. Everyone can do that, regardless of the size of his or her offering. Percentage giving comes next and it brings the key change in thinking. Initially, it is not about the *10* in 10 percent, it's about a *percent*. We have become convinced that percentage giving is *the* major cultural shift in getting our parish on the right track. Then, as people become percentage givers, the "progressive" part takes care of itself. It really does!

People should give in a planned way that is absolutely a priority and at a progressive percentage. And we believe that the very best way to get them involved and keep them giving is through electronic funds transfer or what we call automatic worship offering. While percentage giving is the key change in *thinking*, electronic giving is the key change in *practice*. The more givers a church has giving in this way, the more giving will grow and the more reliable it will become. We experienced a blizzard one weekend a couple of years ago that completely shut the church down. We didn't have a single service. But we still had a decent income because of electronic givers. We have also recently added a giving option on the website and are looking at other ways to make giving easy and accessible (and not dependent on cash and checks that nobody carries around any more).

We only talk about giving to our parish *once* a year. Currently, the weekend before Thanksgiving is designated as "Stewardship Sunday." We make presentations at all weekend Masses in which we respectfully refresh people's understanding of what it costs to run a parish and pay a staff, but never in a needy or nagging way. The focus of the message however, is all about the good and great work that their offering is funding. We want to congratulate and encourage our current givers and inspire and motivate emergent ones. We use Stewardship Sunday to celebrate our parish and the life changing work we do. Far from being an annual exercise only to be gotten over with, for many people it is their favorite weekend of the year.

Want to know more/go deeper?

Watch our Stewardship Sunday video. Go to rebuiltparish.com, click "Chapter 10," then click "Stewardship Sunday."

Following the message, we provide time for everyone to reflect on their giving and make a commitment for the coming year.

We ask them to complete a commitment card, which represents their plan for giving in the coming year. Then we collect cards at the altar as a sign of how important their commitment is. Their giving is a worship offering.

On the same weekend, we also host our annual parish "business meeting." There, members of our Financial Council review the current and past years' budgets, discussing income and expenses. This meeting is open to the parish and the public and promoted as a clear sign of our transparency when it comes to money. Incidentally, in recent years, hardly anybody comes. We view lack of attendance as a sign of church health. Parishioners trust us with their money.

Another way we promote giving is by modeling it not only personally but also corporately. If a natural disaster hits, such as the earthquake in Haiti, the floods in Pakistan, or the Tsunami in Japan, we don't take up a "second" collection, we tithe our collection and send it to Catholic Relief Services or whatever agency is involved.

Over the last few years, we have helped members of our parish go deeper in understanding what God says about money by making solid resources available to them. We very much like Dave Ramsey's Financial Peace University, an extremely effective approach that helps people improve their personal finances that in turn will help them improve their giving. There are also other great teaching resources available. The point is to help people manage their money more effectively and in a way that honors God, improves their lifestyle, and increases their giving.

However, the most significant way we encourage discipleship with finances is through preaching. We talk about giving to the parish only once a year, BUT we don't hesitate talking about money anytime it comes up in the lectionary. In some recent years we've devoted whole message series to the topic. The first time we did that it took considerable courage and brought a lot of criticism, because consumers don't want to hear it. But as we've presented a consistent message over the course of several years, it has become easier to do, gains a better hearing, and yields ever-stronger results. People's hearts certainly won't change overnight, but if you really live out what God teaches about money personally and then preach it, God will begin to change people's hearts.

> *You get what you give.*
> —The New Radicals[6]

Today, despite the worst economy since the Depression, our income has been growing substantially. Meanwhile. we've eliminated all our debt, continued to increase staff and staff salaries, set aside money for upgrades in the facility as well as repairs, and have been building a reserve for some bigger projects we know are coming our way. Obviously, our increased income means we're supporting our diocese in a bigger way and are able to expand charitable assistance and outreach.

Don't Go Limping Along

In First Kings, Elijah asks the people of Israel, "How long will you straddle the issue? If the LORD is God, follow him; if Baal, follow him" (1 Kings 18:21).

The people wanted to serve God *and* a false god named Baal. Elijah told them you can't serve both. Choose one; otherwise you are just limping along in your faith. Next, he challenges the prophets of Baal to a contest, essentially to prove the truth of the living God. It's a funny story, but bottom line: Elijah wins, the people come to faith, and they give up their false god.

Don't go limping along, straddling the issue. Fundraisers are easy, expedient, and time-tested methods to raise money. They may seem essential. If you're a school or a hospital or some other kind of charity, they are. But for churches, they're a debilitating crutch, and when we use them in place of offerings and tithes, we're just limping along and crippling ourselves and our ministry efforts. The Church of Christ is not a casino, caterer, or carnival. Our mission is making disciples, and fundraisers don't help. They foster the consumer mentality that keeps demanding consumers consuming instead of growing disciples giving.

YOU CAN DO THIS!
Steps You Can Take in Your Parish

- *Step One:* As parish leaders, start obeying God's word when it comes to your own personal finances, beginning with the tithe. Give back to God your first 10 percent.
- *Step Two:* Reconsider fundraisers and competing systems that send confusing messages to members about how they should be supporting the parish. If your budget relies heavily on fundraisers, start weaning yourself off them, even if it means delaying projects or temporarily cutting programs. To the extent possible, reduce special appeals and "second" collections or any collection besides your worship offering.
- *Step Three:* Pray over your offering as it is taken.
- *Step Four:* Live within your means when it comes to how you are spending your offering. Be good stewards of whatever is given.
- *Step Five:* Preach about *money* as often as it comes up in the lectionary. Preach about *giving to the parish* once, and only once, a year. Ask for parishioners' commitment, based not on *your need for money*, but on *their need to give*.

Repeat these steps year after year in a disciplined manner. Through each of these steps, always teach your congregation to give in their place of worship as an act of worship. Help them learn to do it for no other reason than to honor God and grow as a disciple. Don't keep limping along with fundraisers while saying you trust God. Raise disciples, and God will send the money.

Worship is the act of giving value to something. It is what God wants from us, and God himself has taught us how to do it. Repeatedly he admonishes: "No one shall appear before me empty-handed" (Exodus 23:15).

From the beginning of the Church, every gift to the Church and everything given to the poor was understood as gifts to God, as an "offering" to the Lord. In the first few centuries, as the liturgy began to take shape, these gifts of Christian charity became associated with the ritual preparation of the gifts of the Eucharistic sacrifice. In this way the faithful could place their offering with the Lord's.[7]

Today, we make an offering in the middle of Mass; we give money in our place of worship as an act of worship. It doesn't cost us *everything*, as did Jesus' offering, but it should cost us *something*.

King David, who knew more about worship than anybody else before him, *insisted* that his worship cost him something significant and sacrificial (2 Samuel 24:24). Same for us—worship must cost us something.

> The Church of Christ is not a casino, caterer, or carnival. Our mission is making disciples, and fundraisers don't help.

But, on the other hand, it's also an investment. The wisest thing we can do with our money is to fund the work of God's kingdom. It is obviously the best long-term investment strategy there is. As Jim Eliot wrote, "He is no fool who gives what he cannot keep, to gain that which he cannot lose."[8] Use your money to fund the work of his kingdom and your future.

> I tell you, make friends for yourselves with dishonest wealth,
> so that when it fails, you will be welcomed into eternal
> dwellings. (Luke 16:9)

You've Just Got to Do It

Money is a big commitment on the part of growing disciples. But, as we'll see, another commitment is also required. Without this additional commitment, your church will be filled with consumers and your disciples won't be growing. It's difficult, it's labor intensive, and nobody is going to thank you for it (at first); but as a church leader, you've just got to do it.

11

GET THE PARISH OUT OF THE PEWS

Everyone, not just the Missionaries of Charity, can do something beautiful for God. . . . This is the future—this is God's wish for us—to serve through love in action.

—Blessed Mother Teresa[1]

Father Michael: My first year here, I stood by the front door before and after every weekend Mass. I was there to answer questions, field requests, and generally make members feel appreciated for showing up. On the weekends I was also the person who unlocked the building, opened the doors, made the coffee, sold the Mass cards, and changed the toilet paper in the men's room (not sure who did it in the ladies' room).

During the week, I felt compelled to try to visit anyone who might be in the hospital, see everyone who wanted to see me about anything (pretty much on their schedule not mine), manage the office, serve as director of operations, director of marketing, communication director, chief financial officer, and chief of staff. I also headed up the customer complaint department.

The expectation, indeed the *demand*, was that I—and by extension whatever staff I had—would do everything. And, if there were any kind of gathering or meeting for any purpose, I was expected to be there, too. Events were somehow always inauthentic and incomplete without my presence. My absence from a ladies club luncheon, or middle school mixer was more than bad manners, it was considered a disrespectful affront. And when, inevitably, I failed to meet these relentless demands, I was accused of being lazy, incompetent, or "unpastoral."

I recently called a colleague and friend. He was not in, but on his answering machine was his cell phone number and a complete list of other numbers where he could be reached the rest of the day. The message was clear: Whoever you are and whatever you want, call me.

Don't Pamper; Prepare

This level of consumer care is not uncommon among the clergy. It's generous and selfless and we've all been taught to do it. It's also crazy. If a dissatisfied consumer calls to complain and can complain directly to the boss, why wouldn't they? If an inquiry on your website can be sent to the top, that's where it will go. If you can have the pastor do everything from offer the final blessing to throw out the first pitch, you won't settle for less. It's a scenario that leads to expanding demands and inevitable burn out, as we sadly see so often—sometimes even more commonly among religious and lay pastoral ministers than among the clergy. But there is actually an even sadder consequence. This kind of approach, on the part of the parish staff, *guarantees* parishioners will remain demanding consumers rather than engaged disciples.

> There is still a long way to go. Too many of the baptized do not feel part of the ecclesial community and live on its margins, only coming to parishes in certain circumstances to receive religious services. Compared to the number of inhabitants in each parish, the lay people who are ready to work in the various apostolic fields, although they profess to be Catholic, are still few and far between.[2]

The word ministry derives from the Latin *ministerium* or *servitium*, which is translating the Greek *diakonia*, a word for household service, like serving at table. The Bible is clear as can be when it comes to who does this kind of service in the household of the Lord:

> And he gave some as apostles, others as prophets, others as evangelists, others as pastors and teachers, to equip the holy ones for the work of ministry, for building up the body of Christ. (Ephesians 4:11–12)

If you're a pastor, read that again. No, really. Read it again. Pastors should be *preparing* the members, not pampering them—preparing them for the works of ministry.

Jesus *insisted* on the support and assistance of his disciples through-out his ministry. From the miracle of the loaves and fish, to raising Lazarus from the dead, those around him were pressed into service to help him. They were expected to assist. Consistently, he would do his part only *after* the disciples did what *they* could do. Ministry is sup-posed to be a team sport.

The same thing was true in the early church—the apostles filled their role and looked to the church members to take an active part of their own. In fact, they were adamant about it. Paul says, "See that you fulfill the ministry that you received in the Lord" (Colossians 4:17).

The eventual centralization of the roles of bishop and presbyter, and the expansion of consecrated religious life, seems to have absorbed much of the ministry in a way that was not seen in the New Testament Church. Thus, the emergence of a professional ministry class. According to Thomas O'Meara,

> Other baptized Christians might help in the physical support, . . . but they were kept at a distance from the real, public ministry just as they were kept from the sanctuary. There were overtones that ministry was largely about the methods of spirituality and the rubrics of liturgy, that the fallen world could receive only so much redemption, and that all not under orders or vows remained in a secular sphere capable not of ministry but of a vague witness.[4]

The Church has rightly corrected that course. Because who does the "work" of the church is probably *the* most critical question when it comes to changing the

> Indeed, "the more the lay apostolate develops, the more strongly is perceived the need to have well-formed holy priests. Thus the very life of the People of God manifests the teaching of the Second Vatican Council concerning the relationship between common priesthood and the ministerial or hierarchical priesthood. For within the mystery of the Church the hierarchy has a ministerial character (cf. Lumen Gentium, 10). The more the laity's own sense of vocation is deepened, the more what is proper to the priest stands out."
> —Blessed John Paul II[3]

consumer mentality. It's obvious: If people are only being served, they're consumers; if they're working, they're ministers. Our churches will be unhealthy consumer-driven assemblies if people are not pressed to get involved and help out. Just like a family, the only people who don't help are the babies. Christians who don't serve their church family are, at best, baby disciples.

The Second Vatican Council set a new direction that was recently given renewed emphasis by our own bishops. They help us understand that what has been called "lay ecclesial ministry" is not a Plan B for the dearth of vocations, but the mature fruit of the baptized:

> The ministry is lay because it is service done by laypersons. The sacramental basis is the Sacraments of Initiation, not the Sacrament of Ordination. The ministry is ecclesial because it has a place within the community of the Church, whose communion and mission it serves, and because it is submitted to the discernment, authorization, and supervision of the hierarchy. Finally, it is ministry because it is a participation in the threefold ministry of Christ, who is priest, prophet, and king. "In this original sense the term ministry expresses only the work by which the Church's members continue the mission and ministry of Christ within her and the whole world."[5]

> Christians who don't serve in their church family are, at best, baby disciples.

Every Member a Minister

Ministry goes deeper than just helping out. It expresses the work by which Christ's mission continues, so it is basic to discipleship and evangelization. To create the vibrant environment that motivates our members to grow, they've got to serve. To be a place of energy and excitement that is irresistible to outsiders we've got to get the insiders out of the pews. Visitors, guests, and newcomers are served. Members are serving them, as well as one another. Not instantly, not initially, but eventually, we want every member to join a ministry team and serve our church family and our community. Our goal is simply, *every member a minister*.

An obvious question is: "How do you get people to serve?" We preach it, all the time. Not when we need help, not just when we're desperate: all the time. But, we don't nag. No one wants to join a losing team; people aren't motivated to fill holes. They want to follow a vision and make a contribution to a winning effort. That's how we preach ministry. Serving is what a disciple does. And to grow as a disciple, to make more disciples, you've got to keep serving. As ministers, our members get to be on the winning team.

One for One.
—Tom's Shoes
Company Motto[6]

We preach the availability of different ministries to fit the various gifts and talents of our parishioners. We want them to recognize how God has shaped them to serve:

> There are different kinds of spiritual gifts but the same Spirit; there are different forms of service but the same Lord; there are different workings but the same God who produces all of them in everyone. To each individual the manifestation of the Spirit is given for some benefit. (1 Corinthians 12:4–7)

On the other hand, we limit the ministries people can get into when they first sign up. If there are too many options, they might not do anything. It makes it confusing for them to commit and impossible for us to manage toward successful outcomes. Eventually we want to use our ministers' gifts, in a full way, but when starting out, new ministers choose from only a few simple ministries, like making coffee or emptying trashcans. No one is too big or important to start small. By the way, nobody can begin in a liturgical ministry. They have to begin with simpler, humbler tasks. Only ministers who are already successfully serving are invited to liturgical ministry.

To help make ministry accessible, we have a program called "First Serve," a title we borrowed from Willow Creek Community Church. It's simply a chance to try one of our ministries on a single serve, one-time only basis with no obligation to join. If you like it, you come back; if you don't, you can try something else.

Another way we get people to volunteer is to make not only the *job*, but also the *commitment*, small and easily manageable at first. Then, as people see that they really can do ministry and enjoy their experience, they'll often commit to more.

> Our goal is simply, *every member a minister.*

The initial commitment we request is usually two hours, twice a month. That's simple to understand, easy to remember, and not in the least intimidating. This is an extremely important cultural shift. Because churchworld is often about saddling a small circle of people with huge commitments. It's frightening and dysfunctional.

For instance, one reason Nativity could never find enough religious ed teachers was that we were seeking so much from people who weren't giving *anything*. It required expertise they did not have and a time commitment that could involve a significant weekend lifestyle change. There was no "farm system" to feed in new people.

Father Michael: And on the other side of the commitment, there was no end to it. We just plugged people into slots that needed to be filled and then hoped they'd stay in place until Jesus comes. I remember vividly one Sunday my first year here visiting the classes in the religious education program. After meeting with a somewhat chaotic seventh grade class and their clearly bewildered teacher, she pulled me aside and desperately entreated, *"You gotta get me out of here. I stepped in as a sub ten years ago and they've never found a replacement for me. I'm no teacher!"*

> There was no "farm system" to feed in new people.

The initial commitment we ask members to make is our farm system to greater commitment, and sometimes, eventually, to leadership.

On the Team

To get on the team, every minister receives child protection training and background checks. They are asked to provide application information and complete an orientation.

We try to take care of ministers by showing that we value their service and honor their efforts. We want to set them up for success. That includes providing schedules for them in a timely manner; making sure everyone has a supervisor, who is also a volunteer, for support and accountability; and supplying the tools they need. When they succeed, they enjoy their service more and often expand their commitment.

We're working on a program of simple annual reviews so that ministry leaders can make sure ministers are performing well and are still happy in their service. We encourage ministers to take breaks when needed or change ministries when desired.

Many of our weekend ministers wear some identifiable uniform, mostly t-shirts, as well as name badges. This makes them more accessible to members and visitors. But we also like the distinctive garb, because wearing it is an obvious statement that they're on our team. That, in itself, is an additional commitment and a sign of that commitment.

In addition to the weekend ministers, we have dozens of member ministers who work throughout the week. As mentioned previously, we currently have no parish secretaries on staff; most all of the office work is handled by parishioners. They also take care of ordering and stocking supplies for the café as well as looking after supplies and resources for student and kids' programs. More and more of the maintenance is increasingly accomplished by member ministers (one day we hope it all is). Like many parishes, we have a pastoral visitors program that ensures most everyone who is sick at home or in a hospital will get care and prayer (even if they're not in a small group). These volunteer ministers regularly conduct prayer services in the many assisted living centers in our community as well.

Volunteers, as a wise person once said, are not free. We make sure there are snacks and drinks for our weekend ministers in our "volunteer lounge" (which sounds fancy but is just what our front office becomes on Saturday and Sunday). We give them a place to hang their coats, stash pocketbooks, and just hang out with other ministers, which creates fellowship and friendship. We encourage ministry teams to socialize together regularly, reward each other, and celebrate their wins together as a team. We have a full-time staff person, Maria, who is the leader of all the ministry leaders. She shepherds them, holds them accountable to our mission and values, and makes sure they're appreciated. Sometimes she also has to remind us on staff, "Stop, don't do that, let the ministers do that instead."

On the other hand, we do not, as a church, spend a lot of time publicly thanking them, because we don't want church to be about insiders. It's boring when you're in a self-congratulatory church, and it definitely takes the focus off newcomers and puts it on us. Besides, that kind of recognition isn't why ministers should be serving anyway. This past Easter Sunday morning we had 600 members, serving in t-shirts, who hosted our services for about 6,000 parishioners and guests. Behind the scenes we encouraged our ministers and thanked them (and made sure they got breakfast and lunch), but from the altar we thank our guests—for coming. This shift alone would make a huge cultural change in your church.

Want to know more/go deeper?

Meet our director of adult ministries and learn more about attracting and maintaining ministry teams. Go to rebuiltparish.com/chapter11 and watch the video "Building Ministry Teams."

Just because volunteer ministers are working for free doesn't mean they do it on their own terms. That's a commonplace attitude in churchworld and it always creates problems—eventually. Instead, we have values and standards that ministers must fulfill beyond the obvious safety standards and background checks that are now mandatory everywhere. These values and standards were developed by Maria and her team, and are explained and discussed at "First Serve" before anyone begins serving. Disregarding them can lead to a minister being asked to step down.

> **Value #1.** Ministers recognize that they are working for God. Besides praying as a team, our members are asked to approach their service prayerfully and see themselves as servants of the Lord.
>
> **Value #2.** Ministers work together as a team and maintain clear, respectful communication with their teammates and leaders.

Value #3. Ministers share a common sense of purpose, recognizing that, in some specific way, what they are doing is serving our church-wide purpose. There is no unimportant ministry, no matter how modest or simple the task. Ministers are stewards of their ministry and remain accountable for it. Ministers, regardless of their ministry, serve with an attitude that is welcoming, friendly, and accepting of everyone, but especially of "Tim" and his family. They prioritize their tasks from the lens of the newcomers' experience; they carefully avoid becoming the servants of demanding regulars.

Value #4. Ministers are sensitive to physical and emotional obstacles, and real or imagined roadblocks that prevent guests from having a great experience. They take pride in a clean, attractive environment that minimizes distractions from the church-wide message. Everybody, from the pastor to the operations minister who cleans the bathroom (and now changes the toilet paper), takes responsibility and, when needed, lends a hand when it comes to how the place looks.

> There is no unimportant ministry, no matter how modest or simple the task. Ministers are stewards of their ministry and remain accountable for it.

Value #5. Ministers aim at shaping environments that are reliably excellent; they share best practices and work to continue to raise the standard of our service.

To make sure we're holding these values, ministers also agree to the following standards:

Standard #1. Show up for ministry.

We expect ministers to be responsible for doing their job and being where they agree to be, when they're supposed to be there. They need to replace themselves when they can't serve; that's their responsibility, not ours.

Standard #2. Minister casually.

As noted, many of our ministers wear distinctive shirts, t-shirts, vests, or aprons. Beyond that, we ask them to dress casual/business casual, because that's how "Tim" is going to dress for church.

Standard #3. Minister prepared.

We have in-week, electronic communication that aims at focusing ministers' attention and prayer on what's coming up over the weekend and what we're trying to accomplish. We're still experimenting with the most effective methods for doing this, but, bottom line: We want to communicate with them sometime mid-week to help them arrive for their weekend service equipped and ready for what's going on. As full time church ministers, we are very much aware that next weekend is Palm Sunday or Advent. It's likely your volunteer minister isn't.

Standard #4. Minister and worship.

The old *Everybody Loves Raymond* episode, where Ray discovers that being an usher means you don't have to go to Mass, gets it exactly right. So often in churchworld tasks replace worship. A special class of people busy themselves during Mass rather than offering God honor and praise. Wrongly they believe what they do is more important than worship. We ask our ministers to make a commitment to serve one Mass and attend another. We don't have complete buy-in with that yet, but we're working on it. Ministry is a form of honor and worship before God, but it is not an alternative to prayer within the assembly of the faithful at the Eucharist. Disciples do both.

Standard #5. Minister to win.

We ask our ministers to be on the lookout for what God is doing through them and around them, as well as in the bigger church community. We encourage them to name and celebrate their wins as a team, share their wins with team leaders, and make winning a part of the whole church culture.

YOU CAN DO THIS!
Steps You Can Take in Your Parish

- Start a ministry (not a liturgical ministry): a host team to greet guests at your front door or a hospitality team to serve coffee in your lobby after Mass. Try to invite some new people who have never served before, in addition to regulars. Appoint a team leader you know and trust. Give him or her real authority as well as responsibility.
- Invest in your leader and team, give them lots of your time as you launch your ministry. Together, reflect on your standards and values, what you're looking for in terms of wins. Decide what you're going to wear. Get t-shirts, badges, lanyards, or whatever works best in your setting and culture.
- When you do launch, don't make a big deal out of it with the larger congregation. If *they* do, fine, but you don't. This

is about under-promising and over-delivering: You might still have a long way to go in sustaining your new ministry.

- Prepare for the inevitable setbacks (your leader quits; your team doesn't show up on Sunday; someone complains about the effort itself). Don't get discouraged and don't give up. Keep turning the flywheel even if, from time to time, it's all on you. But most of all keep investing in your team. That will ensure it's not all on you all of the time.
- After you've got your team solidly established, start a second team to serve in some other way (parking or ops). It will be easier the second time.

The "There" There

The writer Gertrude Stein once quipped about Oakland, California, "There's no there, there."[7] Unfortunately, the same can be said of many church experiences. People come, people go, it begins to feel like there's no there, there. For newcomers and guests, our ministers are the "here, here."

Pastor Bill Hybels, who has assembled one of the largest volunteer church ministry staffs in the country at his truly amazing church outside of Chicago, writes,

> Imagine what would happen if people in our world—by the masses—took up serving towels, draped them over their arms and willingly (even joyfully!) served other people in their everyday lives. Such attitudes and actions would change our world! I believe a volunteer revolution can happen and that the church should set the pace and energetically lead the way. In my view, people are never closer to

living out the teachings of Christ than when they are adding value to someone else's life. And people who are far from God are rarely more impacted than when they see twenty-first-century Christ-followers behaving as Christ behaved.[8]

Ministers in the Church, for the Church

It's great to get members to do the ministry *of* the church, *in* the church. But even that is not enough when it comes to growing the healthy church culture Christ wants us to be. Your parishioners have got to be ministers of the Church, in the Church, and *for* the Church—and they've got to be ministers *for* the Church *in* the world. Out there in the world, we want our church ministers to . . .

12

BE RESTORERS

We urge you in the Lord, again and again, to spare no labors and let no difficulties conquer them, but rather to become day by day more courageous and more valiant for arduous indeed is the task we propose.

—Pope Pius XI[1]

From the very beginning, God gave human beings a job to do in service to his creation. Throughout the Old Testament we read about that role as an expanding one, more and more with a special attention to the poor, the widow, and the orphan. A relationship with God demands justice and right relations among peoples and care for others. God desires only worship that is accompanied by such work.

In his inaugural sermon in the Gospel of Luke, Jesus places Isaiah's vision at the center of his mission. "The Spirit of the Lord is upon me, because he has anointed me to bring glad tidings to the poor" (Luke 4:18). For his disciples, Jesus makes service to others the second greatest commandment, and he closely associates it with their basic mission of evangelization: "Your light must shine before others, that they may see your good deeds and glorify your heavenly Father" (Matthew 5:16).

Jesus also erases any boundaries or limits to the kind of service his disciples will undertake in the world. And, he makes it clear that their service will be the number one criterion for their performance evaluation. "Amen, I say to you, whatever you did for one of these least brothers of mine, you did for me" (Matthew 25:40).

Why Did He Say That?

The heart of Jesus' teaching and preaching is the announcement of the arrival of what he calls "the kingdom of God." This kingdom is not so much a destination to which we should be heading as it is a *movement* now moving in the world and in human hearts that are open to it. Foundational to this movement is the reordering of our world, the reconciliation of creation, and a return to what the creator intended. The kingdom of God is restoring what God intended from the beginning.

Here's the deal: The redemption won for us, Christ's saving victory on our behalf, is a once-and-forever, for everyone event. But it doesn't mean we're done. The redemption of creation is the work of Christ; and its *restoration* is a work we share with him.

> This, rather, is the fasting that I choose: releasing those bound unjustly, untying the thongs of the yoke; setting free the oppressed, breaking every yoke.
> —Isaiah 58:6

Think of it this way: You lose your house through foreclosure because of stupid choices and bad debt; someone else buys it, but allows it to fall into disrepair; then someone else buys it back and returns it to you. They have redeemed it for you, but it's still a wreck. It is still in need of restoration. Redemption and restoration are two different, though intimately related, exercises. Christ redeems, and *in Christ* Christians restore.

From the beginning, the life of the Church illustrates this restoration movement. In the Acts of the Apostles, just days after Pentecost, Peter and John are on their way to worship when they come across a man crippled from birth who, in his brokenness, must beg for a living. Here's what happened:

> Peter said, "I have neither silver nor gold, but what I do have
> I give you: in the name of Jesus Christ the Nazorean, walk."
> Then Peter took him by the right hand and raised him up,
> and immediately his feet and ankles grew strong. He leaped
> up, stood, and walked around, and went into the temple
> with them, walking and jumping and praising God. (Acts
> 3:6–8)

More than mobility, the man is given a new life: He can rejoin society instead of just watching it walk by, give up begging and get a job, worship again in the temple. It is a restoration.

Restoration is a kingdom movement. When we join in mission service, we are joining in the movement of Christ's kingdom, announcing and extending his lordship over the earth. Of course, this work will not be complete until the Lord comes in glory, but it has begun, and it is our responsibility to advance in his grace.

> Christ redeems, and in Christ Christians restore.

False Distinction

The modern missions movement, as we know it, was born during the Enlightenment in the eighteenth century, the fruit of modernity's newfound sense of freedom and hope. Later in the United States, special impetus was provided by a "great awakening" in the Protestant community. This movement encouraged Christians to embrace their faith with vigor, to reform the world, and help usher in a new age characterized by justice and prosperity. The industrial age that followed introduced urban poverty on a new scale and made this effort more urgent than ever.

In the early decades of the twentieth century, American Protestantism started drifting in two distinctly different directions. One branch (soon to be labeled liberal) became more and more consumed with social change and transformation. Meanwhile their enthusiasm for old-fashioned evangelization waned, and began to give way to what became known as the "social gospel."[2] The other branch, fundamentalism, responded in opposite fashion by stressing "the dangers of the world, the comforts of a separated piety, the centrality of evangelization, and an expectation of the end."[3] Thus a dichotomy between evangelization and mission-service was introduced.

The origins of Catholic service in this country were mostly a matter of expediency arising from the poverty of the immigrant Church. This service, which parallels the development of the "social gospel" in the Protestant community, was undertaken foremost and most fearlessly by the many communities of women religious that populated the Church and whose example should be everywhere celebrated and never forgotten.

Later, as Catholics became more affluent, they looked beyond taking care of their own. "Labeled progressivism, it was a reform movement made up principally of the new middle class emerging at the turn of the century: educated men and women, they believed in progress and the ability of people to fashion a better world."[4]

This development would lead to amazing programs of poverty reduction, family and social services, health and human services, disaster relief, education, advocacy, and so much more ultimately under the direction of world class networks of Catholic healthcare and charity agencies in this country and abroad.

But, like the pattern experienced among Protestants, this work gradually seemed to some to grow apart from the Church's more deliberate disciple-making work. Many efforts began to look like they were not only administratively but also missionally distinct.

> *Make poverty history.*
> —Bono

Today it is imperative that any distinction or division should be overcome, because the choice between *saving the world* and *changing it* is a false one. They are intimately related, the work of redemption and the work of restoration.

Restoration is an authentic witness and expression of our Catholicity. It fuels parish renewal because this work helps shape disciples. And there is growing consensus that Christian unity and rebuilding will start here, too. In his book *The Next Christians*, Gabe Lyons puts it powerfully this way:

> I've observed a new generation of Christians who feel empowered. Restorers exhibit the mind-set, humility, and commitment that seem destined to rejuvenate the momentum of the faith. They have a peculiar way of thinking, being, and doing that is radically different from previous generations. . . .
>
> I call them restorers because they envision the world as it was meant to be and they work toward that vision. Restorers seek to mend earth's brokenness. . . . Through sowing seeds of restoration, they believe others will see Christ through us and the Christian faith will reap a much larger harvest.[5]

Our parishioners should be serving and our parishes should be models of service in our communities and beyond. Service needs to be integrated into the mainstream life of the parish, rooted in prayer, and flowing from the Eucharist as an essential response to what we have received. It should be an essential part of how we are who we are.

But how do you make that happen in a big church, or even in a big way in a small church? How do you get it off the shoulders of the few and into the hands of the many—and keep it there? Here are some steps we try to keep taking.

1. **Have a Purpose; Plan a Partnership**

   If there is any confusion about what exactly mission-service is (and is not), or why you're doing it, your very best efforts could fail. For simplicity's sake, we're distinguishing "missions" as service *outside* the parish, as distinct from service for other parishioners *within* the parish, which we are calling "ministry." Obviously they're interchangeable words but two different things, and it's our contention disciples have an obligation to undertake both—at least from time to time.

   Missions are the work of restoration:

   • Outside our congregation
   • In partnership with others
   • Undertaken to love God

   A car wash to raise money for the youth group is not mission service. It's fundraising. Assisting at your neighborhood polling place on Election Day is community service, but not the service we mean. What we're talking about is the work of returning God's people and God's creation to what he intended, as a way of serving his kingdom and growing in love for him.

   Perhaps the key word is *partnership*. Our mission-service must be a *partnership*. Whatever we do is only *part* of what God is doing. Wherever we go, God is already there, inviting us to join him in his work. And wherever we go, God's people are already there, too, and he is at work in them as well. Mission service is not about paternalistic generosity, it is about joining a team that includes God and the people we are going out to serve alongside.

A partnership approach also guards against actually doing harm in the course of doing good; making ourselves feel good and others feel needy. Authors Steve Corbett and Brian Fikkert offer this challenging assessment: "One of the biggest problems in many poverty alleviation efforts is that their design and implementation exacerbates the poverty of being of the economically rich—their god-complexes—and the poverty of being of the economically poor—their feelings of inferiority and shame."[6]

Plan all your mission efforts from the perspective that it's a partnership. It's about a partnership of mutual respect and support, fueled by faith, and leading to love.

2. **Find a Leader; Build a Team**

Missions are like evangelization, at least in a middle-class community such as ours, because it's hard to stay focused on who's not here, like the homeless and the hungry. But, while evangelization can be driven through the entire organization, missions cannot. It's always a specific and deliberate exercise, and if it doesn't have a champion, with a voice at staff meetings and in strategic discussions, it will suffer, all your hard work notwithstanding.

Without a specific point leader, missions, if it happens at all, will be a "silo" ministry, isolated from the larger church and competing for resources and support with other ministries (maybe even working against them). Where there is no leadership, parish efforts only happen from time to time, with no real impact beyond stand alone projects themselves. They come and go—parishioners expect them to—and the result is tepid support. In the absence of effective, empowered leadership, missions always become the province of the few who can grow to resent the apathy of the many.

When we came to Nativity there were some stouthearted souls who undertook missions in the name of the parish (God bless them). But here was the problem: Too much was on the shoulders of too few, making the work burdensome and even onerous. And when they simply gave up or died, their mission projects died with them.

There was a parishioner here who had a heart for the hungry in Baltimore City and took the initiative in a monthly canned food drive. He worked long and hard at it, but the poor fellow had an uphill battle from the beginning. His pantry was regularly disrupted by other parish organizations who encroached on his space, his bulletin announcements got lost, and, saddest of all, as a staff we more or less ignored him. Unfortunately, he never really tried to build up a team of people to help him, and his collection and distribution system was erratic. His disappointment and frustration with the project grew as his energy waned. One day, he showed up in the parish office and quit . . . the parish! He blamed us for this failed enterprise and, in a sense, he was right. There was no leadership and there was no support.

You need a point leader to keep missional service in the place it should hold in your parish—an essential discipline of discipleship. Currently, we have a fairly large staff (for a Catholic church) and we have a staff position dedicated to missions. Brian's job number one is keeping missions a top priority for the rest of us.

But if you're like we were not so long ago, you can't afford to do that. That need not be an obstacle. There is probably someone in your parish who would do this for free, maybe they're already involved. Find them, recognize them, and raise them up to the level of your other staff. Include them in meetings (as well as staff parties or lunches). Give them the support they need to serve like staff.

And then make sure they don't try to do it all alone. Encourage them to build a team to support, sustain, and advance parish missions. Then the team makes sure the next steps happen.

3. Focus Your Efforts for the Greatest Impact

> **Father Michael**: At a parish where I worked for a
> little while, there was a very active group of people
> who supported a soup kitchen. They made casse-
> roles and collected food and regularly went there to
> serve meals. There was another group who helped
> out at a homeless shelter. They collected and dis-
> tributed socks, toiletries, and warm clothes. One
> weekend, just before Thanksgiving, each group was
> posted on opposite sides of the front door seeking
> support for *their charity*. As the weekend wore on,
> they became more and more aggressive in pro-
> moting themselves, with less and less effect. It was
> counterproductive. When people are unclear what
> you want them to do, they do nothing. When they
> are unsure who to support, they support no one.

Sometimes the problem isn't doing too little; it's doing too
much. Churches, large and small, have mission and service projects
all over the place and nobody really knows what's being accomplished . . . maybe not much considering all the effort. When
Brian first started as director it took him a few months just to track
down the various efforts that were already being undertaken by our
parishioners and in our name. We didn't know what was going on.

Start focusing your efforts. Determining to do so will be difficult, maybe even painful because no one wants to give up the
good work they're already doing. And its difficult to *stay* focused
because there are always more requests for assistance. But, focusing
your efforts will make a greater impact on those you serve and on
your parish. And those outcomes will, in turn, motivate more of
your members to step up and get involved.

The missions team should begin in prayer and look for direction there. Of course they need to proceed with the greatest respect for what is already going on and the past efforts of others. But, at the end of the day, the parish might need to kill some project or programs in order to achieve focus.

When it comes to the "where" of missions, Rick Warren, among others, helped us find inspiration in Jesus' parting words to his friends: "You will be my witnesses in Jerusalem, throughout Judea and Samaria, and to the ends of the earth" (Acts 1:8).

If you think about it, that's three distinct destinations. Jerusalem is where the disciples were living, the most immediate vicinity. Judea-Samaria was their native land, their part of the world. And then, there's the rest of the planet. He's actually giving us three commissions . . . don't know why exactly, perhaps because he wants his Church to be universal, and he wants us to care about everyone. A single community can't do everything, but we can do three things, and we decided that's what we wanted to do. We formed the goal that our mission efforts would try and address all three of those commissions.

Currently, we have a partnership with two communities in Nigeria, and several dozen parishioners have already gotten involved in travel teams. Many more have served in the stay-at-home support we call our home team. Their initial missional effort is to learn more about and learn to love the community they seek to serve. Only secondarily are they there for specific missional service.

More recently we have established a sister-parish relationship with a church in Haiti, where we are helping to rebuild their earthquake-damaged school and support their educational and nutritional efforts in other ways, too. We use the same arrangement of travel teams and home teams, which allows for people who can't travel to also get involved. Of course, it is in local missions where most people will serve, and we are currently developing or building partnerships with several agencies whose work address poverty, violence, fatherless kids, human trafficking, and pro-life advocacy. These are all places that deserve our help here in our community.

Want to know more/go deeper?

Meet Brian and learn all about our missions projects, what we're currently learning about missional service, and how we fund and staff missions. He'll talk about opportunities available to your parish to send a representative or a delegation on mission nationally and internationally. Go to rebuiltparish.com, click "Chapter 12," and then click "Meet Brian."

---

4. **Get Everyone Involved**

Part of our plan for the discipleship of our members is missions. Everybody, at least everybody who is physically able, is challenged to serve. But not all the time, just from time to time. As long as parishioners see missions as someone else's job, they're acting like customers. Everyone has to serve. And it should not be as simplistic as writing a check to fund the effort of others. Our members need to roll up their sleeves and get involved.

We want to motivate and mobilize members to love others and make disciples through accessible service locally, nationally, and internationally. To motivate our members, the work of restoration has to be preached. Like everything else, it will not happen if it doesn't come from the pulpit. And the message has to be consistent, clear, and challenging.

But the preaching will go nowhere if missions aren't accessible. What you're doing and when and how you're doing it have to be clear. How to get involved should be the easiest thing imaginable in your church. It should almost be easier to do it than not to do it.

Besides being clear about what *you're* doing, you have to be clear about what *they'll* be doing, step by step. Break it down into little tiny pieces. If you say, "We're renovating a house," I can't help you because I don't know how to do that. If you say, "We're going to Africa to promote clean water initiatives," it's out of my league. On the other hand, you can say, "We're painting a house on Saturday morning from 9 to noon," or "Two weeks this summer, we're bringing medicine to a village in Nigeria and learning more about some of their challenges," then I can begin seeing myself as part of that project.

Provide all the practical details they need to get involved: what to wear, where to park, that kind of thing. Our current thinking is that people pay for their own travel expenses to serve, but we provide, as applicable, the refreshments, meals, and lodging. Funding is an obviously important question to answer. Since we don't do fundraisers, what money our parish gives to missions comes out of our operating budget. We give a percentage.

Other objections might raise additional considerations. Besides the expense, there are travel, logistical, and safety issues related to mission service in other communities, especially in other countries. Here the value of "partnership" is particularly evident. There are myriad organizations your parish can partner with who take care of making service safe, affordable, and accessible so that you actually can send missionaries into the world.

At one time it was the case, in both the Catholic and Protestant communities alike, that mission work was the province of professional missionaries who devoted their lives to it. The parishioner's role was just to pay for it. Most Catholics are familiar with the pulpit appeals from visiting missionaries who tell exotic stories of far-away places.

But today, modern travel makes a two-week mission to Nigeria or a long weekend trip to Haiti, not to mention an afternoon trip into the city, a reasonable commitment of time. Many people in the congregation can do it.

We're also increasingly interested in what can be done *among* communities and congregations. Currently, we are involved in discussion with a neighboring evangelical church, as well as some Catholic pastors in Baltimore city churches, about what we can do together across denominational, racial, and socio-economic lines.

Currently we are participating in prayer walks in particularly violent urban neighborhoods. The goal is for the Church to be an agent of peace. This spring we joined forces with our evangelical neighbor engaging hundreds of our members in a one-day service event. Through simple good works, the goal was to humbly stand together as the Body of Christ in our community. While these are just first steps for us, others have more to teach us. One important initiative in Portland illustrates this exciting trend and its potential outcomes when it comes to the work of restoration:

> Rather than retreat into their churches and conduct business as usual, these restoration-minded Christians engaged their city as the countercultural hands and feet of Jesus Christ. Over time, the church has earned a seat at the table. They are included in serious discussions about the future of Portland and illustrate well the difference a countercultural community for the common good can make on the place they call home.[7]

Blessed John Paul II taught that Catholics should be *completely* willing to collaborate in this field with other churches and ecclesial communities, as well as invite them to share our initiatives.[8] Together, obviously, we can do more.

5. **Celebrate It**

If you get serious about missions, engage a majority of your congregation, and focus your efforts for the greatest impact. You will see fruit for your efforts. And you need to go ahead and celebrate, not in a self-congratulatory way, but definitely in a way that honors God for what he is doing through you.

A couple of years ago, we undertook a terrific program called Advent Conspiracy. This is an effort that many churches have embraced. It's all about doing Christmas with more focus on God and greater investment in people through "relational" gift giving. The suggestion was made that the relational giving (i.e., time spent together and time invested in a relationship) replaces just one store-bought gift. And then we invited everyone to give whatever money that one gift represented to our water project in Nigeria. A lot of money came in, about five times the amount we needed for the wells. Later, a missions group went to help set up the wells and record the event. Today, 90,000 people enjoy fresh, clean, and accessible water because of that effort.

But here's the point: The weekend we showed the video of the missions trip, with the Nigerian children splashing and playing in the fresh water, was one of the most powerful, emotional events in the life of this parish. When people realized the difference they made in the lives of those kids, they were deeply moved. Something in our congregation's culture changed profoundly that day. There is a lot to celebrate when you get missions going in your parish and look up to see what God can do through your efforts.

> The parish dimensions of social ministry . . . [are]
> a part of what keeps a parish alive and makes it
> truly Catholic. Effective social ministry helps the
> parish not only do more, but be more—more of a
> reflection of the gospel, more of a worshiping and
> evangelizing people, more of a faithful community.
> It is an essential part of parish life.[9]

YOU CAN DO THIS!
Steps You Can Take in Your Parish

- Look around for a leadership-level person who has a heart for the work of restoration. Maybe they're already doing something on their own at your parish and would love to step up to a new level of service. Make sure they have access to the pastor and all the privileges of the staff.
- Help that person build a leadership team.
- Charge the team with assessing all the parish's current and past efforts: what's working and what isn't; who's involved; what resources are available. They will want to gather all the information available and be honest about what they learn. They should also consider opportunities not currently being pursued. Who exactly you are partnering with in current or potential projects needs to be carefully understood. They should make recommendations to the pastor and parish leadership on which programs to focus on (and which ones to kill). The pastor should take their recommendations.
- With a clear decision about when, where, and how your parish is going to reach out beyond your congregation, the pastor needs to start preaching it from time to time. Meanwhile, the team is shaping accessible opportunities for people to get involved.
- Pray for your partners. Celebrate your wins.

My Neighbor Can Open My Eyes

Father Michael: Our very first foray into missions far from home came following Hurricane Katrina. In the aftermath of that heartbreaking disaster, it was easy to raise money for emergency relief. But we determined this time would be different, and I announced we would be going to the region to actively help. We had no idea how, who, where, or what, but I went ahead and made the public commitment that we would. In the next several years that followed, dozens of parishioners got involved, but getting started was the trick.

As with so many things, if it were easy everybody would do it. And it definitely was not easy. We put together a team of some smart people, and after a lot of dead ends they eventually identified a parish in Pass Christian, Mississippi, where we could help. That first trip down was an unforgettable experience for the half dozen of us who went. It was like the hurricane had hit the day before. Though the streets were clear, devastation and debris were everywhere else: cars in trees, trees in houses, some blocks demolished, others washed away with only their foundations remaining. The parish church was an empty, muddy shell. The school, improbably, more or less sat on its side. The rectory looked like it had been squashed.

Never in my life had I seen an entire town so utterly destroyed. There was little sign of any progress or hope.

But that experience taught us an important lesson that has influenced all of our subsequent efforts. The only thing we did on that first trip was listen to the people and their pastor as they told us about what happened to them. On and on, all that long day, they effusively told us their story.

Before we left, I remember apologizing to one of our hosts for not actually *doing* anything. She looked at me with astonishment and began to cry. It took her some time to compose herself. Finally she managed to say, "You don't understand; you just don't understand."

Then suddenly I did. On the surreal landscape of their wrecked community, we were standing with them—to simply stand with them, to be with them, and to love them.

The movement of the kingdom of God is the movement of love. Ultimately we're helping to restore the reign of love. And we won't see it—we'll miss it—unless we're serving one another.

> Only if I serve my neighbor can my eyes be opened to what God does for me and how much he loves me. The saints—consider the example of Blessed Teresa of Calcutta—constantly renewed their capacity for love of neighbor from their encounter with the Eucharistic Lord, and conversely this encounter acquired its realism and depth in their service to others. Love of God and love of neighbor are thus inseparable.[10]

Christian service is about more than proper care of another's needs. It isn't necessarily *doing* anything for those in need. It is about recognizing the image of God in others through our service. It is about allowing our service to open our eyes to God himself and fall more deeply in love with God. Mission work is the practice or program of love by the Church as a community of love.

You Can't Do It Alone

Growing a healthy parish is about growing disciples. Growing disciples are growing in the Word of God and the Eucharist, sharing their lives with one another, doing what God wants us to do with money, and serving others.

Whatever size parish you have, you cannot do it all alone. You need a team. And not just a team, a group of people who are willing to . . .

13

FALL IN LOVE

He went up the mountain and summoned those whom he wanted and they came to him. He appointed twelve, whom he also named apostles, that they might be with him and he might send them forth to preach and to have authority to drive out demons.

—MARK 3:13–15

Father Michael: In the grocery store, I ran into a priest I know who had just been appointed a pastor for the first time. He was understandably excited and wanted to talk about it. His first question to me was, "What is going to be my biggest challenge?" Without hesitation I answered, "Your staff." And I said that not knowing a single person on his staff. One month later, I ran across him again (again at the grocery store). I asked him how it was going. He told me, "I feel like firing them all."

Staffing Headaches

Once there were two part-time secretaries at Nativity who sat across from one another in the main office area. They did not speak to each other. They glared at each other, and it seemed like they hated each other (and it felt like they didn't like us very much either). Their former boss had given them a slender list of tasks, and that's what they did. And they made it quite clear they were unavailable to help us.

There was also the accountant. He was ninety (no, really, he was). He was a kindly gentleman who held the steadfast view that money was not to be spent. It was to be counted and saved and carefully accounted for in the giant ledger books he'd inherited from Ebenezer Scrooge. Of course, he must have been very frustrated because Nativity had no savings. Then there was a breezy youth minister, although there were no youth ministry programs. Her job seemed mostly about providing day care for her three-year-old. There was a friendly, easygoing maintenance man who, in his generosity, everyone took advantage of, and a foreign-born housekeeper whom everyone ignored.

And then there was the de facto chief of staff, the religious education director. Inexplicably, this lady kept the group together through an elaborate web of gossip, intrigue, and drama that she constantly spun. It gave her something to do.

The workday unfolded according to a time-honored template. Things got started around 9:30 a.m. when the former pastor's acolytes rolled in from daily Mass for their morning coffee klatch with the staff. This was the absolute zenith of office activity as the news of the day was exchanged. Eventually, the focus of office discussion turned to the business of the day: lunch. It was provided by the parish and ordered out daily.

If you wanted to capture the quintessential moment when this parish culture was most authentically itself, it would have been the staff lunch. It was a catered gossip session. The discussion emphasized *us* and *them* divisions, and, if you left the room, you immediately became one of *them*.

As a group, our staff was unhealthy. And far from working together as a team, we often worked against one another. Nor were we acting like leaders because we weren't leading anyone anywhere, certainly not into discipleship.

We were lucky because within our first two years most of these people were gone. Both secretaries just stormed off at different points (not sure why, guess they really didn't like us after all). The accountant retired, and we helped the youth minister find a more appropriate job, given her family demands. The religious ed lady got another job behind our backs and then quit at the moment of maximum inconvenience, creating as much collateral damage as she could on the way out.

Since then, we've made some good hires, and we've also made some serious mistakes. As mentioned earlier, a big problem was always trying to hire too fast, not taking the necessary time to find the right person while often not even understanding what we really wanted from that person.

It also needs to be stated that, increasingly in churchworld, hiring is complicated by the dearth of available candidates. Besides the "vocation crisis" to the priesthood and religious life, there is another crisis of lay vocational workers. The generation or so of DREs and youth ministers who sprouted up after the Second Vatican Council are now retiring, and it is not at all clear who will replace them. It is beyond the scope of this book to get into why that is so—we're not even sure we *know* why, though we will return to this topic again. One important study sums up what we are facing:

> The profession of lay ministry needs more young people. The average age is too high now. Young people would bring new vigor and would be a sign that lay ministry has a future. They would also be key for better ministry to youth

and young adults. The most valuable young people would
be persons who see ministry as a calling and a long-term
career.[1]

We were surprised to learn that this situation has also led to a lot
of "poaching" of other people's staffs, which is currently an entrenched
part of the culture in churchworld. It sometimes looks like musical
chairs—directors of religious education and youth ministers moving
around from parish to parish. They show up, like Mary Poppins, with
their bag of tricks; they do what they do. Then, they move on after
they've done it, only to do it again in another parish. Some eventually
graduate out of the system and take a job in a Catholic school, which
pays more and offers better hours, or they take a job with the diocese,
which pays more and offers better hours.

> **We were not leaders because we weren't leading anyone anywhere, certainly not into discipleship.**

The constant changes erode volunteer
ministers' commitment and weaken programs. On the flip side of this approach are
the staffers who settle into their positions
as if they were lifetime entitlements. They
manage their ministry into almost effortless
maintenance and then proceed to retire in
place. When they finally go, there is usually
a lot of mopping up that has to be done.

Many dioceses now offer ministry formation programs, which is a very positive
step. But it is not clear how successful these programs are or will
become or just *who* they will attract. Besides, if the formation is only
theological, if it is all presented by theologians or religious professionals
who are not grounded in the workings of a local parish church, it will
be of limited assistance in raising up parish ministers.

At Nativity, the major criterion for our hires was availability and a
willingness to work for next to nothing. Then we held our breath and

hoped for the best. And oftentimes, this, in turn, yielded dysfunction. The dysfunction of many church communities begins with a dysfunctional staff. On the other hand, a healthy staff culture will go a long way toward building a healthy church culture.

Hiring Strategies

Here are the strategies we have adapted from others and currently use to make the right hires that have built our team in the past few years.

Strategy #1. *Hire people of good character.*

A great team is only as great as its individual members. So build a team made up of people of character: not perfect people, not people of blameless backgrounds, but people of good character. As the saying goes, character is "who you are when no one's looking." Or, as Thomas Paine expressed it, "Reputation is what men and women think of us; character is what God and angels know of us."[2]

Character is about the core, things like self-control, discipline, respect, kindness, honesty, integrity, trustworthiness, and humility. It takes a great deal of humility to be successful in churchworld these days. At the same time, humility is balanced with confidence, not hubris or pride, just the positive demeanor that should accompany faith. St. Paul teaches that character comes from perseverance and leads to hope, so it's a fundamental requirement for working for God (cf. Romans 5:4).

Don't compromise on this one, because it's the critical piece. The other strategies won't work out long term if this one isn't foundational. Without good character all the other attributes the person brings to the job will eventually be worthless to you. When character is wanting, your hire will eventually become too expensive for you, in one way or another. And hiring a person with character issues will ensure that problems will develop among your other team members. Bill Hybels believes,

> Good character is tough to discern in a fifteen-minute interview. You have got to do your due diligence to be sure the person you're about to invite onto the team has a proven track record of being a truth-teller, a covenant-keeper, ... someone who manages relationships well, and one who credits the efforts of others when a victory is won.[3]

And since we're in the disciple-making business, good character in church ministry must also include discipleship in Christ. Don't hire anyone who isn't serious about his or her discipleship. Doesn't matter where they started, or where they *are* in that process, but it matters a lot that they are *in* the process. In fact, keep an eye out for the formerly dechurched in your midst who might be your next best hire. They'll be in a better position to communicate with people outside the Church than you are.

Barry is a great example of what we're talking about. He would willingly describe himself as a true "Timonium Tim," whose journey took him away from the Church after his Catholic school education but eventually back by way of Nativity. Barry got into a small group, started serving in our café, and really doing discipleship in his life. In his case, small groups and service were the path back to weekly worship at Mass. When a staff position became available and Barry applied, it was a no-brainer—the job was his. Today, he is our weekend director, a kind of engineer of weekend operations, making sure all the trains run on time and problems are handled in an efficient manner.

Strategy #2. *Hire people with ability.*

Typically, hires are asked about their experience. Experience is usually desired, required, and rewarded. We actually believe that, at this point in time, churchworld is changing so quickly that "know-how" might just be a liability—nobody knows how anymore. Your staff's previous experience won't necessarily translate into useful insights in doing church today and tomorrow. And if they've got the "that's the way we always do it" mentality, it could slow your team down. Sure, people skills, a work ethic, and knowledge of process and procedure gained by work in the field can add value to any team. But experience isn't the first thing we look for.

We look for ability. Can this person learn, grow, adapt, and change in fast-paced, changing circumstances? Does this person have *that* ability? Of course, we also look at specific *skills* the person needs to do a specific *job*, though not having them isn't necessarily a deal breaker if we believe he or she has the motivation to go out and get what is needed.

Lucas is in this category. He started out working for us a few hours a week in college and kind of grew up with us, though he wasn't yet a Christian. After college, Lucas entered the Church and joined our team full-time. As he grew in faith, he was also growing in knowledge of our purpose and mission and how it can be advanced through technology. His ability is obvious in all our creative tech efforts.

Kristin is in this category. Fresh out of college, she had no background in what she would be doing. But her natural ability and disciplined approach to learning what she needed to know eventually allowed her to apply creative talent to our communication efforts.

Father Michael: Another part of ability is passion. My axiom is, "I want them to care about this more than I do." When I get a person in charge of kids' ministry, or tech, or the website, who's more passionate about those things than I am (and I care passionately), then I know I've got the right person.

Brian is a great example here. He followed a typical trajectory of Catholic school education and church attendance followed by a college experience wandering away from the Lord. He eventually came back around and started working on our staff as a volunteer. When we could, we hired Brian full-time, and, for a while he did some different things; but meanwhile, he awakened to his passion in life—missions. Today Brian is our mission and service director and makes sure the topic stays front and center in the parish's agenda.

Strategy #3. *Hire people you like.*

When we first came to work at Nativity, the staff didn't like one another and they didn't get along. Infighting and gossip were a big part of the culture. We learned a hard but valuable lesson through that experience. It is no fun to work with people you don't like; it takes a lot of the joy out of life, makes workdays very long days, and easily contributes to burn out. On the other hand, working with people you *do* like or even love is a joy and a blessing, and nothing will knit a team together more effectively.

This is a gut thing; obviously, you can't see into the future and know for certain that your hire will be a "fit" with your team. You have to go on instinct, and if you don't have good instincts on this, then you probably shouldn't be the one hiring in your organization.

After our original religious ed director bailed, we went through a succession of others who didn't work out either, for one reason or another. But truth be told, we didn't really have chemistry with *any* of them (not their fault, but ours). Lisa started volunteering in our kid's ministry a couple of years ago, and it was amazing to us how much kids liked her. Today Lisa is director of all of our children's ministries, and we like her, too. When Lisa is around everyone is smiling.

Strategy #4. *Hire from within.*

The easiest way to make sure you accomplish strategies 1–3 is to use this strategy. That's why your best volunteer is your next best hire. Look around for who is already working for you for free: Do you like them; do they have ability and good character; do they understand your mission and your church? When it comes time to hire, hire them!

We have followed this rule for the past few years, and now we live by it. It's possible we could make an exception for some special or extraordinary reason . . . but we can't even imagine what that exception would be.

Jeremy is a great example of our hiring from within, and so is Maggie. Jeremy was working closely with our tech team on weekends. We learned that he's smart and funny, and we liked having him around. Maggie was a super volunteer in the nursery, and we learned she has a beautiful heart for little children. So, when we had the opportunity, we just gave Jeremy and Maggie desks and a salary and said, "Now you're on staff."

We can remember a time when we couldn't find anyone to hire, despite our very best efforts.

Currently, we could easily name a long list of people we would bring on our team today if we had the money. And maybe, one day, they will be a part of our full-time ministry team. Meanwhile, they're already unpaid staff.

Strategy #5. *Hire people who have fallen in love with your church.*

Sometimes people have come to work for us who we liked and who seemed to have good character and ability. But it didn't work because they didn't *get* it; they didn't *get* us. Sometimes they thought they did, but they didn't. What they got was a single slice of what we do that appealed to them, and they equated it with the sum total of the place. As they eventually learned about the rest of the organization, they realized it wasn't for them.

We had a music director who was an awesome musician. He built a choir of unrivaled excellence, and at Christmas and Easter he could blow the roof off the place. But he didn't really feel comfortable with our changing church culture and he grew distant and detached from us as it changed. Eventually he left. No hard feelings; we're all still friends. We just don't belong on the same team.

Don't hire anyone, however talented, who isn't completely sold on the mission of your parish. The person on our staff who probably "gets it" the most is Maria. She came to us out of college and was the first hire we made after we began developing our new strategy. The original disciple of our changing church culture, Maria, has matured into a leader for

> *When I hire somebody really senior the real issue for me is, are they going to fall in love with Apple? Because if they fall in love with Apple, everything else will take care of itself.*
> —Steve Jobs[4]

our staff. At the same time, as director of adult ministry, she is moving more and more parishioners down
the path of discipleship. Maria loves our parish, and
the parish has fallen in love with her.

Investing In Your Staff

Building a team takes a lot of work and perseverance, over an extended
period of time. After you start fielding your team, it requires constant
maintenance and support. And, it is going to be a work in progress,
never really finished because human beings are never really finished.
There will always be departures and newcomers, and every time there
are, the group dynamic changes; you've got a new group. Here are a
few things that have helped us.

1. **Prayer**

   Each week we pray together as a staff. We pray for one another
   and for what we are working on that week. Throughout the week
   we try to hold one another up in personal prayer.

2. **Respect and Trust**

   If you hire people you know and like, and they are people of
   character, it will be easy to respect them. Trust is more complicated
   because it depends on competence as well as character. Most people
   can be trusted in some things. As a team member shows competence, it becomes easier to trust them in more things. Likewise, as
   a team member's actions and words line up, it becomes easier to
   more and more trust his or her character.

   Lack of trust is that gap between what is expected and what
   is given, and it will inevitably pop up from time to time. And it
   needs to be addressed every time it does. That's demanding work,
   and nobody wants to do it. But if it's not done, we start keeping
   "lists" on one another. Any remaining trust is eroded, and a team

can be destroyed. Invest the effort in being honest and up-front; keep "short lists"; let others know when you're hurt, annoyed, or angry; and keep talking to one another.

3. **Consistent Communication**

> **Father Michael**: I know it is popular to view meetings as boring and unproductive, which all too many meetings are. Frankly, we've really struggled to figure out the meetings we want and need, which ones we find useful and productive and which ones are unproductive. Perhaps the key is to constantly evaluate the *purpose* of your meetings. I am a big fan of meetings *with a purpose.* The excellent book *Death by Meeting,* by Patrick Lencioni, is an especially helpful guide for churches on this topic.[5]

Back a few years ago, when we were still trying to figure out our strategy as a parish, we had to have meetings about strategy. Those were big, open-ended discussions that oftentimes went nowhere, sometimes created more confusion than clarity, and every once in a while struck gold. We don't have a lot of those kinds of meetings anymore for the whole staff because generally we don't need them, and it would be a waste of many people's time.

As we became clearer about our strategy, we found ourselves having meetings about implementation of our strategy, everyone around the table methodically working out the management of what we were trying to do. Those were important meetings for the team at the time, in learning about *how* to do what we were trying to do. We don't really have those kinds of meetings much anymore either.

Now that our strategy has been clarified and the methodology is established *and* our staff has grown, our meetings have changed again. We have organized our team into working groups who meet together weekly. These groups are organized around adult ministry, family ministry (kids and students), creative tech, and administrative. The group leaders meet together each week. We try and rely on collaboration and consensus in these meetings.

The whole staff meets only twice a week. On Mondays we meet for lunch (yes, we've re-instituted the Nativity staff lunch, but with a new purpose). This meeting is more of a fellowship-style event, with opportunity to share wins and success stories from the past weekend, discuss what we learned or got wrong, and celebrate the work God is doing among us. It also serves to punctuate the past week's efforts, allow us to take a breath, and relieve the sometimes-creeping feeling that we're on a treadmill.

> **Father Michael**: On Tuesdays I meet with the whole staff to share with them what's going on, what I'm working on, and what's happening. This is also their chance to give me feedback. By the way, this meeting and the weekly group-leaders meeting are the only two I chair. The pastor does not have to chair every meeting he sits in—and probably shouldn't.
>
> We also have brief check-in meetings at midweek and a few times during the course of the weekend, too, bringing together whoever is here, merely for information sharing and communication on what's going on.

Twice a year we also host staff retreats—a time for prayer, discernment, and planning for what's ahead. We invest a lot in making these events productive and energizing. Most recently we've launched a one-day conference for all our ministry leaders to share vision, mission, and strategy.

Whatever the purpose of the meetings, their bottom- line is communication. And the communication needs to be consistent and honest. You will never have a great staff without great communication.

Want to know more/go deeper?

Watch Michael and Tom discuss meetings and how they currently run them. Go to rebuiltparish.com, click "Chapter 13," and then click "Meetings."

---

4. **Fun**

We recognize the value of making sure our team has fun and enjoys themselves. This is a huge part of the culture in some of today's most successful churches and corporations. We both willingly acknowledge that neither of us is particularly gifted at encouraging fun, but we're working on it. Fun builds respect and trust; it strengthens communication.

5. **Growth**

Besides our regular meetings, each of our departments gathers every other week for learning sessions. They choose their own reading assignments and then discuss what they've read: theology, church history, ecclesiology, leadership. All these are topics for our discussion. We want our team to keep learning and growing.

6. **Compensation**

You don't have to pay your staff anything. Jesus didn't. Our sister parish in Haiti doesn't have any paid staff, beyond the pastor, but they have several volunteer staff members. A pastor we know showed up at his new parish day one, learned he had no staff, and announced to his small congregation, "Okay, you're my staff."

Our point here is: If you do pay your staff, make every effort to pay them a salary that is fair and consistent with community standards. We made a strategic decision a few years ago to invest in our staff by investing in staff salaries. We want young people to be able to come to work here and have a family and a life outside of Nativity. And we want successful career people to be able to comfortably make the transition to church ministry without risking hearth and home, not to mention health insurance. Many of us suspect that the simple reason people don't want to work in churchworld today is because we don't pay people fairly.

> Many of us suspect that the simple reason people don't want to work in churchworld today is because we don't pay people fairly.

Of course this is tied to church finances, as we have already discussed. Unless church-wide giving is addressed, you won't be able to pay your staff.

Our staff knows that staff salaries are a priority. So does our congregation, because we always include it in our annual stewardship appeal. No nagging, no guilt, just a reminder of a simple fact: This is your church, they're your staff, and it's your responsibility to pay them.

YOU CAN DO THIS!
Steps You Can Take in Your Parish

It doesn't matter what the size of your staff is—full time, part time, stipendiary, or volunteer—they can be a great staff if you get the right people on board, then find the right job for them.

If you have a staff:

- Challenge everyone to write a job description for themselves. Review it together as a team.
- Set a weekly one-on-one meeting with each person who
  reports to you. Use this time to check in personally as well
  as professionally. Get updates on projects, but also use the
  time to build relational trust.
- Begin to gather your staff for learning meetings. Choose
  a topic that is of mutual interest to all.
- Pray together.
- Have fun! Schedule it if you have to.

*If you don't have a staff (and you don't have any money to
hire staff):*

- Make a list of everything you do that someone else could
  easily do. Make a second list of everything you do that
  someone else could do with a little training.
- Take both lists to prayer and begin to ask God to give you
  the people you need to fill those roles. You don't want one
  person doing it all (that just perpetuates the old problem).
  You're praying to find a team.

Give Me the People I Need

Father Michael: At one particularly low point
early on, after our original staff was gone *and* after
we had parted company with many subsequent
hires, I had determined to swear off hiring anyone.

I was done. I took the pledge. I had gotten to the point where I would rather work alone and try to do everything myself (or leave it undone) than deal again with the heartbreak of wrecked staff relationships.

This resolve of mine was formed, coincidently, just as Tom had met a young man he thought would be a perfect fit for us. I refused to interview him (Chris), even though we desperately needed the help. Tom continued to lobby, and I continued to resist. Finally, he asked me if I would at least pray about it, which, remarkably, is exactly what I had not done. I took the weekend and prayed about Chris and our neuralgic staffing problems. Through the course of that weekend I raised this problem up to the Lord and begged for guidance, "Why won't you give me the people I need to do the job you want me to do?" Persistence in prayer works because somewhere that weekend God came thundering back, "I'll send you the right people when you are ready to treat them right."

As pastor, I have no more important job than taking care of our team. They are not here to serve me. I am here to serve them and make it possible for them to lead others in ministry and service. My job is to be their champion when it comes to compensation, getting them the resources they need, setting them up for success in every way I can, and always watching their back. With that conviction so clearly given, that day I set out on a new road.

Later that evening, preparing to leave, I remembered that I had promised Tom to make some kind of decision about Chris. I said to God, "Okay, what do you want me to do? Show me." It was late. I was exhausted; and I didn't know what to do. I was in the sacristy, and I remember literally throwing my head down on the vesting cabinet. "What do you want me to do? Show me!"

And, in the clearest, most efficient answer to a prayer I have ever received, at that precise moment, for no apparent reason, Chris walked in the door and said, "Here I am." He's been here ever since, and he is one of the most awesome and effective people I've ever worked with.

In the intervening years, we have been abundantly blessed as God has built up an amazing group of young leaders who are creative, hard-working, highly motivated, and have fallen in love with Christ and his Church. And they're not "my" staff. They're our leadership team.

Invest in your staff, or volunteer staff, and get them invested in being the lead agents in your mission. Love them and help them fall in love with the Church of Christ, so there is nowhere else they'd rather be, nothing else they would rather be doing. Help them fall in love with what they're doing for Christ.

14

LEAD WHERE YOU SERVE

The LORD brought David victory in all his undertakings. David was king over all Israel; he dispensed justice and right to all his people.

—1 CHRONICLES 18:13–14

The writers of the Bible weren't particularly creative when it came to book titles. Not surprisingly, the First and Second Books of Kings are about the kings of Israel and Judah. More than their histories or deeds, the Books of Kings describe the *hearts* of the leaders.

Far and away, Israel's greatest leader was David. And the Bible describes many of the attributes that qualified him for that title: courage, conviction, determination. But more than anything else, David was distinguished by a heart that was fully devoted to God. In other words, he followed God's leadership.

Unfortunately, many of the subsequent kings failed to do that. Over and over again the Books of Kings tell us that the hearts of the leaders were often far from God. Instead they followed their own hearts and got into a lot of trouble.

And as the king went, so went the nation. The kingdom of David split when his grandson, Rehoboam, ignored the advice of his elder counselors, listened to people who told him what he wanted to hear, and made the terrible decision to increase taxes, even though the people desperately needed relief. The eventual result was civil war. The two poorer, weaker kingdoms that followed both suffered unfaithful king after unfaithful king and eventually fell victims to their enemies.

Throughout both books, it is the kings' failures and idolatry that bring about the ruin of the nations, not the failures of the people. First and Second Kings make clear a fundamentally important principle: Everything rises or falls on leadership.

> Everything rises or falls on leadership.

What is leadership? As authors and management experts Ken Blanchard and Phil Hodges point out, it's basically a process of influence. Any time you're trying to influence the thoughts and actions of others toward a new place or different outcomes, in either their personal or professional life, you're engaging in leadership.

History is shaped by leaders. Nothing great ever gets accomplished without great leadership. And lots of bad stuff happens in the absence of it.

God has created the gift of leadership, and he's shaped all of us to lead, because bringing lost people to Christ is an exercise in leadership. Disciples are leaders, and discipleship is all about leading. And, of course, it's a hierarchy. It begins with God. God wants leaders in his church who are like David, in other words, fully devoted to him. God uses and blesses people who accept his leadership over their lives.

If you are reading this book (or *still reading* this book), God wants you to lead where you are. It's the pope's job to lead the Roman Catholic Church; it's your bishop's job to lead the diocese; but that doesn't mean God isn't calling you to be a leader, too. He actually intends to use you to awaken others to the purpose of their lives. He expects you to help people follow him. He's calling you to lead. Wherever and however you serve, he wants you to lead.

Want to know more/go deeper?

Listen to Michael and Tom discuss the priest's unique role in the parish as spiritual father. Avoiding both clericalism on the one hand and a false egalitarianism on the other, the priest exercises an authority of service. Go to rebuiltparish.com, click "Chapter 14," and then click "The Unique Role of the Priest."

Some Leadership Charges

1. **Be a servant leader.**

As you consider the heart of leadership, a primary question you will continue to have to ask yourself is, "Am I a servant leader or a self-serving leader?" It is a question that, when answered with brutal honesty, will go to the core of your intention or motivation as a leader. One of the quickest ways you can tell the difference between a servant leader and a self-serving leader is how they handle feedback, because one of the biggest fears that self-serving leaders have is to lose their position.[1]

At one point in Mark's Gospel, Jesus was trying to stay out of sight, so he could spend time teaching and investing in the disciples closest to him. He was training them to lead the Church after his death, so that they would understand what their leadership would require and accomplish. In that context, his warning came, "the Son of Man must suffer greatly and be rejected by the elders, the chief priests, and the scribes, and be killed, and rise after three days" (Mark 8:31). Now that was some pretty big news. What kind of a reaction did it get? Well, here's what happened:

> They came to Capernaum and, once inside the house, he began to ask them, "What were you arguing about on the way?" But they remained silent. They had been discussing among themselves on the way who was the greatest. (Mark 9:33–34)

> *Do nothing out of selfishness or out of vainglory; rather, humbly regard others as more important than yourselves, each looking out not for his own interests, but also everyone for those of others.*
> —Philippians 2:3–4

There are a lot of people in leadership positions, including some pastors and parish leaders, who approach their job with the attitude that being in charge means "I don't have to do anything (and I get to tell other people what to do)." They're self-serving leaders only interested in preserving their position, advancing their agenda, and getting what they want.

Jesus isn't just a *spiritual* leader. Jesus is the model for *all* leadership. And he leads from the Cross. If we want to be great before God, we have to be like Jesus and put other people's interests ahead of our own. It's not just service; it's becoming a servant. It's a role, not simply an activity. That's the path to great leadership.

That's servanthood. A servant's first job is to look out for the interests of others, even anticipating their needs. But Paul doesn't stop there:

> Have among yourselves the same attitude that is also yours in Christ Jesus, Who, though he was in the form of God, did not regard equality with God something to be grasped. Rather, he emptied

> himself, taking the form of a slave, coming in
> human likeness. (Philippians 2:5–7)

We say someone is "full of himself" when we're talking about pride. To explain the opposite of that, Paul says Jesus "emptied himself" and poured out his whole life. He took all his rights—the right to be worshiped, the right to rule, the right to the perfection of heaven—and gave it all up. He emptied himself to become not just a servant but a slave. Paul goes on to describe his life that way, too, "poured out as a libation" (Philippians 2:17).

That's servant leadership. Pouring out selfishness and pride in order to have the capacity to receive the wisdom, knowledge, understanding, right judgment, and all the other gifts the Holy Spirit offers. And then, it is about emptying even these gifts into the lives of those you serve. Andy Stanley talks about mentoring his staff as emptying his cup into their cups.

In *Good to Great,* author Jim Collins sets out to show why some companies greatly improved their performance while others, in similar circumstances, did not. He found that one essential element of a good to great company was what he called a "level 5 leader."[2] These leaders all demonstrate the same qualities:

> Jesus is the model for all leadership. And he leads from the Cross.

- They blend extreme personal humility with intense professional will.
- They're ambitious, but their ambition is directed toward their company, not themselves.
- They attribute successes to others and take responsibility for failures themselves.

2. **Be a wise leader.**

Lots of parishes suffer because the pastor is surrounded by people who foolishly flatter him and tell him exactly what he wants to hear. That was the mistake of Rehoboam, in I Kings.

> Jesus summoned them and said, "You know that the rulers of the Gentiles lord it over them, and the great ones make their authority over them felt. But it shall not be so among you. Rather, whoever wishes to be great among you shall be your servant; whoever wishes to be first among you shall be your slave. Just so, the Son of Man did not come to be served but to serve and to give his life for the many."
> —Matthew 20:26b–28

A fool is just a silly person who lacks good judgment, and for some reason churchworld seems to have its fair share. Fools want attention they haven't earned, credit they don't deserve, and influence they shouldn't be given (though they'll always rush in to get it). Parish leaders need to be on their guard against acting foolishly or allowing foolish people to dominate.

At the same time, wise counselors have to be sought out. Whatever kind of parish you have, there are very successful people in your pews who can teach you lots of leadership lessons. There are parishioners you know who have good judgment that they can bring to many of the decisions you have to make. A wise leader will seek those people out, invite them to get involved, make sure they have a voice, *and* listen to them. Some people are wise, some people are not. But nobody has all the wisdom they need. That's why wise leaders are people who surround themselves with wisdom.

As our parish has grown, the number of people we have involved in leadership roles has grown. It's not about meetings and committees for their own sake; rather, it's about gathering the wisdom that is around us. Currently, we have teams of advisors for finances, maintenance, technology, development, human resources, and strategic planning. We don't have any elections—notice how they don't really do elections or take votes in the Bible. Instead we're very careful about selecting the advisors we assemble. We don't necessarily want the most *popular* people; we seek the most *talented* people. And, in turn, we take their advice very seriously. We have also developed "accountability" teams who speak wisdom into our own lives. Once a month we open up about what is going on in our lives, professionally and personally, and they hold us accountable for the goals we set for ourselves and the changes we need to make.

3. **Be a leader who learns.**

Acts 19 tells a humorous story, but it is also tragic because it depicts what happens so often in parish life. Paul is living in a town called Ephesus. In fact, he's planting the Church in Ephesus by preaching God's word there. Because Paul is Paul, his preaching is accompanied by extraordinary miracles that cure the sick and drive out evil spirits. This power springs from his intimate relationship with Jesus Christ. Others see him at work and, impressed with the results, decide to give it a try, even though they don't know what they're doing.

> *The way of fools is right to their own eyes, but those who listen to advice are the wise.*
> —Proverbs 12:15

> Then some itinerant Jewish exorcists tried to invoke the name of the Lord Jesus over those with evil spirits, saying, "I adjure you by the Jesus whom Paul preaches." When the seven sons of Sceva, a Jewish high priest, tried to do this, the evil spirit said to them in reply, "Jesus I recognize, Paul I know, but who are you?" (Acts 19:13–15)

Then the evil spirit proceeds to beat them up and they run away naked; in other words, they are completely defeated. They were aping Paul's practices without understanding how they worked.

Plans fail when there is no counsel, but they succeed when counselors are many.
—Proverbs 15:22

How often does that happen in ministry? We certainly did it for years. Witnessing others' successful efforts, we copied the details without even trying to understand what they were doing (never mind what God wanted *us* to be doing). And then we were surprised when we failed.

Father Michael: A pastor I didn't know very well called me to say he was angry with me. I asked him why and he told me "You ruined my Sundays." How did I do that? Well, apparently he had gotten pressure from parents in his parish to have a Sunday evening "youth" Mass ("just like Nativity has"), and he reluctantly agreed. "We even had pizza," he complained. The problem was that he didn't understand the principles on which we built our youth program, and he wasn't interested in learning. He just copied details, and then there he was, stuck, with a program he didn't want, that didn't work . . . and a lot of cold pizza.

It was not and never is about the pizza. It's about learning what God is calling *you* to do and then doing it. The power in a program or an event or any ministry is never on the surface or even in the details. It's not that method doesn't matter or that details are unimportant. But, the power in our ministry efforts comes from our close association with the Lord and, first of all, learning *what* he wants us to do, and then learning how to do it.

As others have joined our staff or gotten involved in parish leadership, we find ourselves enjoying their surprise as they learn about the complexity of leading a parish church. We've already talked about the myth that church is easy. That is a seriously debilitating lie. And by the way, it's not easier to run a smaller church; it can actually be harder. These days, successfully leading a church community of any size requires focused study matched with disciplined deliberation. We have to be concerned about educational, liturgical, and musical programs; services for every age group; making and keeping budgets; raising money; communication; copyright laws; building and maintaining organizational systems and structures; human resources; marketing; plant management; and security. The list goes on and on.

We need to continue to learn more about what we're trying to do, which means growing beyond our assumptions or superficial understanding to deep knowledge about:

- the place our parish holds in people's lives and why it might fail to interest outsiders;
- what makes for effective communication in our community;
- what motivates people to get involved or give.

We need to ask questions about *why* we do what we do. What is a particular program trying to accomplish? What, specifically, is a win? How will people's lives be changed as a result of this effort? Why is it worth our time and money? How does it fit in with the unique calling God has for our community? And we need to *keep* asking those questions, because what works today will probably not work tomorrow.

We have to cultivate humility and enthusiasm to learn from others who are successfully doing what we're trying to do and avail ourselves of the resources that are available. The term "learning organization" was coined by Peter Senge and seems basic to the way successful organizations will be operating in the future in our world of ceaseless, accelerated change. The principles are simple to state but challenging to keep in focus: the interconnectedness of team members; an environment of coaching and learning; permission to fail in order to learn; and most of all, good communication.

Currently we build in learning time to our weekly meeting schedule, and encourage staff to take *work time* for *study time* and personal development, even if that means not doing other things. We also budget as much money as we can put aside to get our staff and volunteer ministry leaders exposed to some of the energizing and inspiring church conferences that so many of the largest evangelical churches in the country increasingly offer (often at only nominal fees). Just getting staff into vibrant church settings where they can see and learn from successful church leaders is motivating. Always viewed through the lens of our Catholic faith, these experiences can sometimes even be transformational (as it was for us at Saddleback).

There are lots of ways to learn, but the place to start is always humbly before God, grounded in his word, attentive to his instruction.

> Let the wise listen and add to their learning,
> And let the discerning get guidance . . .
> the fear of the Lord is the beginning of knowledge,
> but fools despise wisdom and discipline. (Proverbs
> 1:5, 7)

4. Be a leader of courage.

Actually leading anybody anywhere requires a certain amount of courage. And being the lead agent in changing a church culture these days will require a lot of it. Fortunately, that's the way we're made. Gary Haugen, founder of International Justice Mission, writes:

> When it comes to being brave, we should picture
> the courage of Jesus—power to fearlessly speak the
> truth, freedom to selflessly love, the strength to
> unflinchingly stretch oneself on the cross. And the
> truth is that in our deepest core we were actually
> made to be like that.[3]

Courage in parish leadership means, first of all, preaching the whole message of the Gospel, not just the parts people like to hear. It also means:

- Speaking the hard truths, in a loving way.
- Confronting the facts, even when they're brutal.
- Making the tough calls—the ones nobody else wants to face, let alone make.
- Really loving the people in our parish, even when they're not in our church and sometimes when they're not lovable.

5. **Be a leader of faithfulness.**

Some things just take time. Ministry is one of those things. It is a marathon, not a sprint. Leadership in ministry is a long-term project. Author and business blogger Seth Godin says it well:

> It's a myth that change happens overnight, that
> right answers succeed in the marketplace right away,
> or that big ideas happen in a flash. They don't. It's
> always (almost always, anyway) a matter of accre-
> tion. Drip, drip, drip. Improvements happen a bit
> at a time, not as grand-slam homeruns that are easy
> to get. . . . If your organization requires success
> before commitment, it will never have either.

Part of leadership (a big part of it, actually) is the ability to stick with the dream for a long time. Long enough that the critics realize that you're going to get there one way or another . . . so they follow.[4]

You will not change the culture of your parish overnight or all at once. It happens slowly, so it just takes time. Give it the time it takes and needs. You've just got to keep going and not give up. Even when things are not going well and people are beginning to question you or leave, you can't quit. You cannot abdicate your leadership role just because you're frustrated when people don't follow you.

> *Leadership is not about titles, positions, or flowcharts. It is about one life influencing another.*
> —John C. Maxwell[5]

Be a leader who perseveres. And let your faithfulness be founded in and fueled by faith. Be faithful in the Lord Jesus. Keep faith in his leadership and the work he has given you. As Paul instructed the leaders of the Church at Ephesus before he bid them farewell, "If only I may finish my course and the ministry that I received from the Lord Jesus, to bear witness to the gospel of God's peace" (Acts 20:24).

Aim to finish the race you have set out on, to complete the work God has given you and the share you have in testifying to the gospel of God's grace. Elsewhere Paul perfectly summed up leadership in the Church of Christ. If you're working with children or students or in outreach or service, if you're answering the phones or leading the music ministry, if you're an usher or a greeter, if you're doing it in Christ's Church, then you're called to be a leader, in just the way Paul spoke of leadership, "Be imitators of me, as I am of Christ" (1 Corinthians 11:1).

YOU CAN DO THIS!
Steps You Can Take in Your Parish

If you're a pastor, pastoral life director, pastoral associate, director of religious education, or youth minister:

- Honestly examine your motives when it comes to your ministry. Take a look at why you do what you do.
- Take a look around for the leadership people already in your pews, the people smarter than you who know stuff you don't. Whatever your structure or governance, invite them to form an advisory group that speaks truth into your life and your stewardship of the parish.
- Look beyond your parish to the resources available from other churches, even if they're Protestant churches.
- Start evaluating opportunities, problems, and fears when it comes to your ministry.
- Pray about those fears, lean into those problems, and pursue those opportunities.

15

YOU CAN DO THIS!

For the vision is a witness for the appointed time; a testimony to the end; it will not disappoint. If it delays, wait for it, it will surely come, it will not be late.

—HABAKKUK 2:3

Vision is an image or picture of what could be and should be. It is a preferred future in which life is better. Vision says that that the status quo isn't good enough any more; there is a better way. When pastors and parish leaders don't urge people on to a greater future in service to the Lord Jesus, they languish. If you're serving in a parish, then there are probably lots of things you see that should or could be, even though they're not actually there. That's vision. Vision matters. Your vision can inspire you, but first of all, it is probably going to anger you. Good. Feel the anger; it can be fuel.

Bill Hybels writes about "holy discontent," the frustration you feel when the vision God is giving you grows too far from the reality at hand.[1] Sometimes we reach what Hybels calls the "Popeye" moment. The famous comic book character would only take so much and then explode with the phrase, "That's all I can stands, I can't stands no more."

The heroes of the Bible were fueled by a discontent that led them to a decision to do great things for God. Moses became murderously angry about Israel's enslavement in Egypt. David was so offended that Goliath would mock God, he went to war. Nehemiah wept that the walls of Jerusalem had fallen into disrepair, and he set aside everything else to do something about it. They all caught a vision of what God wanted them to do, and, after that, they just had to do it. In fact, Nehemiah is a model for determination when it comes to visionary leadership. His critics threaten and oppose him and insist that he step down, but he answers them: "I am engaged in a great enterprise and am unable to come down" (Nehemiah 6:3).

Getting Started

No matter what kind of parish you're in, where you're located, or what your resources are right now, you can begin to grow a healthy parish exactly where God has placed you.

1. **If you're the pastor of a large suburban church—you can do this!**

   Chances are there is also a large evangelical church somewhere in your region. And chances are, it is filled with more than a few former Catholics, maybe some of them your former parishioners. Here's what you can do: Reach out and start learning from the people of that church. They have a lot to teach you, and they will very likely be glad to talk. If you need to, you can first repent of all the uncharitable things you've said about that church.

2. **If you're a pastor of a small rural or urban church and you don't have any money and staff—you can do this!**

Start tithing yourself and begin challenging everyone in the pews to get involved to serve and to give (use something like our "Five-Step Process" from page 174 to help get moving). Get to know your community, not just your congregation, and craft your weekend homilies with them in mind.

3. **If you're a deacon or pastoral life director with responsibility for multiple sites—you can do this!**

Study your weekend experience from the perspective of the dechurched in your community. What does it feel like, sound like, and look like to them? Honestly evaluate your music and start praying about what needs to be done there. Take a look at the entrance to your church or your lobby. Can you make it better, clean it up, and make it more inviting, maybe even irresistible?

4. **If you're the DRE, the youth minister, the parish secretary— you can do this!**

Pick two or three people you respect and trust, who are not currently running or leading anything in your parish, and begin a quiet evaluation process of all your programs. Don't forget to evaluate *all* of them, everything that is going on in your parish and vying for your space and resources as well as your parishioners' attention, time, and money. Put together a comprehensive list and try to identify the *purpose* of each program or event. Then start the discussion about what you should stop doing because it doesn't align with God's purpose for your church.

> No matter what kind of parish you're in, you can begin to grow a healthy parish.

5. **If you're a parishioner, alarmed and concerned for your parish and perhaps for your pastor and the demands placed on him—you can do this too!**

Ask your pastor if you can greet people at the door for weekend Masses. Ask others to help you, too. See how many people you can get to join you. Start generating energy and excitement that others can catch. Form a prayer team to support your pastor.

These are obviously first steps—baby steps—but that's where every journey begins. Begin somewhere, and ask God for the vision he wants to give you.

For Such a Time as This

The Book of Esther takes place during the heartbreaking exile of the Jews. At that point in the story they've lost their hallowed Temple, their beloved homeland, and their precious freedom. But worse things still are in store for them. An evil counselor to the ruler of the land, the king of Persia, plots the extermination of the entire Jewish people.

But God raises up Ester, a simple Jewish girl, and places her in the unlikely position of Queen of Persia. And then he plants a vision in Esther to save his people. It comes in the words of a friend who tells her she must go to the king and intercede, a dangerous thing for even the queen to do. Her friend tells her:

> Even if you now remain silent, relief and deliverance will come to the Jews from another source; but you and your father's house will perish. Who knows—perhaps it was for a time like this that you became queen? (Esther 4:14)

Other translations say, "And who knows whether you have not come to the kingdom for such a time as this?" Of course, she gets to work and literally saves the day. God placed her in a position of influence and gave her a vision for exactly the time and the circumstances she was in. That's you. And you are not alone!

You are not alone in your heartbreak as you watch people walk away from the Church in droves. You are not alone in your sadness to see it drift into irrelevance in the lives of so many people including your own family and friends. You are not alone in feeling frustrated about the current state of the local parish enterprise you serve. You are not alone in wanting things to go better.

You are not alone in believing that the Church should be a place where people connect with their heavenly Father, come to know their Savior, and learn to walk in step with the Holy Spirit. You are not alone in seeking to help lead people into a joyful and loving celebration of the Eucharist. You are not alone in your desire for the Church to provide meaning, purpose, and direction in people's lives. You are not alone in expecting life-changing outcomes from the incredible work you're

You are not alone!

already doing. You are not alone in wanting your congregation to have a greater impact on your community, connecting more people to Christ.

You are not alone. God is with you. God desires these changes even more deeply than you do. And perhaps he has placed you exactly where you are "for such a time as this." And more than that, he's raising up still others who share that same passion to provide the vitality for a movement whose moment has come. Obedient to the Magisterium, this moment is all about giving fresh impetus to the directions set by the Second Vatican Council, reinvigorating the noblest efforts of the Catholic Church, and returning to what God's word itself tells us—his Church—to do.

We are called to give leadership to a movement whose moment has arrived: to rebuild parish life in the Catholic Church in the United States. It is a movement of the whole Body of Christ as well, to take back our Church from casual consumer Christians and put it in the hands of humble and bold believers transformed by their faith and transforming society.[2]

> *Start by doing what's necessary; then do what's possible; and suddenly you are doing the impossible.*
> —Saint Francis of Assisi[3]

And when you move, others will, too. Because people are hardwired to get into a movement, people love movements. God made us that way. Even if the desire is dormant, it is there, and you can awaken it.

We can call our congregations to the challenge of discipleship and get them growing as fully devoted followers of Jesus Christ. We can make our parishes wellsprings of vitality and spirit that energize our disciples to help them become more convincing witnesses in the community. We can make an impact on the next generation for Christ. Instead of a stumbling block and obstacle course, people far from God can begin to see the Church as a great place to come to know him. Our growing disciples can joyfully serve one another and model missions that aim at restoring creation and renewing the face of the earth.

This book is not just about doing church differently. This is about being part of a movement to change people's experience of the Church so that our society is more and more transformed by Christ. It is not only something worth dying for, it is something worth living for— something worth giving your life to. And *that* is the movement of the kingdom of God. It is not a "religious" movement; it is a "kingdom movement." It's about the movement of the kingdom of God.

> The LORD's acts of mercy are not exhausted,
> his compassion it not spent;
> They are renewed each morning—
> great is your faithfulness! (Lamentations 3:22–23)

Every day there are new waves of mercies and grace God is sending your way. God wants to do something in your local church community that he is not doing anywhere else. There is a great work through you and your people he will not repeat, a unique story that he will never tell again.

Great parish leadership demands the vision to see that. And that means you've got to be looking for it, hungering for it, fasting and praying for the great work God wants to do through you. There is a mission, but he is waiting on a leader. God is waiting on you to raise your hand and say, "I'll step up. I'll do the heavy lifting and the hard work. I'll take the bullets and the criticism, but I can't take mediocrity and irrelevance anymore. I can do this!"

> We are called to give leadership to a movement whose moment has arrived: to rebuild parish life in the Catholic Church in the United States.

Think about it. This is the Church that Christ founded and died for. This is the Church that holds the fullness of the faith and teaches with uncompromising authority on moral matters. This is the Church that serves as steward of the Eucharist and the other sacraments. This is the Church that blessedly preserves and everywhere promotes devotion to our Savior's Blessed Mother. This is the Church of the apostles and their successors, the martyrs, and the heroes of the Christian centuries: Peter and Paul, Jerome and Augustine, Francis of Assisi, Thomas Aquinas, Catherine of Siena, Thomas More, Ignatius Loyola, Mother Teresa, and Pope John Paul II.

This is the Body that Christ forms as his own and charges to transform society through the introduction of the kingdom of heaven on earth. It is quite simply the hope of the world. And believe it or not, you hold that hope in your hands in your local parish church. Use it.

Make church matter.

Appendix A

A DETAILED EXAMPLE OF CHANGING OUR CULTURE

In our part of the world, everyone wants church as early as possible on Christmas Eve. No matter how many other Masses we had, 4:00 afternoon Mass was always absurdly jammed every year. It was the annual, ultimate example of "get it over with." The congregation overflowed from the church into the church hall and beyond. The parking lot and adjoining streets where tempers flared became hopelessly gridlocked. It was an annual exercise of frustrated efforts, hurt feelings, and failed expectations.

It was just a terrible experience for everyone (except, of course, the insiders who knew how to make the dysfunction work for them). Beyond the chaos was the lost opportunity of connecting positively with people who didn't have a church but came to church that night. Christmas Eve was their yearly reminder why they didn't want to be here.

There had to be a better way to do this. Year after year, we tried everything we could think of to relieve the early congestion and make the experience better. Nothing worked. Until . . .

> **Father Michael**: One summer evening I was stopped at a light, on York Road, just up the street from our church. I was in front of the main entrance to the Maryland State Fairgrounds here in Timonium. It wasn't fair season but the gates, I noticed, were open. I had never been inside, and, with no pressing engagements and totally on impulse, I drove in. There was a sea of parking and several large buildings, one of the largest of which, for some reason, was also open. I parked and went inside. In an instant, I knew I wanted to do Christmas there.
>
> Why not just get off the treadmill of an unsuccessful exercise, stop the ridiculous multiplication of Masses, gather everyone together for a real parish celebration, and have space for visitors as well. It would be a dramatic illustration of our changing culture: doing church differently by getting out into the community and being accessible to them at the time they actually want to visit us. We could make Christmas Eve absolutely *not* all about us and positively all about the people who aren't in the pews. I *loved* the idea.
>
> **Tom**: I thought it was crazy. I mean *really*, who would go to the "cow palace" on Christmas Eve? And I was sure my reaction would be the typical one (and, just for the record, *it was*).

But, as we discussed the idea and prayed about it, it seemed like a calculated risk we should take. First step was to find out what it was going to cost and if the place was available. We had an intern named Bob working for us that summer, and after discreet inquiries he learned that the rental was only a nominal fee and they would be happy to have us. We were good to go. We didn't take a vote, once we were prayerfully sure this was where God was leading, we followed. We did, however, develop a deliberate strategy.

Moving forward, it looked as if we had *two* projects to tackle. Logistically, the exercise was about moving our entire church up the street for a single evening. That seemed like a big deal, but the public relations exercise before us was even more daunting. We not only wanted to convince people to go, but we wanted them to go enthusiastically and bring their friends.

We met with two of our strongest parish leaders. Before asking for their help, we asked for their advice, and they gave it to us. They were startled and concerned with the idea, and we let them have some time to feel those feelings. But after they had processed their emotions, they both came back to us with enthusiasm and support. *Then* we asked them to lead *our* efforts. Mitch would run the logistics and Roni would help us sell it to the people.

In turn, they both invited others onto their teams and built a solid core of support for this project before we ever shared it with the rest of the parish. Most of our volunteers moved from skepticism to support in a reliable pattern that taught us more about how we should introduce it to the congregation. Before the general announcement, we made sure that the parish council, our staff, and the volunteer leaders understood and bought into the idea.

We announced the plan in a letter from the pastor in the bulletin, about two months before Christmas. We thought the written format would be best, since the idea was so unexpected that it could easily be misunderstood if only announced in church. We already knew most everybody would respond with confusion, so we wanted it clearly spelled out in black and white.

The letter set the record straight about the real problems with Christmas Eve (which are easy to forget from year to year) and the advantages of moving. It discussed the opportunity the plan provided when it came to the dechurched in our community.

We also announced another decision at that time, too, and it was a big one. We were *not* going to give people a choice between the fairgrounds and the church. We were going to have one Christmas celebration. That was a very difficult decision to make, but we were convinced it was critical for the success of the plan.

There was a huge response, mostly running from cautiously curious to openly hostile. We just let people sit with it for a few weeks, and then we followed up with a video we showed at the end of weekend Masses to try to change people's minds. The video featured two high school students, Billy and Gair, poking fun at all the problems on our campus in previous years, playfully romping around the fairgrounds, and then celebrating all the available parking. This was spliced between clips of a lovely, distinguished lady, Elaine, describing her own original distaste for the idea and subsequent conversion. It's hard to be angry when you're laughing, and this video made people laugh. It was a huge hit and won over lots of hearts. (It has subsequently become something of a Christmas cult classic around here, known affectionately as the "More Parking!" video).

Of course, not everyone was laughing. One of our major donors told us flat out that if we followed through on the plan, he was cutting us off. At that point his annual contribution was just about what we were anticipating Christmas would cost us. So, in effect, his announcement doubled the cost. Just for the record, he did withdraw his contribution and, unfortunately, left the parish. That was intimidating. Of course, there were calls, complaints, and all the predictable difficulties that change always unearths. But we held to our resolve.

We showed two more videos in the following weeks: One was just a practical piece about where to go and what to expect when you got there. The final pitch, the weekend before Christmas, was an emotionally uplifting appeal connecting our celebration to the higher purposes

God has given the Church. At that point, we probably weren't changing anybody else's mind, but we were helping our "converts" to appreciate the good thing we were all doing together.

All the logistics of moving out and setting up went according to plan, thanks to a really super team of young leaders—Bob, Joe, and Brian—who caught the spirit of the project and made it happen.

Want to know more/go deeper?

Listen to Bob, Joe, and Brian discuss changing the culture of Christmas. Go to rebuiltparish.com, click "Appendix A," and then click "Changing the Culture."

Christmas Eve 2005 was a long day as we stared at the 1,500 empty seats in our venue, the Exhibition Hall. That's a lot of chairs. And nobody was rushing to take them, that was for sure. Twenty minutes before the Mass, it was still mostly empty. But minutes later, people started to come, and they kept coming and we more or less filled the place. In the last five years, Christmas Eve at the fairgrounds has grown to become one of our most revered traditions. At this point, we have already expanded to a larger facility on the same campus with 3,200 seats and two Masses back-to-back. This spring we did Easter at the fairgrounds. People who never come to church are very comfortable in that setting, and many who join our church start there.

The point isn't Christmas Eve; it's about effecting cultural change.

YOU CAN DO THIS!
Steps You Can Take in Your Parish

If you have responsibility in your parish for anything, and it's not going well:

- Acknowledge what is not working. Discontent and frustration can give birth to new ideas.
- Think differently; apply yourself creatively to the problem. When brainstorming, no idea is a bad one. That doesn't mean that there are no bad ideas. Clearly there are, but don't kill an idea too quickly before it's completely studied and discussed. Through prayer and honest internal discussion, make sure the idea isn't just your impulse or your will; make sure it's a God thing.
- Share your idea in a small but growing circle and get them to invest; in fact, make them the leaders and the sales force for your cultural change.
- Be collaborative, be inclusive, and show care for people's emotions in the face of change. But don't let the critics and the naysayers slow you down, and don't compromise your idea to accommodate them either, even when there is a financial cost.
- Create a sense of movement. Get people to see the change as a mission connected to the great big mission of Christ's Church. It's a movement . . . that means sometimes it's got to MOVE!

Appendix B

A FEW OF THE (MANY) THINGS WE STILL DON'T KNOW

For the past several years we have been struggling with the (admittedly) happy problem of overcrowding on Sunday mornings. The crowds are such that it's kind of silly and unproductive to encourage parishioners to invite guests or newcomers to join us. But to discourage invitations more or less undermines our basic purpose.

We began strategic planning to look at what could be done long term. Meanwhile, we introduced some small steps to relieve the problem short term (like encouraging parishioners to park off campus or give up their seats at optimum times). Yet we kept wondering, was there anything *else* we could do more immediately and effectively to address this critical challenge?

We decided to try something we've seen an increasing number of large, successful evangelical churches doing: "video venues." Basically it was about making our weekend service available at peak times to newcomers and visitors *off campus*, with the help of video technology.

Instead of joining us on our home campus, they'd join us elsewhere. Video venues can easily provide extra seats with no new construction.

> **Father Michael**: After consultation with the Archbishop's office, it was decided that this service would not be a Mass, since it was designed for dechurched people in our community. Instead we would use the old idea of the "Mass of the Catechumen," essentially a Liturgy of the Word (without a Liturgy of the Eucharist), with the same homily I was giving in church, prerecorded, and presented via video.

> **Tom**: The rest of the service (music, readings, and prayers) would also be the same service as experienced in our church but presented live. I conducted the service. We decided to replicate other elements of our weekend experience: host team, nursery, even a small "café" coffee service. After considering a number of different sites, we chose a local hotel, the Crowne Plaza. We invested energy, staff, and volunteer time, and, of course, money in this experiment (not a lot but it was money that obviously could have been used elsewhere).

And it didn't work.

Aside from people who were just being nice and doing us a favor by attending, as well as few curiosity seekers, not many people came. We certainly didn't attract large numbers of the dechurched as we were hoping. Since we had undertaken the project as a limited exercise, when our contract at the hotel was finished, so was the exercise.

Naively we had broken one of our own rules and just copied what others were doing without any real understanding of *how* to do it. Following the experience, we took a hard look at what we got wrong (which was very painful after having begun with such high hopes).

We came to the conclusion that probably it was a matter of marketing more than anything else. People in our community didn't really know about the Crowne Plaza experience, and it was over before they had time to learn. And given that it is such an unexpected approach in churchworld, it could take them a long time to learn.

> **Father Michael**: I very much wanted to try again, and prove we could do it.

> **Tom:** I did not. It was a labor-intensive exercise that seemed beyond our strength at that point. And to attract the numbers that would make it worth the effort, and do it in a timeframe that would make it worth the expense, seemed to require a marketing campaign we couldn't afford.

The point is that we didn't know what we were doing, and we *still don't* when it comes to "video venues." We know that they can be done successfully, because others do them; we just don't know how to do it here. We decided not to repeat the Crowne Plaza experience, for the reasons given above, but we didn't give up on looking for ways to make our weekend experience more accessible.

Currently on Sunday mornings at 10:30 (and again at our 5:30 p.m. Mass) we are live streaming our weekend service on our website. Initially we were bedeviled by technical problems and for months actually attracted smaller numbers than the video venue, which was disappointing. But unlike Crowne Plaza, this exercise involves less work and money, so it can be more easily sustained.

The online campus has recently begun to really take off with hundreds of online visitors and worshipers weekly. There is a chat function, a prayer request feature, and donations can be made (to date, we've collected $25 from one woman in Dallas). The primary audience remains dechurched Catholics in Timonium, Maryland, and it looks as if more and more of them are tuning in. "Give us a try online" is certainly an easy invitation for our parishioners to make to their friends and family. It turns out there are unintended benefits to the site, too. Parishioners who are traveling, or on vacation, can still join us. College students can stay in contact with their church family wherever they are at school, and those who are homebound or sick need not be alone. A local hospital has even contacted us about dedicating a channel on their in-house network to broadcast our Sunday morning service. While it's not an acceptable alternative to Mass attendance, it's a great alternative to doing nothing at all (and a first step back to church). Meanwhile, it allows us to continue to grow.

To be the healthy culture that we want to be, we need to know what we *don't know* and what we need to learn. To be a growing church, we need to acknowledge what we're currently getting wrong, what is inhibiting growth, and where we have to keep growing.

Want know more/go deeper?

Try our online campus Sunday mornings at 10:30 am and again at 5:30 pm. Go to our website, churchnativity.tv, and click "online campus."

Our Current Standouts

When it comes to the local parish church there are many things we don't know. Here are some of the current standouts that we're trying to learn more about:

1. **Communication**

   We know how to communicate clearly, coherently, and consistently the steps we want parishioners to take on their discipleship path. We don't know how to manage this process or keep track of it.

2. **Small Groups**

We know the value of small groups and the need for relationships to grow in faith. We don't know how to involve the substantive majority of our congregation in small-group life *and* keep them there. We do not know how to measure the lifecycle of our small groups, and when it's time to multiply, merge, or disband.

3. **Testimonies**

We have discovered the power of parishioners sharing their stories of life change through a relationship with Christ. We don't know how to motivate parishioners to talk about their faith in more public ways, give witness to life-change, or share stories about their discipleship.

4. **Young Adults**

We're still trying to figure out young adult ministry. We're attracting young adults, but we're not sure *how many or how* we're attracting them. We want to be better at helping our teens to know the Lord in a way that will shape their decisions, preserve their purity, and direct their path.

5. **Tech**

We don't know how to gather and maintain up-to-date census data about our congregation. Neither do we know how to gather feedback and information from them. And we really don't know what to do with it when we *do* get it.

Like everyone else, we do not know where technology is going or how we can keep pace with it. We do not yet understand how to integrate the various forms of communication we've already got going. And we really don't know what to do with social media.

6. **Managing Growth**

We don't know how to continue to grow, given the limitations of our campus. We are struggling with what *can* be done, but also with what *should* be done in bricks and mortar. We know the last thing Baltimore needs is another church building, but we also know that we need more space. On the other hand, can our church growth also happen in other ways, too, like online? What will a church "campus" even be in the future? We don't know.

7. **Achieving Balance**

And, believe it or not, we still don't always know the difference between meeting the legitimate needs of our congregation and pandering to consumers. We know there's a line between the two; we just don't where it is.

It has become axiomatic for us to say, "We don't know what we're doing." We used to be embarrassed about that. It sounds like an excuse for failure. Sometimes it's the first step forward. No matter the particular challenge, it's always going to be the same disciplined exercise in naming the problem, finding a way forward, and developing a consistent strategy.

Appendix C

NAMING THE CHANGE: MISSION, VISION, AND STRATEGY

O ver the past few years, we have clearly identified our mission, seen God's vision for our parish take shape, and developed a successful strategy to make it all happen. Articulating all of these in a clear and simple way that staff, volunteers, parishioners, and newcomers can understand and remember has turned out to be unexpectedly challenging. We still struggle with getting it right and keeping it in focus for our parishioners.

Most parishes and church communities have a mission statement, but how often is it ignored or unknown, and how frequently does it belie what is really going on? The culture of every organization is shaped by the values out of which the individuals in the organization operate. But sometimes those values are unintentional. How often do leaders in an organization, of any size, discover that even their best employees and biggest fans can't really tell you what it is that the organization is about?

We have also found that even after people have been invested in the vision, it needs constant maintenance because, in Bill Hybels analogy, vision "leaks."[1] People forget or get confused. They become distracted and look elsewhere. You've got to keep infusing your congregation with God's vision and mission for your parish.

Below are the statements we have formed to give words to who we are and what we understand God is doing through us. Currently we make sure that this material is regularly reviewed in our annual staff retreat. It is introduced as new staff members are welcomed; it is relied on as programs are formed. And, it is used as a critical measurement for wins and successful efforts.

Our Faith

I believe in God, the Father almighty,
Creator of heaven and earth,
and in Jesus Christ, his only Son, our Lord,
who was conceived by the Holy Spirit,
born of the Virgin Mary,
suffered under Pontius Pilate,
was crucified, died and was buried;
he descended into hell;
on the third day he rose again from the dead;
he ascended into heaven,
and is seated at the right hand of God the Father almighty;
from there he will come to judge the living and the dead.
I believe in the Holy Spirit,
the holy catholic Church,
the communion of saints,
the forgiveness of sins,

the resurrection of the body,
and life everlasting. Amen.
    —Apostles' Creed

Our Mission

Love God • Love others • Make disciples

Your shall love the Lord, your God, with all your heart, with
all your soul, and with all your mind. You shall love your
neighbor as yourself.

    —Matthew 22:37, 39

Go, therefore, and make disciples of all nations, baptizing
them in the name of the Father, and of the Son, and of the
Holy Spirit, teaching them to observe all that I have commanded you.

    —Matthew 28:19–20

Our Vision

Make church matter
by growing disciples who are *growing disciples*
among dechurched Catholics in north Baltimore
and influencing churches to do the same elsewhere.

Our Strategy

Currently one in three people raised as Catholics is no longer connected to the Catholic Church. Our strategy is to reach out creatively to dechurched Catholics in our north Baltimore community with a fresh and relevant presentation of the life-changing message of the Gospel. We want to take them on a journey to become fully devoted followers of Jesus Christ.

Our weekend experience is central to our strategy and the weekend message is central to the experience. Music, message, and ministers work together to create an irresistible environment of energy and excellence in which newcomers feel welcome. Equally important strategically are excellent weekend programs for kids and students where the messages usually parallel the adult message.

Newcomers are encouraged to come back. Regular weekend attendees are invited to become members. Members are challenged to take their next steps: get to know the centrality of the Eucharist, serve in a ministry, join a small group, worship through their tithe or offering, support our missions, spend daily quiet time with God, and increasingly honor God in all areas of their lives, for example personal morality. Members are also encouraged to invest in and invite their dechurched friends to our weekend experience.

Our strategy is to try to meet people exactly where they are in order to challenge them to take their next step.

Our Values

Worship

We believe in orthodox Christianity, as taught by the Magisterium of the Roman Catholic Church. The Eucharistic celebration is the source and summit of our faith that we seek to live and serve with the whole of our lives in vibrant ways. We value this "dynamic orthodoxy." Excellence in our worship honors God. *We value excellence.*

Discipleship

We believe the Bible is the inspired, infallible Word of God. Our preaching and messages strive to break open the relevance of the Bible to our daily lives.

Changing and growing into the likeness of Christ is not just about greater knowledge of our faith, it's doing what God's word says we must to do. *We value life-change.*

Fellowship

We believe that our Baptism forms us into a family that is constantly nourished and renewed by all the sacraments, which teach us to love one another as Christ loved us.

We strive to build a church culture through small groups where people are open and authentic, especially about their need to grow and change. *We value doing life-change together.*

Service

We believe that the Holy Spirit has prepared works for us to do that will advance the kingdom of Christ. We recognize God's call to our church to serve both within our parish and also beyond: in our city, our country, and the world. In the service of the Lord we can always do more. *We value that challenge.*

Evangelization

We believe that Jesus came to seek and save the lost. We heed God's command to share his name with the world. We look for the opportunity to invite dechurched Catholics to join us. As a parish church, we want insiders to reach outsiders. *We value growth and health.*

NOTES

Epigraph

1. National Conference of Catholic Bishops, *Communities of Salt and Light: Reflections on the Social Mission of the Parish* (Washington, DC: United States Catholic Conference, 1994), #1.

Preface

1. John Paul II, "I Shall Give You Shepherds" *Pastores Dabo Vobis* (Vatican: The Holy See, March 25, 1992), 18.

2. Thomas J. Reese, "The Hidden Exodus: Catholics Becoming Protestants," *National Catholic Reporter*, April 28, 2011, http://ncronline.org/news/hidden-exodus-catholics-becoming-protestants. For specific data, see the US Religious Landscape Survey by the Pew Research Center's Forum on Religion and Public Life, Washington, DC: Pew Research Center, 2008.

3. Samuel R. Chand, *Cracking Your Church's Culture Code: Seven Keys to Unleashing Vision and Inspiration* (San Francisco: Jossey-Bass, 2011), 2.

4. Gabe Lyons, *The Next Christians: The Good News About the End of Christian America* (New York: Doubleday Religion, 2010), 165.

Introduction: Convenient Parking

1. The Beatles, "Hello, Goodbye," written by Paul McCartney and John Lennon, recorded October–November 1967 on *Magical Mystery Tour*, Capital Records, 1967.

2. Lewis Carroll, *Through the Looking-Glass and What Alice Found There* (New York: Bloomsbury, 2001), 42–43.

3. Vincent J. Miller, *Consuming Religion: Christian Faith and Practice in a Consumer Culture* (New York: Continuum, 2005), 210.

4. Rodney Clapp, ed., *The Consuming Passion: Christianity and the Consumer Culture* (Downers Grove, IL: InterVarsity Press, 1998), 190–91.

1. Church Is Not Easy

1. Second Vatican Council, "Dogmatic Constitution on the Church" *Lumen Gentium* (Vatican: the Holy See, November 21, 1964), sec. 8, http://www.vatican.va/archive/hist_councils/ii_vatican_council/documents/vat-ii_const_19641121_lumen-gentium_en.html.

2. Miller, *Consuming Religion*, 6.

3. "US Catholics Attending Mass Weekly," Center for Applied Research in Apostolate (CARA), accessed February 10, 2012, http://cara.georgetown.edu/CARAServices/FRStats/massattendweek.pdf.

4. Dallas Willard, *The Divine Conspiracy: Rediscovering Our Hidden Life in God* (San Francisco: Harper San Francisco, 1998), 342.

5. Malcolm Gladwell, *The Tipping Point: How Little Things Can Make a Big Difference* (Boston: Little, Brown, 2000), 98–99.

6. Perry Noble, "Six Leadership Mistakes I've Made," *Perry Noble: Leadership, Vision & Creativity*, May 11, 2010, accessed November 8, 2011, http://www.perrynoble.com/2010/05/11/six-leadership-mistakes-ive-made.

2. Pharisees at Heart

1. Jesus Jones, "Right Here, Right Now," written by Mike Edwards, recorded May 1990 on *Doubt*, Matrix Studios, 1990.

2. Rick Warren, *The Purpose Driven Church: Growth without Compromising Your Message & Mission* (Grand Rapids, MI: Zondervan Pub., 1995), 14–16.

3. C. S. Lewis, *Mere Christianity: A Revised and Amplified Edition, with a New Introduction, of the Three Books Broadcast Talks, Christian Behaviour, and Beyond Personality* (San Francisco: Harper San Francisco, 2001), 124.

4. Avery Dulles, *The Resilient Church: The Necessity and Limits of Adaptation* (Garden City, NY: Doubleday, 1977), 33.

5. Second Vatican Council, "Decree on Ecumenism" *Unitatis Redintegratio* (Vatican: Herder and Herder, New York, 1966), #3, 346.

6. Michael Scanlan, T.O.R., and James Manney, *Let the Fire Fall* (Ann Arbor, MI: Servant Books, 1986), 68–69.

7. Cathy L. Grossman, "Most Religious Groups in USA Have Lost Ground, Survey Finds." *USA Today*, March 17, 2009, accessed February, 10, 2010, http://www.usatoday.com/news/religion/2009-03-09-american-religion-ARIS_N.htm.

8. Thomas Reece, "The Hidden Exodus: Catholics Becoming Protestants." *National Catholic Reporter*, April 18, 2011, accessed February 3, 2012, http://ncronline.org/news/hidden-exodus-catholics-becoming-protestants.

9. Doug Fields, *Purpose-Driven Youth Ministry: 9 Essential Foundations for Healthy Growth* (Grand Rapids, MI: Zondervan, 1998), 43.

10. Ibid., 17.

3. Lost People in *Churchworld*

1. Robert S. Rivers, *From Maintenance to Mission: Evangelization and the Revitalization of the Parish* (New York: Paulist Press, 2005), 23.

2. Andy Stanley, *The Grace of God* (Nashville, TN: Thomas Nelson, 2010), 126.

3. Paul VI, "On Evangelization in the Modern World" *Evangelii Nuntiandi* (Vatican: The Holy See, December 8, 1975), http://www.vatican.va/holy_father/paul_vi/apost_exhortations/documents/hf_p-vi_exh_19751208_evangelii-nuntiandi_en.html.

4. National Conference of Catholic Bishops, *Go and Make Disciples: A National Plan and Strategy for Catholic Evangelization in the United States* (Washington, DC: United States Catholic Conference, 1993), 3.

5. Edward P. Hahnenberg, "Sell Your Soul: Catechesis in Consumer Culture," *Catechetical Leader* 18 (September/October 2007): 5.

6. John Paul II, "Mission of the Redeemer" *Redemptoris Missio* (Vatican: The Holy See, December 7, 1990), #2, http://www.vatican.va/holy_father/john_paul_ii/encyclicals/documents/hf_jp-ii_enc_07121990_redemptoris-missio_en.html.

4. War In Heaven

1. Niccolò Machiavelli, *The Prince*, trans. W.K. Marriott (Campbell, CA: FastPencil, 2010), 21.

2. Thom S. Rainer, *Surprising Insights from the Unchurched and Proven Ways to Reach Them* (Grand Rapids, MI: Zondervan, 2001), 93.

3. Robert S. Rivers, *From Maintenance to Mission: Evangelization and the Revitalization of the Parish* (New York: Paulist, 2005), 22.

4. Brad Powell, *Change Your Church for Good* (Nashville: Thomas Nelson, 2010), 137.

5. Second Vatican Council, "Decree on Ecumenism" *Unitatis Redintegratio* (Vatican: The Holy See, November 21, 1964), http://www.vatican.va/archive/hist_councils/ii_vatican_council/documents/vat-ii_decree_19641121_unitatis-redintegratio_en.html.

6. Seth Godin, *Tribes: We Need You to Lead Us* (New York: Portfolio, 2008), 113.

7. Rivers, *From Maintenance to Mission*, 196.

5. Pretty Churches and Other Lies

1. Dietrich Bonhoeffer, *The Cost of Discipleship* (New York: Touchstone, 1995), 59.

2. Avery Dulles, *A Church to Believe In: Discipleship and the Dynamics of Freedom* (New York: Crossroad, 1982), 7–11.

3. For further discussion, see Andy Stanley, Reggie Joiner, and Lane Jones, 7 *Practices of Effective Ministry* (Sisters, OR: Multnomah Publishers, 2004), 86–97.

4. Erwin Raphael McManus, *An Unstoppable Force: Daring to Become the Church God Had in Mind* (Loveland, CO: Group, 2001), 71–72.

5. Matthew Kelly, *Rediscover Catholicism: A Spiritual Guide to Living with Passion & Purpose*, 2nd rev. and exp. ed. (Cincinnati: Beacon Publishing, 2011), 55–56.

6. Warren, *The Purpose Driven Church*, 51.

7. Stanley, Joiner, and Jones, 7 *Practices of Effective Ministry*, 146.

8. Kelly, *Rediscover Catholicism*, 300–303.

9. Brainyquote, "Mickey Mantle quotes," accessed March 26, 2012, http://www.brainyquote.com/quotes/authors/m/mickey_mantle.html.

10. Bonhoeffer, *The Cost of Discipleship*, 43–45.

6. "It's the Weekend, Stupid!"

1. John Paul II, "The Lord's Day" *Dies Domini* (Vatican: The Holy See, July 5, 1998), http://www.vatican.va/holy_father/john_paul_ii/apost_letters/documents/hf_jp-ii_apl_05071998_dies-domini_en.html.

2. Neil Postman, *Amusing Ourselves to Death: Public Discourse in the Age of Show Business* (London: Penguin Books, 2006), 87.

3. Ed Young, *The Creative Leader: Unleashing the Power of Your Creative Potential* (Nashville, TN: B&H Publishing Group, 2006), 52.

4. John Paul II, "Church of the Eucharist" *Ecclesia de Eucharistia* (Vatican: The Holy See, February 22, 2007), http://www.vatican.va/holy_father/special_features/encyclicals/documents/hf_jp-ii_enc_20030417_ecclesia_eucharistia_en.html.

5. Ibid.

6. Benedict XVI, "The Sacrament of Charity" *Sacramentum Caritatis* (Vatican: The Holy See, February 22, 2007), http://www.vatican.va/holy_father/benedict_xvi/apost_exhortations/documents/hf_ben-xvi_exh_20070222_sacramentum-caritatis_en.html.

7. Quoted in James C. Collins, *Good to Great: Why Some Companies Make the Leap . . . and Others Don't*, 1st ed. (New York: Collins, 2001), 98.

8. United States Conference of Catholic Bishops, *Sing to the Lord: Music in Divine Worship* (Washington, DC: USCCB Publishing, 2008), 1.

9. Ibid., 38.

10. Thomas Day, *Why Catholics Can't Sing: The Culture of Catholicism and the Triumph of Bad Taste* (New York: Crossroad, 1990), 64–65.

11. Joseph Ratzinger, *The Spirit of the Liturgy* (San Francisco, CA: Ignatius, 2000), 136.

12. United States Conference of Catholic Bishops, *Sing to the Lord*, 32.

13. Second Vatican Council, "Constitution on the Sacred Liturgy," *Sacrosanctum Concilium* (Vatican: The Holy See, December 4, 1963), http://www.vatican.va/archive/hist_councils/ii_vatican_council/documents/vat-ii_const_19631204_sacrosanctum-concilium_en.html.

14. Ratzinger, *The Spirit of the Liturgy*, 136.

15. United States Conference of Catholic Bishops, *Sing to the Lord*, 32.

16. Ibid., 36.

17. Augustine, "Saint Augustine: Let Us Sing to the Lord a Song of Love," *Letter* (Vatican: The Holy See, accessed February 13, 2012, http://www.vatican.va/spirit/documents/spirit_20010508_agostino-vescovo_en.html.

18. Andy Stanley, "Creating an Irresistible Environment," *Ministry Today*, March 23, 2010, accessed February 13, 2012, http://www.ministriestoday.com/index.php/ministry-news/18862-creating-an-irresistible-environment.

7. Mobilize the Next Generation

1. John Paul II, "To the Youth of the World" *Dilecti Amici* (Vatican: The Holy See, March 31, 1985), sec. 15, http://www.vatican.va/holy_father/john_paul_ii/apost_letters/documents/hf_jp-ii_apl_31031985_dilecti-amici_en.html.

2. "Walt Disney," BrainyQuote.com, Xplore Inc, 2012, accessed August 20, 2012, http://www.brainyquote.com/quotes/quotes/w/waltdisney131640.html.

3. Quoted in David Kinnaman and Gabe Lyons, *Unchristian: What a New Generation Really Thinks about Christianity . . . and Why It Matters* (Grand Rapids, MI: Baker Books, 2008), 142.

8. Make the Message Matter

1. Quoted in St. Augustine, *Augustine De doctrina Christiana*, ed. and trans. R. P. H. Green (Oxford University Press, 1985), 229.

2. Second Vatican Council, *Sacrosanctum Concilium* (Vatican: The Holy See, December 4, 1963), http://www.vatican.va/archive/hist_councils/ii_vatican_council/documents/vat-ii_const_19631204_sacrosanctum-concilium_en.html.

3. "Quotes from Bishop T. D. Jakes," *It's Your Time*, accessed December 15, 2011, http://www.itsyourtime.co.za/bishops-quotes.

4. "Ethos, Pathos, and Logos." Durham Technical Community College, *Durham Tech Courses Server,*. accessed January 27, 2012, http://courses.durhamtech.edu/perkins/aris.html.

5. Hippocrates, and Mark John Schiefsky, *On Ancient Medicine* (Leiden: Brill, 2005), 28, eBook.

6. Gabriel Moran, "Augustine Despite Aquinas," *Speaking of Teaching: Lessons from History* (Lanham, MD: Lexington, 2008), 35.

7. Andy Stanley, *Deep and Wide: Creating Churches Unchurched People Love to Attend* (Grand Rapids, MI: Zondervan, 2012), 117.

8. Rainer, *Surprising Insights from the Unchurched*, 218.

9. Build from Below

1. Robert D. Putnam, *Bowling Alone: The Collapse and Revival of American Community* (New York: Simon & Schuster Paperbacks, 2000), 367.

2. Gary Portnoy, "Where Everybody Knows Your Name," written by Gary Portnoy and Judy Hart, recorded 1982, Angelo Addax Music Company, Inc., 1982.

3. John Paul II, "On the Vocation and Mission of the Lay Faithful" *Christifideles Laici* (Vatican: The Holy See, December 30, 1988), http://www.vatican.va/holy_father/john_paul_ii/apost_exhortations/documents/hf_jp-ii_exh_30121988_christifideles-laici_en.html.

4. C. S. Lewis, *The Four Loves* (New York: Harcourt Brace Jovanovich, 1991), 61.

5. "Catholic Data, Catholic Statistics, Catholic Research," Center for Applied Research in the Apostolate (CARA), accessed February 10, 2012. http://cara.georgetown.edu/CARAServices/requestedchurchstats.html.

6. Bernard J. Lee and Michael A. Cowan, *Gathered and Sent: The Mission of Small Church Communities Today* (New York: Paulist, 2003), 11.

7. Karl Rahner, *The Shape of the Church to Come* (New York: Seabury Press, 1974).

10. Don't Rob God

1. Council of Trent, "Tithes Are To Be Paid In Full; Those Who Withhold Them Are To Be Excommunicated. The Rectors Of Poor Churches Are To Be Piously Supported," session 25, chap.12.

2. Amiram D. Vinokur, Richard H. Price, and Robert D. Caplan, "Hard Times and Hurtful Partners: How Financial Strain Affects Depression and Relationship Satisfaction of Unemployed Persons and Their Spouses," *Journal of Personality and Social Psychology* 71, no. 1 (1996): 166–79, accessed February 1, 2012, http://www.isr.umich.edu/src/seh/mprc/PDFs/Vin_jpsp96.pdf.

3. Pastor Rick Warren speaking at his "Purpose Driven Church" Conference, Saddleback Church, Lake Forest, California (various years).

4. The Irish were no longer obligated to fund the Church of England as of 1869, the eventual result of the Tithing War. Irish Church Act, § 20 (1869).

5. Andy Stanley, *Fields of Gold: A Place beyond Your Deepest Fears, a Prize Beyond Your Wildest Imagination* (Wheaton, IL: Tyndale House, 2004), 92–94.

6. The New Radicals, "You Get What You Give," written by Gregg Alexander and Rick Nowels, *Maybe You've Been Brainwashed Too*, MCA Records, 1998.

7. J. A. Jungmann, *The Mass of the Roman Rite* (New York: Benziger Brothers, Inc., 1955), 19–20.

8. Jim Elliot and Elisabeth Elliot, *The Journals of Jim Elliot* (Old Tappan, NJ: F. H. Revell, 1978), 174.

11. Get the Parish Out of the Pews

1. Teresa of Calcutta, *A Simple Path*, comp. Lucinda Vardey, 1st ed. (New York: Ballantine, 1995), 137.

2. Benedict XVI, *Church Membership and Pastoral Co-Responsibility* (Vatican: The Holy See, May 26, 2009), http://www.vatican.va/holy_father/benedict_xvi/speeches/2009/may/documents/hf_ben-xvi_spe_20090526_convegno-diocesi-rm_en.html.

3. John Paul II, "I Shall Give You Shepherds" *Pastores Dabo Vobis* (Vatican: The Holy See, March 25, 1992), 18.

4. Thomas F. O'Meara, *Theology of Ministry* (New York: Paulist Press, 1999), 31.

5. United States Conference of Catholic Bishops Committee on the Laity, *Co-workers in the Vineyard of the Lord: A Resource for Guiding the Development of Lay Ecclesial Ministry* (Washington, DC: United States Conference of Catholic Bishops, 2005), 11.

6. Tom's Shoes, http://www.toms.com/one-for-one.

7. Gertrude Stein, *Everybody's Autobiography* (New York: Cooper Square Publisher, 1971), 289.

8. Bill Hybels, *The Volunteer Revolution: Unleashing the Power of Everybody* (Grand Rapids, MI: Zondervan, 2004).

12. Be Restorers

1. Pius XI, "In the Fortieth Year" *Quadragesimo Anno* (Vatican: The Holy See, May 15, 1931), http://www.vatican.va/holy_father/pius_xi/encyclicals/documents/hf_p-xi_enc_19310515_quadragesimo-anno_en.html.

2. Jay P. Dolan, "Toward a Social Gospel," *The American Catholic Experience: A History from Colonial Times to the Present* (Notre Dame: University of Notre Dame, 1992), 321–26.

3. James F. Engel and William A. Dyrness, *Changing the Mind of Missions* (Downers Grove, IL: InterVarsity, 2000), 61.

4. Dolan, *The American Catholic Experience*, 340.

5. Lyons, *The Next Christians*, 47.

6. Steve Corbett and Brian Fikkert, *When Helping Hurts: How to Alleviate Poverty without Hurting the Poor—and Yourself* (Chicago, IL: Moody, 2009), 65.

7. Lyons, *The Next Christians*, 183–184.

8. John Paul II, "The Concern of the Church for the Social Order," *Sollicitudo Rei Socialis* (Vatican: The Holy See, December 30, 1987), http://www.vatican.va/holy_father/john_paul_ii/encyclicals/documents/hf_jp-ii_enc_30121987_sollicitudo-rei-socialis_en.html.

9. National Conference of Catholic Bishops, *Communities of Salt and Light*, 1.

10. Benedict XVI, "God Is Love," *Deus Caritas Est* (Vatican: The Holy See, December 25, 2005), http://www.vatican.va/holy_father/benedict_xvi/encyclicals/documents/hf_ben-xvi_enc_20051225_deus-caritas-est_en.html.

13. Fall in Love

1. Dean R. Hoge and Marti R. Jewell, *The Next Generation of Pastoral Leaders: What the Church Needs to Know* (Chicago, IL: Loyola, 2010), 114.

2. "Thomas Paine," BrainyQuote.com, Xplore Inc, 2012, accessed August 15, 2012, http://www.brainyquote.com/quotes/quotes/t/thomaspain117868.html.

3. Bill Hybels, *Axiom: Powerful Leadership Proverbs* (Grand Rapids, MI: Zondervan, 2008), 75.

4. Steve Jobs, TopTen.com, accessed August 16, 2012, http://www.toptentopten.com/topten/steve+jobs+quotes+of+all+time.

5. Patrick Lencioni, *Death by Meeting: A Leadership Fable . . . about Solving the Most Painful Problem in Business* (San Francisco, CA: Jossey-Bass, 2004).

14. Lead Where You Serve

1. Ken Blanchard, *The Servant Leader* (Nashville: Thomas Nelson, 2003), 17.

2. Collins, *Good to Great*, 21–22.

3. Gary A. Haugen, *Just Courage: God's Great Expedition for the Restless Christian* (Downers Grove, IL: IVP, 2008), 104.

4. Seth Godin, *Tribes: We Need You to Lead Us* (New York: Portfolio, 2008), 131–132.

5. John C. Maxwell, Goodreads.com, August 16, 2012, http://www.goodreads.com/quotes/230972-leadership-is-not-about-titles-positions-or-flowcharts-it-is.

15. You Can Do This!

1. Bill Hybels, *Holy Discontent: Fueling the Fire That Ignites Personal Vision* (Grand Rapids, MI: Zondervan, 2007), 23.

2. David Kinnaman and Gabe Lyons, *Unchristian: What a New Generation Really Thinks about Christianity—and Why It Matters* (Grand Rapids, MI: Baker, 2007), 83.

3. St. Francis Assisi, accessed August 20, 2012, http://www.brainyquote.com/quotes/authors/f/francis_of_assisi.html.

Appendix C. Naming the Change: Mission, Vision, and Strategy

1. Bill Hybels, *Axiom: Powerful Leadership Proverbs* (Grand Rapids, MI: Zondervan, 2008), 52.

MICHAEL WHITE received his bachelor's degree from Loyola University Maryland and his graduate degrees in sacred theology and ecclesiology from the Pontifical Gregorian University in Rome. After being ordained a priest of the Archdiocese of Baltimore, he worked for five years as personal secretary to Cardinal William Keeler, who was then archbishop. During that time, he served as the director of the papal visit of Pope John Paul II to Baltimore.

During his tenure as pastor at Church of the Nativity, the church has almost tripled in weekend attendance from 1,400 to over 4,000. More importantly, the commitment to the mission of the Church has grown, evidenced by the significant increase of giving and service in ministry.

TOM CORCORAN received his bachelor's degree from Loyola University Maryland and completed his graduate work in theology with Franciscan University of Steubenville. Corcoran has served Church of the Nativity in a variety of roles that give him a unique perspective on parish ministry and leadership. Beginning as a youth minister, Corcoran later held positions as coordinator of children's ministry and director of small groups. He currently serves in the position of associate to the pastor and is responsible for weekend message development, strategic planning, and staff development.

AVE

Ave Maria Press

Founded in 1865, Ave Maria Press,
a ministry of the Congregation of
Holy Cross, is a Catholic publishing
company that serves the spiritual and
formative needs of the Church and its
schools, institutions, and ministers;
Christian individuals and families; and
others seeking spiritual nourishment.

For a complete listing of titles from

Ave Maria Press

Sorin Books

Forest of Peace

Christian Classics

visit www.avemariapress.com

Ave Maria Press
Notre Dame, IN
A Ministry of the United States Province of Holy Cross